WITH THE MASTER

BEFORE THE MIRROR

of God's Word

By
Susan J. Heck

With the Master Before the Mirror of God's Word
A Ladies' Bible Study on First John
By Susan J. Heck

Focus Publishing, Bemidji, Minnesota

Cover design by Melanie Schmidt

ISBN 978-1-885904-04-1

Printed in the United States of America

Dedication

To my children and their spouses:

My son, Charles Heck, and his wife Andrea

and

My daughter, Cindi Gundersen, and her husband David (Gunner)

Their lives mirror the Master!

Endorsements

Susan Heck adds another volume to her excellent series of meaty studies for thinking women. First John is one of the most convicting yet uplifting epistles in the New Testament. It is profound and pithy; rich with doctrine and pathos; full of insight and inspiration. This wonderful survey of the epistle carefully and skillfully reflects all those balances, unfolding the apostle's message with the straightforward simplicity that has become the trademark of Susan's teaching.

Phil Johnson—Executive Director,
Grace to You Radio Ministry with John MacArthur Jr.

Susan Heck writes this scholarly, yet simple-to-understand commentary on 1 John from a heart that has grasped the message of that book and thus convicts the reader (she has memorized 1 John, just as she has most of the New Testament). *With the Master Before the Mirror of God's Word* is well documented with footnotes that the more scholarly among women will greatly enjoy. As the title suggests, the diligent reader will be able to evaluate herself through the "mirror" of 1 John and come not only into a genuine assurance of salvation, but into practical holiness strongly rooted in the truths of Scripture. The Appendices at the back of the book are particularly enlightening and I found the *Questions to Consider* at the end of each chapter (an aid to Group Studies) a great help to ensure the reader applies the truths taught. Susan Heck is a great communicator and her book, like the others she has written, will be a great blessing to our women and through them strengthen our homes and local churches. I heartily recommend this book!

Chris Williams—Grace to You, India

In a day and age in which almost all of the prominent female Bible teachers will readily accept and even target male audiences, Susan stands as a breath of fresh air against this increasingly popular, but decidedly unbiblical practice. She is the beautiful embodiment of the Titus 2 woman.

It is with great and hopeful enthusiasm that I commend this study to you. Read it and take notes. Study. Ponder the depths of what the Apostle John has to say to his readers and ask God's Holy Spirit to illumine the riches of this epistle to your mind and implant them within your heart. When our knowledge of God is deepened, our love for God is deepened. It is my prayerful expectation that this study into which you are about to embark will deepen your knowledge of our great God and thereby deepen your love for Him, resulting in a life of joyful obedience to His commands.

Justin Peters—Justin Peters Ministries

Foreword

That there is a "famine in the land ... of hearing the words of the Lord" (Amos 8:11-12) has oft been discussed, pontificated and lamented. It is undeniably true that among the professing Christian world there is a famine in the land of sound, biblical preaching and teaching. There is no shortage of biblical teaching in general. Churches abound and teaching is abundant. Christian bookstore shelves are filled with books from popular teachers and authors, most of who claim to have new insight into how to have a more prosperous and fulfilling life, marriage, or career. With the advent of the internet and its accompanying blogs and podcasts, never has there been more information more readily available than there is today.

And yet with all of this, people are spiritually starving. Most of them do not even know it. They are starving because they are feeding upon spiritual junk food. They are reading and watching teachers who use an abundance of Christian terminology but provide a paucity of biblical truth. We are seeing the fulfillment of the Apostle Paul's warning that the time will come when people will "no longer endure sound doctrine" but will rather opt for those who "tickle the ears" (2 Timothy 4:3-4). This dearth of sound doctrine is rampant in all of Christian media genres, but is especially acute in those designed for female consumption.

Happily, all is not lost. There are a select few God-called female Bible teachers who are theologically sound and who do raise the doctrinal bar. One of these is Mrs. Susan Heck. My wife and I were privileged to meet Susan and her husband, Doug, in 2012 when we visited the church he pastors in Broken Arrow, Oklahoma. My wife describes Susan as a female version of Dr. John MacArthur. In other words, she is a Bible expositor. In her numerous Bible studies, CDs, and booklets, Susan employs sound hermeneutics and carefully exegetes the Scriptures. She, rightly, does not concern herself with the supposed "felt needs" of the masses but rather thoughtfully exposits the text, thereby bringing her readers to engage its truth.

Susan has committed to memory at least 23 books of the Bible. To say that she is a student of the Word would be quite the understatement. She is a force with which to be reckoned. Our churches would be in a far better state than what they are if more pastors had Susan's level of biblical knowledge. The fruits of her diligent study are evident in the work you are about to read. Be forewarned: If you are looking for a typical, sappy, emotionally driven, feel-good devotional, then this study is not for you. First John is both a deeply theological and deeply practical book. It deals with false teachers, warnings of false conversions, marks of being a true believer, the deadly consequences of sin and the imperative of obedience. Cotton candy theology it is not.

Then again, maybe this work is *exactly* that for which you are looking, or, at least, exactly what you are *needing*. Susan's work will confront the reader with biblical truths that are hard and sobering and yet encouraging and comforting at the same time. It has been said that soft teaching produces hard hearts but hard teaching digs deeply into the human heart and softens it toward the Truth.

As I, accompanied by my wife, travel around the country preaching and teaching, I am struck by the epidemic lack of biblical knowledge and, consequentially, biblical discernment among the great majority of professing believers. This sad state is especially acute among ladies. This is not, however, entirely their fault, for few Christian women have husbands who are adequately fulfilling their roles as the spiritual leader of the home.

I was greatly honored when Susan asked me to write the foreword for this work. After having read it, the honor has only deepened. Susan is not only an able Bible teacher, but she is also imminently qualified for her task. In addition to rightly dividing the Word of Truth (2 Timothy 2:15), she also fulfills the biblical role for a woman. Specifically, she teaches women and women *only*. In a day and age in which almost all of the prominent female Bible teachers will readily accept and even target male audiences, Susan stands as a breath of fresh air against this increasingly popular, but decidedly unbiblical practice. She is the beautiful embodiment of the Titus 2 woman.

It is with great and hopeful enthusiasm that I commend this study to you. Read it and take notes. Study. Ponder the depths of what the Apostle John has to say to his readers and ask God's Holy Spirit to illumine the riches of this epistle to your mind and implant them within your heart. When our knowledge of God is deepened, our love for God is deepened. It is my prayerful expectation that this study into which you are about to embark will deepen your knowledge of our great God and thereby deepen your love for Him, resulting in a life of joyful obedience to His commands.

Justin Peters
July, 2013

Chapter 1

Facts, Fellowship, and Fullness of Joy

1 John 1:1-4

Many years ago I came across a book that my husband had recommended to me, entitled *The Prince of the House of David.* A best selling novel first published in 1855, this book is written as a series of letters from a Jewish girl to her father during the reign of Tiberius Caesar and during the time of Christ's earthly ministry. The letters cover the time from the ministry of John the Baptist until the ascension of Christ into heaven, and were written in order to inform her father of the events of this man named Jesus and His claim to be Christ the Messiah. If you have never read this book, it is one I would highly recommend. It makes the time when Christ lived here on earth come alive in a way that will excite and warm your heart! I want to begin our study of John's first epistle by sharing a small portion of this young girl's seventh letter to her father. It begins this way:

> My Dear Father, My trembling fingers scarcely hold the light reed with which I am about to write you concerning the extraordinary things I have seen and heard; but they tremble only with joy. Oh, my father, my dear father, Messiah has come! I have seen Him! I have heard His voice! He has truly come! Oh joy, joy, joy! My eyes have beheld Him of whom Moses and the Prophets did write![1]

And so Adina, a young Jewish maid, begins to expound on the events that led her to see with her own eyes and hear with her

---

1 J. H. Ingraham, *The Prince of the House of David, or Three Years in the Holy City* (New York, NY: Pudney & Russell, 1855), pp 53, 54. Also included in the author's trilogy are *The Pillar of Fire,* covering the time of the exodus and Moses (which inspired the film *The Ten Commandments*, by Cecil B. DeMille), and *The House of David*, covering the time of David's reign. As with *The Prince of the House of David*, each book in this trilogy is written as a series of letters.

own ears Christ Jesus, the promised Messiah of the Jewish people. John, the aged old apostle, by the enabling of the Holy Spirit, writes something very similar in his first words to the churches in Asia Minor.

> That which was from the beginning, which we have heard, which we have seen with our eyes, which we have looked upon, and our hands have handled, concerning the Word of life— [2]the life was manifested, and we have seen, and bear witness, and declare to you that eternal life which was with the Father and was manifested to us— [3]that which we have seen and heard we declare to you, that you also may have fellowship with us; and truly our fellowship is with the Father and with His Son Jesus Christ. [4]And these things we write to you that your joy may be full (1 John 1:1-4).

Background

In this lesson, we'll cover the first four verses of John's epistle, but before we do so it is imperative that we understand some background and other information about this epistle. This information will help us to better understand what John is saying as he writes this letter. The first question that should be on our minds when we consider a book of the Bible is, *Who wrote it?* John the apostle wrote 1 John. As one of the three disciples who was closest to our Lord (Peter and James being the other two) John was known as the apostle of love and also as the disciple whom Jesus loved (John 13:23). He was the disciple reclining on Jesus' breast during the last supper (John 13:23-25), as well as the disciple to whom Jesus committed the care of His mother from the cross as He was dying (John 19:25-27). Even though John was the disciple whom Jesus loved, he was also known as one of the Sons of Thunder along with his brother James. In Mark 3:17 we read that Christ gave these two this name—perhaps because at one time they wanted to call fire down from Heaven to destroy a Samaritan village for its rejection of Christ. In that instance, Jesus replied to them, "you do not know what manner of spirit you are of" (Luke 9:51-56)! The Apostle John was also the only apostle who escaped a violent death. Even though he was cast into a cauldron of boiling oil, church history records that he escaped by a miracle, without injury. In addition to 1 John, the Apostle John also wrote 2 John, 3 John, the Gospel of John and the Book of the Revelation.

The similarities between the Gospel of John and 1 John are pretty amazing, which is another proof of John's authorship of 1 John. I remember several years ago, after I had memorized both the Gospel of John and 1 John, that as I reviewed one book, I would suddenly find myself quoting from the other one. For example, in 1 John 1:4 John writes, "And these things we write to you that your joy may be full," and then in John 15:11 he writes, "These things I have spoken to you, that My joy may remain in you, and that your joy may be full." Or 1 John 3:13, "Do not marvel, my brethren, if the world hates you," and then John 15:18, "If the world hates you, you know that it hated Me before it hated you." In fact, there are well over 100 similarities between the two books. It is amazing!

Another question we want to ask is, *When was it written?* It was likely written between 85 and 95 AD. This would mean that the believers John writes to were second and third generation Christians. The excitement of the early church had somewhat faded, and Christianity had become a habit, a traditional thing to do, much like it is in our day. John was concerned as he wrote this book that the flame would be rekindled. The Christian life had become a more difficult burden for many, and some were growing weary of it. That's why John writes in 1 John 5:3, "For this is the love of God, that we keep His commandments. And His commandments are not burdensome." John says the commandments of God are not irksome, they are not heavy, they are not oppressive, and yet John knew that for some they had become just that. This is an important fact to keep in mind as we study this book.

You might also be asking, *Where was John when he wrote 1 John?* John was in Ephesus when he wrote this epistle, and it is interesting to note that after John wrote this epistle he was exiled to the island of Patmos, where he wrote the book of the Revelation, and later returned to Ephesus for his final years. Another important question to consider is, *Who is this book written to?* According to tradition, this letter was written to the churches in Asia Minor, and especially to the church at Ephesus, where John himself lived for many years.

But probably the most important question to consider is, *Why did John write this epistle?* Let's look at 1 John 5:13 for John's purpose statement: "These things I have written to you who believe in the name of the Son of God, that you may know that you have eternal life, and that you may continue to believe in the name of the Son of God." John's main purpose for writing this epistle is that believers might know for certain—without a doubt—that they are born of God. If you struggle with the assurance of your salvation then 1 John is the book for you. When we have finished this epistle we will have discovered 20 tests of assurance—20 ways in which to know for sure if you are redeemed. I encourage you to examine yourselves in light of the 20 tests that John will give. John says you can know for sure that you are saved—you never have to doubt again!

It is interesting that John also has a purpose statement in the Gospel of John. In John 20:31 John writes, "but these are written that you may believe that Jesus is the Christ, the Son of God, and that believing you may have life in His name." Whereas John's purpose in writing the Gospel of John is to prove the authenticity of Christ, to prove that He was the Son of God, and to convince others to believe that they might have life, in the epistle of 1 John, his purpose is to provide assurance of salvation by valid tests that he will give. In addition to this, John also has other purposes for John writing 1 John: 1 John 1:4, "And these things we write to you that your joy may be full"; 1 John 2:1, "My little children, these things I write to you, so that you may not sin. And if anyone sins, we have an Advocate with the Father, Jesus Christ the righteous"; 1 John 2:21, "I have not written to you because you do not know the truth, but because you know it, and that no lie is of the truth"; 1 John 2:26, "These things I have written to you concerning those who try to deceive you." These all fall under the category of John's main purpose, stated in 1 John 5:13, as a genuine believer will have joy, will not practice sin, will seek the truth, and will be discerning of false teachers and not be seduced by them.

And while we are on the subject of false teachers, this is a theme that is spoken of much throughout the epistle of 1 John, and for good reason. False teachers were invading the church and were teaching a heresy called Gnosticism (a heresy which also invades our churches today). Gnosticism was a very dangerous heresy and John writes to warn them of it (see 1 John 2:18-22; 4:1-3). You might ask, "Well, what is Gnosticism? Why was it so bad?" The term Gnosticism is derived from the Greek word gnosis, meaning knowledge. The first Gnostic according to church history was Simon the Sorcerer. It is said of him in Acts 8:10 that he claimed that he was someone great, to whom they all gave heed, saying that this man was the great power of God. Simon claimed that he had some power that could reach up to God, and that's where Gnosticism appears to have had its beginning. The Greeks loved knowledge, and to them the gospel message was too simplistic. To them Jesus was not enough, and so they added Christ plus knowledge. They were in the know, or so they thought, and in order to carry out their ridiculous theology they had to come up with some pretty strange ideas.

For example, they believed that anything created was evil and that only spirit was good. Because of this, they could not reconcile the creation of the world, because all that stuff was matter and it was evil. How could a holy God create a world that has sin in it? God was good, yet matter, they said, was evil. The Gnostics, who were thought to have all that superior knowledge (they were in the know, you know), had to have an explanation for it. The Gnostics believed that God's energy must have been limited and thwarted, and that God limited Himself in the act of creation. There was a germination of God, and then another and another and so on—thousands of lesser gods, until there was one god created so distant from Him that this god could touch evil, and this god created the world. Of course this god was so far removed from The True God that this little god became feebler, therefore he could make contact with evil, and so then creation took place. Now, as you can imagine, this led them into all sorts of other heresies. In their thinking, Jesus, if he really was the Son of God, could not possibly have taken on a human body because the body is matter and therefore the body is evil.[2] To them, Jesus Christ being human was evil because he was material. That is why John warns them,

> Beloved, do not believe every spirit, but test the spirits, whether they are of God; because many false prophets have gone out into the world. By this you know the Spirit of God: Every spirit that confesses that Jesus Christ has come in the flesh is of God, and every spirit that does not confess that Jesus Christ has come in the flesh is not of God. And this is the spirit of the Antichrist, which you have heard was coming, and is now already in the world (1 John 4:1-3).

They denied that Jesus Christ was part of the Godhead; therefore, they taught that Jesus Christ died in appearance only, not in reality. One form of heretical Christology was Docetism (from the Greek word dokein, meaning to seem, to appear). Docetism taught that Jesus Christ only appeared as a man but actually had no physical reality; they taught that Christ didn't have a human body; they denied his incarnation. This view was later condemned by such

---

2 One particular false Gnostic teacher in Ephesus at this time, when the Apostle John was living in Ephesus and wrote this epistle, was Cerinthus. Church Father Irenaeus, in his work *Against Heresies*, summarized: "Cerinthus, again, a man who was educated in the wisdom of the Egyptians, taught that the world was not made by the primary God, but by a certain Power far separated from him, and at a distance from that Principality who is supreme over the universe, and ignorant of him who is above all. He represented Jesus as having not been born of a virgin, but as being the son of Joseph and Mary according to the ordinary course of human generation, while he nevertheless was more righteous prudent, and wise than other men. Moreover, after his baptism, Christ descended upon him in the form of a dove from the Supreme Ruler, and that then he proclaimed the unknown Father, and performed miracles. But at last Jesus suffered and rose again, while Christ remained impassable, inasmuch as he was a spiritual being." cf. Alexander Roberts and James Donaldson, *The Ante-Nicene Fathers: The Writings of the Fathers Down to A. D. 325*, vol.1 (Grand Rapids, MI: Eerdmans, 1975), pp 351-352.

church fathers as Ignatius, Polycarp and Tertullian. John confronts this error in: 1 John 1:1-3; 2:22-23; 4:1-3, 14-15; 2 John 9. The final orthodox statement against the error of denying the incarnation was drafted in AD 451:

> While the framers of the Apostles' and Nicene Creeds were opposed to docetic teaching and clearly assumed the two natures of Jesus, the drafters of the Definition of Chalcedon (AD 451) made explicit the Christian teaching concerning Jesus Christ as "truly God and truly man."[3]

As we'll see in later lessons, John again confronts this in his letter in 1 John 1:2, 3, and 2:22, 23. These false teachers ignored the significance of the ministry, the death and the resurrection of Jesus Christ as being real. They believed it was knowledge, not faith, which was necessary for salvation. This led to denying the sufficiency of Christ. Of course, when one denies the sufficiency of Christ, this leads into all kinds of heresy. They were involved in much of what we see today in the church: legalism, mysticism, astrology, and angel worship. They were involved in rigid asceticism (the doctrine that by abstinence and self-denial a person can train himself to be conformed to God's will). This fleshed out with such acts as abstaining from marriage and strict dietary restrictions. (By the way, Paul confronts this same heresy in Colossians and deals with these issues there.) Some Gnostics accepted marriage as necessary to preserve the race, but regarded it as evil, and so they would adopt children. Other Gnostics thought that this was too extreme—because one cannot escape evil—so they cultivated an indifference to the world of sense. They would just follow their impulses; they would treat matter as foreign, and as something to which they had no responsibility. This belief led them to lead immoral lives because they claimed that the spirit was entirely separate from the body; therefore, in their opinion, they were not responsible for the acts of the body. That's why, in 1 John 3:3, 9, John stresses holiness and purity for all men.

---

3 G. L. Borchert, *Evangelical Dictionary of Theology*, edited by Walter A. Elwell (Grand Rapids, MI: Baker, 1984), p 326.

The Gnostics also did not believe that Jesus was the Christ, and John confronts this error in 1 John 2:1, 2. They did not believe in the resurrection of the body. Their ridiculous theology regarding the person of Christ led them to attitudes of arrogance and snubbing their noses at others who did not have their "superior knowledge." They, being in the know, looked down upon others as being spiritually inferior. That is one reason John mentions the word *know*, or some form of it, 38 times in this epistle alone, (1 John 2:3, 4, 5, 11, 13, 14, 18, 20, 21, 29; 3:1, 2, 5, 14, 15, 16, 19, 20, 24; 4:2, 6, 7, 8, 13, 16; 5:2, 13, 15, 18, 19, 20). The knowledge that John will write about was not some superior knowledge that was only for a select few, but a knowledge that comes from knowing God and having a personal relationship with Him.

These false teachers lacked humility and love, which is why in this epistle John stresses the importance of loving the brethren more than 10 times (1 John 3:10, 11, 14 ,16, 17, 18, 23; 4:7, 8, 11, 12, 20, 21; 5:1, 2). The attitude of being better than someone else is to be a foreign thought to the child of God. Instead we are to love one another, consider one another, and be willing to die for one another. So you can see why the aged Apostle John writes that he loves these children of God, that he is very concerned for them, and spiritually jealous over them. John is writing as a father to his children. 1 John is one of the most intimate writings we have in the Word of God.

Let's briefly look into the first four verses. I have outlined them in this way:

The Facts of Christ (vv 1, 2)
Our Fellowship with Christ (v 3)
Our Fullness of Joy Because of Christ (v 4)

Let's look at the facts about Christ in verses 1 and 2!

The Facts of Christ
1 John 1:1-2

> That which was from the beginning, which we have heard, which we have seen with our eyes, which we have looked upon, and our hands have handled, concerning the Word of life— (1 John 1:1).

Notice that there are no greetings at the beginning of this epistle. By the way, there are no greetings at the end either, as John will end this letter with, "Little children, keep yourselves from idols. Amen." This is unlike the writings of the Apostle Paul, who is always sending grace and peace and the like. There has even been debate as to what kind of literature of First John is. Because the book lacks a formal salutation and formal conclusion, some have claimed that it is not an epistle, but a written sermon or even a collection of sermons. This is quite probable, but throughout this study I'll refer to First John as an epistle, since that is what it is most commonly called.[4]

What is John talking about when he says *that which was from the beginning*? John tells us at the end of the verse that it was *the Word of life*. The Word of life was from the beginning. You might be asking, "What was the Word of life?" The Word of life is the Son of God, the incarnate Christ, God in the flesh who was from

---

[4] I. Howard Marshall sees First John as a sermon: "We must conclude that the writing is not so much a letter as a written sermon or address" cf. *The New International Commentary on the New Testament: The Epistles of John* (Grand Rapids, MI: Eerdmans, 1978), p 99. Although some reject this view as suspect, because John directly declares this to be a written book instead of an oral address (cf. 1:4; 2:1,12-13,26; 5:13), it does have much to commend it. The Epistle of First John is similar to the Epistle of Hebrews, as they both lack a formal epistolary salutation. Marshall adds a footnote: "See, however, F. O. Francis, *The Form and Function of the Opening and Closing Paragraphs of James and I John*, ZNW [Zeitschrift fur die Neutestamentliche Wissenschaft] 61, 1970, 110-126, who notes that ancient letters could end without a formal conclusion" (*Ibid.*, p 99). However, without a formal introduction the theory that First John is sermonic cannot be ignored. The preface is calculated to capture the reader's attention, like a brief introduction to a sermon during NT times. This study will employ the accepted "epistle" form, but leave open the probability that this is a written sermon.

the beginning, as John says in the Gospel of John, "In the beginning was the Word, and the Word was with God, and the Word was God. He was in the beginning with God" (John 1:1-2). John says this one, this Word of life, we have heard, seen, looked upon and handled. Now why does John use the pronoun *we*? Who is he referring to? John is not just referring to himself, but also to the other apostles. They were eyewitnesses of God in the flesh. They had seen, heard and touched the incarnate Christ (see Acts 1:21, 22). John says *we have heard ... we have seen ... we have looked upon ...* we *have handled* the Word of life.[5]

The verbs that John uses here are in the present tense, which means the effects of the hearing, seeing, and handling are still effective. The Greek is in the instrumental case, which shows that it was not imagination on John's part; it was not an optical illusion as the Gnostics claimed.[6] Jesus had an actual human body. He could be heard and seen. John actually touched him and handled him. We know that was possible because Jesus had flesh like you and me. This looking upon seems to be more than a casual glance; it is an intense and earnest gaze, until the significance of the person has been grasped. As John puts so well in John 1:14, "... the Word became flesh and dwelt among us, and we beheld His glory, the glory as of the only begotten of the Father, full of grace and truth." I would encourage you to read the gospel accounts, especially the Gospel of John, reminding yourself of the numerous times that John and the others intensely watched the life of the Lord. They were with him 3½ years and during that time they saw Him, they looked

---

5 Although the plural "we" is most often interpreted as being John and the other Apostles, a second view sees this as a literary plural which refers to John himself. This editorial "we" is supported by verse 4, for the other Apostles were no longer living when John wrote (compare with 2:1). John's editorial method of communicating is illustrated in 3 John 9, where he uses the plural but has only himself in view. The literary plural is common in the NT (cf. Col. 4:3; 1 Thess. 2:18; 3:1, etc.). Either option is possible.

6 According to the polemical purpose of First John (2:26), the Docetic Gnostic heresy gave challenge to the validity of sense perception, in denial of the true incarnation of Jesus Christ. To them, Jesus Christ only seemed (Greek, dokein) to be a man, but had no actual material or physical body. Because they denied the incarnation, John begins his epistle with a firm affirmation of his own sense experience with Jesus Christ.

upon Him, and they touched Him. Some of us today might shy away from such intense discipleship!

John also may have had in mind the account in John 20:27 when one of the disciples, Thomas, had doubts about the resurrected Christ. Remember what Jesus said to doubting Thomas? "Then He said to Thomas, 'Reach your finger here, and look at My hands; and reach your hand here, and put it into My side. Do not be unbelieving, but believing.'" John is saying, "Christ is not an illusion or some fantasy. We have seen him, we have touched Him!" These words that John uses to begin his epistle are imperative because of the heresy which had crept into the church. He is setting the stage for the entire book which is centered on Christ and a genuine knowledge of Him, and not some gnosis knowledge. John wants to set forth Christ at the beginning! And so he goes on to talk about this Word of life in verse 2.

> the life was manifested, and we have seen, and bear witness, and declare to you that eternal life which was with the Father and was manifested to us— (1 John 1:2).

Some translations have verse 2 in parentheses. When something is put in parentheses it is usually done for emphasis or to explain an important word. Here in verse 2 the word that is being repeated and emphasized is *life*. John is repeating once again that the life, the Word of life, was manifested and that they had seen it and bore witness to it. John even goes on to say I declare that this *eternal life* was with the Father and was manifested unto us. The eternal life that John is speaking about here is a spiritual quality of life, which God gives to every believer. Eternal life is really just another word for salvation. John is saying Jesus Christ is the life eternal, He is the way to salvation, and we are proclaiming this to you. It was made known to us, and now we are making it known to you. John will make this clear again in 1 John 5:11. "And this is the testimony: that God has given us eternal life, and this life is in His Son." And with that, John shifts from the facts regarding Christ to the amazing fellowship believers have with Christ in verse 3.

Our Fellowship with Christ
1 John 1:3

> that which we have seen and heard we declare to you, that you also may have fellowship with us; and truly our fellowship is with the Father and with His Son Jesus Christ. (1 John 1:3).

John again repeats the word *seen*. He has mentioned this fact three times, so we know the fact that the apostles saw Christ was important. He was not a figment of someone's imagination; He was not a phantom. He did come in the flesh, contrary to what the false teachers were saying. And John is not the only one who claims this, as the Apostle Peter also makes this claim in 2 Peter 1:16: "For we did not follow cunningly devised fables when we made known to you the power and coming of our Lord Jesus Christ, but were eyewitnesses of His majesty." John goes on to say *we declare to you*; we are sharing our experience with you. And we are declaring this for a reason and that reason is so that you too may *have fellowship with us* and *with the Father and with His Son Jesus Christ*. We have a living relationship with the living God, and we want that for you too. Isn't that the desire of all of us? That those we know would have life eternal and enjoy life now with Christ and the Father?

Now let's talk a minute about what it means to have *fellowship*. The word for fellowship is partnership. In secular Greek the word meant to have common ownership like a property that a married couple would jointly own together.[7] We say, "Let's get together and have fellowship," and what we mean is, "Let's get together and have coffee and donuts." But that is not fellowship in the biblical sense. Fellowship is something we have because we share something in common. That commonality is our union with Christ. There is no way that you and I can have fellowship with one another in the biblical sense if we do not have fellowship with God. If we do not have a personal relationship with Him and accept the facts of his incarnation, death, burial and resurrection, we have no fellowship with one another and we have no fellowship, no partnership, with Him. It is only possible to have this fellowship with the Father through His Son Jesus Christ. John will say again in 1 John 5:11, "And this is the testimony: that God has given us eternal life, and this life is in His Son." In contrast to what many false teachers are saying today, Jesus says in John 14:6 that no one can come to the Father except by Him. And the Greek tense here means to keep on having fellowship, which would indicate that genuine believers persevere to the end. This is a comfort to the believer, as no man can pluck us out of the Father's hand—it is a forever deal! Now this fellowship with Christ, this partnership that you and I have,

[7] Contemporary usage of the term *fellowship* is mostly limited to relating, but that is only an outcome of biblical fellowship. The word group usage in the NT suggests that partnership is the issue, i.e., something shared in common. For example, the abstract noun koinonia is used 18 times in the New Testament (cf. Acts 2:42; Romans 15:26; 1 Corinthians1:9; 10:16; 2 Corinthians 6:14; 8:4; 9:13; 13:14; Galatians 2:9; Philippians 1:5; 2:1; 3:10; Philemon 6; Hebrews 13:16; 1 John 1:3, 6, 7); the verb koinoneo is used 8 times in the New Testament (cf. Romans 12:13; 15:27; Galatians 6:6; Philippians 4:15; 1 Timothy 5:22; Hebrews 2:14; 1 Peter 4:13; 2 John 11); and the noun koinonos is used 10 times in the New Testament (cf. Matthew 23:30; Luke 5:10; 1 Corinthians 10:18, 20; 2 Corinthians 1:7; 8:23; Philemon 17; Hebrews 10:33; 1 Peter 1:4; 2 Peter 1:4). Out of the 36 usages in the NT, only five passages (cf. 1 Corinthians 1:9; 2 Corinthians 13:14; Philippians 2:1; 2 Peter 1:4; 1 John 1:3) use the word to signify a relationship between the believer and God. And in none of these passages can the word be used as temporary or to express a variation of degrees, as the Fellowship View demands! Fellowship is not "something more" than the new birth or a deeper life of the Christian. As J. V. Campbell has well established, the primary meaning of koinonia is "participation in something in which others also participate" (cf. *Koinonia and Its Cognates in the New Testament,* Journal of Biblical Literature 51 [1934]: 353). McDermott has pointed out that koinonia, as used by Paul and John, refers to the possession of eternal life and the inseparable relationship with God, which is a New Covenant promise (cf. John M. McDermott, *The Biblical Doctrine of Koinonia,* Biblische Zeitschrift 19, {1975]: 65).

has some wonderful benefits. One of those benefits is joy—and not just plain ole' joy, but fullness of joy! John writes concerning our fullness of joy because of Christ in verse 4.

Our Fullness of Joy Because of Christ
1 John 1:4

> And these things we write to you that your joy may be full (1 John 1:4).

What *things* is John referring to here? *These things* is a reference to the entire epistle. As we saw earlier, one of John's purposes in writing this epistle is so that they would have fullness of joy! *Joy* is cheerfulness or calm delight; *full* means to cover over or be complete. So we might say this is a calm delight that is complete. This is an amazing benefit of having partnership with Christ—overflowing joy! The fact that you and I have partnership with the living God and that we have life eternal should bring us joy as nothing in this life can. John writes of this also in John 3:29, where Jesus says "He who has the bride is the bridegroom; but the friend of the bridegroom, who stands and hears him, rejoices greatly because of the bridegroom's voice. Therefore this joy of mine is fulfilled." Also in the Gospel of John Jesus says, "These things I have spoken to you, that My joy may remain in you, and that your joy may be full" (John 15:11). And in John 16:24, "Until now you have asked nothing in My name. Ask, and you will receive, that your joy may be full." Ladies, Christ wants us to have fullness of joy—do you?

Summary

The Facts of Christ (vv 1-2) are this: He was from the beginning; He was seen, heard, and even touched; He was God in the flesh. He and He alone is the Word of life and He and He alone provides eternal life. Do you believe those facts? Do you really believe those facts? Do you believe that God came in the flesh as a baby and that he lived as a man and died for your sins and is now raised and seated at the right hand of His Father? Do you believe that? Those are the facts. If you believe those facts concerning Christ and have committed your life totally to Him, then as John says you have *Fellowship with Christ* (v 3). Are you now in partnership with Christ? I would be negligent if I did not compel you as we begin our study of this wonderful epistle to make sure that you do indeed have fellowship or partnership with Christ. Without a partnership with Christ His Word will not make any sense to you as you study it. And lastly, if you understand the facts concerning Christ, and if you have fellowship with Christ, then I have wonderful news for you: your life is meant to have joy—and not just plain ole' joy, but *Fullness of Joy Because of Christ* (v 4). Are you running over with calm delight and cheerfulness? If not, why not?

What an exciting beginning to a wonderful book! I pray you will continue with me for the entire journey as we feast on the riches of God's Word through this little epistle. Be faithful, be prepared, and be ready for blessings abundant!

Questions to Consider

Facts, Fellowship, and Fullness of Joy

1 John 1:1-4

1. Read 1 John 1:1-4. (a) What is John referring to in verse 1? (b) What had he heard, what had he seen, and what had he handled? (c) How do you know? Memorize 1 John 1:4.

2. (a) According to verse 4, what is one purpose John writes this letter? (b) Should this fruit be evident in the life of a believer? (See Galatians 5:22, 23.) (c) What does it mean to have fullness of joy?

3. (a) What phrase is repeated in verses 1, 2, and 3? (b) Why do you think John repeats this phrase?

4. What do you think John means in verse 3 by the term "fellowship"?

5. (a) Do you have "fellowship with the Father and with His Son Jesus Christ"? (b) How is this evident in your life?

6. According to the following verses, what should bring one fullness of joy? John 3:29; John 15:9-11; John 16:24; John 17:13; Philippians 2:2; 2 John 12. (By the way, who authored most of these verses?)

7. (a) How does your life exhibit fullness of joy? (b) If your life does not exhibit joy, what is hindering that joy? (c) What will you do about it?

8. What would you like to see the Lord do in your life through this study in 1 John? Please be prepared with a prayer request to share.

Chapter 2

Are You Walking in the Light?

1 John 1:5-7

Many years ago I was visiting with a woman who had attended the church my husband was pastoring. She and her family were with us for a brief period of time and then left to go to another church. I remember having a conversation with her after they left the church, specifically asking her why they had left. Her response has often haunted me—she said, "We knew if we stayed at your church we would have to change the way we live our lives—it was too uncomfortable for us to worship there." I was surprised with her answer but also very grieved, as it was a sad commentary on their family life. As time passed by, I learned that sinful behavior was indeed taking place among their family members.

With that story in mind, I would like to pose a question as we begin our second lesson in 1 John. Do you think it is possible for you and me to live a life of sin and still be on our way to heaven? Many Christians unfortunately have bought into a gospel which says, "Come to Christ, believe in Him, but don't worry about changing your behavior. You've still got your fire insurance, and you're on your way to heaven." What would Jesus say to this gospel that we hear today? What did Jesus say through the Holy Spirit and through the Apostle John?

1 John 1:5-7

> This is the message which we have heard from Him and declare
> to you, that God is light and in Him is no darkness at all. [6]If we
> say that we have fellowship with Him, and walk in darkness,
> we lie and do not practice the truth. [7]But if we walk in the light
> as He is in the light, we have fellowship with one another, and
> the blood of Jesus Christ His Son cleanses us from all sin (1
> John 1:5-7).

In the first lesson in our study of 1 John we learned that John writes concerning *The Facts of Christ*, (v 1-2). We learned that Christ was from the beginning, and that John and the other apostles heard him, saw him, and touched Him. In contrast to what the Gnostics were saying, He was not a figment of someone's imagination. He was real. He was God in the flesh. We also learned that John writes concerning *Our Fellowship with Christ*, (v 3). We learned that the Greek term for fellowship means partnership or joint ownership. Those who have a living relationship with God have fellowship with His Son Jesus Christ and with one another. Lastly, we learned that John writes concerning *Our Fullness of Joy Because of Christ*, (v 4). One of John's purposes for writing is that we would have joy, and not just plain ole' joy, but fullness of joy. We saw that fullness of joy means calm delight which is complete, and that this is only possible because of our partnership with Christ. In this chapter we'll see,

The Character of God (v 5)
The Character of Those Walking in Darkness (v 6)
The Character of Those Walking in Light (v 7)

John continues with his declaration of God and elaborates on His character in verse 5.

The Character of God
1 John 1:5

> This is the message which we have heard from Him and declare to you, that God is light and in Him is no darkness at all (1 John 1:5).

John says *this is the message*, this is the announcement, this is the divine communication that *we have heard from Him*. The word for *heard* is akouo, which not only means to hear, but also to obey. It is the same word used in Ephesians 6:1 where Paul commands children to "obey" their parents. They are not only to hear what the parent says, but they are to obey it. It is only as we obey what we hear that we desire to proclaim it. So John says, "You want me to tell you what we have heard from Christ while He was here? Do you want me to share with you what we have heard and obeyed? Here it is: God is light and in Him is no darkness at all. Here is the character of God: He is light and there is absolutely no darkness in Him."

What does it mean that *God is light*? John is not saying that God is a light, or even the light. Instead, he is saying that God *is* light. He is light itself. I might say to you, "There is a light," as I am pointing to it, perhaps in a room or outside of a building. Or I might turn on a light to explain to you what light is. John is not saying anything like that. He is saying God is light. It is His nature; it is who He is. Paul puts it this way in 1 Timothy 6:16: "who alone has immortality, dwelling in unapproachable light, whom no man has seen or can see, to whom be honor and everlasting power. Amen."

You might wonder where John got this information that Jesus is light. On many occasions John heard Jesus make this declaration while He was here on earth. Jesus had declared this and John had heard it. Consider these passages from the Gospel of John, which the Apostle John also wrote:

- "Then Jesus spoke to them again, saying, 'I am the light of the world. He who follows Me shall not walk in darkness, but have the light of life'" (John 8:12).
- John 9:5, "As long as I am in the world, I am the light of the world." (John 9:5).
- "Then Jesus said to them, 'A little while longer the light is with you. Walk while you have the light, lest darkness overtake you; he who walks in darkness does not know where he is going. While you have the light, believe in the light, that you may become sons of light.' These things Jesus spoke, and departed, and was hidden from them" (John 12:35-36).
- John 12:46, "I have come as a light into the world, that whoever believes in Me should not abide in darkness" (John 12:46).

Christ's message to John consisted of two distinct parts: a positive statement of the nature of God, i.e., that "God is light" and a negative emphatic statement of what He is not, i.e., "in Him is no darkness at all."

You might ask, "What is so important about God being light?" The fact that God is light tells us that nothing is secretive about Him. He has nothing to hide. God is unlike the men whom Jesus describes in John 3:19 who love darkness rather than light because their deeds are evil. Jesus has nothing to do with darkness because He has nothing to hide. There is no sin in Him. There are no secrets with God. He is light and His message must be proclaimed openly. This would certainly contradict those who say their religion is a private matter. That idea is foreign to the God we claim to know and love. The fact that God is light also gives me great hope because He can show me how to live and how to walk in the light and can lead me in the way that I should go. As the Psalmist says in Psalm 36:9, "For with You is the fountain of life; in Your light we see light." If you and I are going to have genuine fellowship or partnership with God as we saw in our last lesson, then knowledge of who He is essential. He is light!

Not only is God light, but John also says *in Him is no darkness at all*. This is a double negative in the Greek, to state emphatically that there is no darkness in Him. According to the Greek order, the rendering is: "And darkness there is not in Him, no, not in any way." There is not even a speck of darkness in God. That is an amazing truth! The word for *darkness* here means the consequence or result of sin. God is light and in Him there is no sin. God is absolutely pure and holy. What is the character of God? He is light and He has no darkness in Him! And having declared the character of God, John now moves on to declare the character of those who do not know Him—those who walk in darkness.

The Character of Those Walking in Darkness 1 John 1:6

> If we say that we have fellowship with Him, and walk in darkness, we lie and do not practice the truth (1 John 1:6).

The question might come to mind, "Who are those who are saying they have fellowship with God, but do not actually have it?" John is combating the false teachers and their false teaching that was infiltrating the church, as we have already mentioned in our first lesson. John is referring to the Gnostics who were saying they had fellowship with God but were walking in darkness. May I say that anyone who professes fellowship with God and yet walks in darkness is Gnostic in that they are claiming that believing in Christ does not mean they have to have a changed life. People can say a lot of religious stuff, but Christ *never* measures someone's relationship to Him by what they say but by what they do! Hopefully the truth of that will be clear to you as you look at Matthew 7 in the "Questions to Consider" that follow this lesson. The Scriptures are replete with examples of this truth, but one we would do well to remember is James 2:14-18:

> What does it profit, my brethren, if someone says he has faith but does not have works? Can faith save him? If a brother or sister is naked and destitute of daily food, and one of you says to them, "Depart in peace, be warmed and filled," but you do not give them the things which are needed for the body, what does it profit? Thus also faith by itself, if it does not have works, is dead. But someone will say, "You have faith, and I have works." Show me your faith without your works, and I will show you my faith by my works. You believe that there is one God. You do well. Even the demons believe—and tremble!

Beware of the person that can articulate a good testimony and even speak fluently regarding the Scriptures but does not live a holy life. As John will say in a few verses, "Now by this we know that we know Him, if we keep His commandments. He who says, 'I know Him,' and does not keep His commandments, is a liar, and the truth is not in him" (1 John 2:3, 4). John does *not* say, "this is how we know we know Him, if we *say* we love God," or "this is how we know we know Him, if we *say* we walk in the light," or "this is how we know we know Him, if we *say* we prayed a prayer, or if we *say* religious things." No, John says, "this is how we know we know Him, if we *keep His commandments*. The keeping of God's commandments is an indicator and assurance that we are children of God.

John goes on to say these guys who profess fellowship *walk in darkness*. To walk in darkness means to live without the benefit of the divine light and guidance and so to live in sin. *Walk* here means to walk about, indicating the habitual course of the life, both outward and inward. It describes the process of our living as living in sin and error. There is a vast difference between sinning and walking in darkness. Christians do sin, but they do not walk in sin. Christians do sin, but they hate sin. Christians do sin, but they sin less and less as they are conformed to the image of Christ. Christians do sin, but they do not claim that sinning does not matter, as the Gnostics were claiming. They hate it. They echo the Apostle Paul in Romans 7:24, as he is battling with sin in his members, and cries out, "O wretched man that I am! Who will deliver me from this body of death?" Christians do not walk in darkness.

John gives two characteristics of this one who walks in darkness. The first characteristic is that *they lie*. To lie means to utter an untruth, or attempt to deceive by falsehood. It also refers to lying deliberately. To lie or to be a liar is a serious accusation. (John also uses this term in John 1:10; 2:4; 2:22; 4:20.) John makes it very clear in another book he wrote, the Book of the Revelation, that it is impossible to be a liar and think you will inherit the kingdom of Heaven: Revelation 21:8, "But the cowardly, unbelieving, abominable, murderers, sexually immoral, sorcerers, idolaters, and all liars shall have their part in the lake which burns with fire and brimstone, which is the second death" (Revelation 21:8), and "But outside are dogs and sorcerers and sexually immoral and murderers and idolaters, and whoever loves and practices a lie" (Revelation 22:15).

Secondly, to those who walk in darkness, John says, *do not practice the truth*. What does it mean to not practice the truth? To *practice* the truth means to show in one's conduct, his feelings, his words and even his thoughts that he is doing the truth. The Gnostics had deceived themselves into thinking that they had fellowship with God, and all the while they were practicing sin, not practicing the truth. If we are going to claim we have partnership with God, then we must walk in light. It is about as ludicrous as saying I am in a marriage covenant with my husband, and yet I am going to have relationships with other men. That is absurd! I am in a covenant relationship with my husband; I am committed to him and him alone. When you committed your life to the Lordship of Jesus Christ you entered into a covenant relationship with Him. You are now a part of the bride of Christ. That was the issue with those in Matthew 7. Those people *said*, "Lord, Lord," but Jesus says, "I never knew you. You did not have partnership with me." In fact He tells them that they practice lawlessness.

The Gnostics were great pretenders to knowledge, and claimed they had partnership with God, but their conduct was corrupt. John is confronting those who were claiming that one could have fellowship with God and yet walk in sin. The Gnostics justified their sinful behavior by claiming the body was going to be destroyed anyway. Therefore, to them, it did not matter what evil they committed with their physical bodies. In fact, it was said that the Gnostics declared that a truly spiritual man was quite incapable of ever incurring any pollution, no matter what kind of deeds he did. But John is saying, "No, it does matter what evil you commit with your body!" In fact it would be interesting to see what these guys would say in rebuttal to Paul in the following passages:

- "Therefore do not let sin reign in your mortal body, that you should obey it in its lusts. And do not present your members as instruments of unrighteousness to sin, but present yourselves to God as being alive from the dead, and your members as instruments of righteousness to God." (Romans 6:12-13)
- "I beseech you therefore, brethren, by the mercies of God, that you present your bodies a living sacrifice, holy, acceptable to God, which is your reasonable service. And do not be conformed to this world, but be transformed by the renewing of your mind, that you may prove what is that good and acceptable and perfect will of God." (Romans 12: 1-2)
- "For we must all appear before the judgment seat of Christ, that each one may receive the things done in the body, according to what he has done, whether good or bad" (2 Corinthians 5:10). No wonder Paul goes on to say in the next verse, verse 11, "Knowing, therefore, the terror of the Lord, we persuade men."

So, the two characteristics of those who walk in darkness are that they lie and that they do not practice the truth. Now in verse 7 John gives us the contrast to those who are walking in darkness by describing those who are walking in light. Interestingly, they also have two characteristics according to this text.

The Character of Those Walking in Light
1 John 1:7

> But if we walk in the light as He is in the light, we have fellowship with one another, and the blood of Jesus Christ His Son cleanses us from all sin (1 John 1:7).

The word *but* is used to show a contrast between those claiming to be in the light but yet are in darkness; and those who are indeed walking in the light. What does it mean to *walk in the light as He is in the light*? Walking in the light as He is in the light means that we reflect the Light which is Jesus Christ. This means we are transparent, we are open, we are honest, we are sincere, and we are striving to be like Him in every way. As Peter put it well in 1 Peter 1:15, 16, "... as He who called you is holy, you also be holy in all your conduct, because it is written, 'Be holy, for I am holy.'" That is why I am curious at times with believers who do not want accountability. They don't want anyone knowing what goes on behind closed doors. And we ask, why is that? What are they hiding? As Paul would say in Ephesians 5:8, "For you were once darkness, but now you are light in the Lord. Walk as children of light." Or to the church at Thessalonica, "You are all sons of light and sons of the day. We are not of the night nor of darkness" (1 Thessalonians 5:5).

Now the *walk* that John mentions here is in a Greek tense which means that we keep on walking. God expects His children to stay on the road of light. They don't wander away from the road of light to the road of darkness and go back and forth. They stay on the path of light. The writer to the Hebrews puts it well in 10:38-39: "Now the just shall live by faith; but if anyone draws back, my soul has no pleasure in him. But we are not of those who draw back to perdition, but of those who believe to the saving of the soul." The saved (just) man or woman, does not draw back; they don't wander away into apostasy, but they live and they walk by faith.

The first characteristic of those who walk in the light is that we *have fellowship with one another*. John has already mentioned this fellowship in verse 3. It is impossible for you and me to have fellowship or partnership with one another without first having fellowship with God. John already gave the basis for our fellowship with one another in verse 3, and that basis is our fellowship with Christ and the Father. Without a partnership with Him there is no partnership with each other. A good indicator of our heart on this issue of fellowship is to look at the company we keep. Our closest friends reveal quite a bit about our character. As we walk in the light, a natural outcome of that walking in the light will be fellowship with those who are also in the light. Now I am not saying that we don't keep company with unbelievers and try and win them to the Savior (Jesus Himself was a friend of sinners.) But I am saying that our closest companions, our soul mates, our best buds should be those who are in the light. In fact we know this to be true by the Greek term that John uses here for *one another*. The word for one another means another of the same kind. We should gravitate toward those who are of the same kind, those who are walking in the light. You've heard the saying, "Birds of a feather flock together." That's a true statement isn't it? Light attracts light and darkness attracts darkness.

The second characteristic of those who walk in the light is that *the blood of Jesus Christ His Son cleanses us from all sin*. What does it mean that His blood cleanses us from all sin? The cleansing of our sin took place with the death of Christ on the cross when He shed His blood for our sins. And the cleansing continues for those who are in Christ as we walk through life. We will see this wonderful truth in our next lesson, in 1 John 1:9, "If we confess our sins, He is faithful and just to forgive us our sins and to cleanse us from all unrighteousness." The word for *cleanses* in verse 7 means more than to forgive; it means to remove. It's like when one finds out they have cancer and the doctors remove the tumor to begin the process of healing. Jesus Christ removes the cancer of sin through the shedding of His blood. As the Psalmist says in Psalm 103:12, "As far as the east is from the west, So far has He *removed* our transgressions from us" (emphasis mine). And ladies, the cleansing is continuous. Praise God!

Notice, it is Jesus Christ, God's *Son*, who cleanses us from all sin. This certainly would confront the Gnostics, who said that Jesus Christ was a figment of someone's imagination, or that he was a phantom. John says, "No! He had a real body, and that body had real blood." This was not an ordinary man's blood, but it was the blood of the Son of God. This blood cleanses us from *all sin*. Notice it is *all* sin—not some but all. This means the whole of sin. Christ does not partially cleanse us but He thoroughly cleanses us. We have been cleansed because of the blood of Christ. We have been purified through the blood of Christ. This is an encouragement to me, because it tells me that there is no sin too big for God to cleanse. In fact, Paul gives a list of some pretty gross sins in 1 Corinthians and yet he also gives us hope. Consider 1 Corinthians 6:9-11:

> Do you not know that the unrighteous will not inherit the kingdom of God? Do not be deceived. Neither fornicators, nor idolaters, nor adulterers, nor homosexuals, nor sodomites, nor thieves, nor covetous, nor drunkards, nor revilers, nor extortioners will inherit the kingdom of God. And such were some of you. But you were washed, but you were sanctified, but you were justified in the name of the Lord Jesus and by the Spirit of our God.

Paul echoes the same thing John has said—these sins were from our former life, before Christ. These are not sins fitting for one who claims to have fellowship with God. The fact that Christ has atoned for our sin once and for all should motivate us to live holy each day.

Summary

Here is *The Character of God* (v 5): He is light and there is absolutely no darkness in Him! Here is *The Character of Those Walking in Darkness* (v 6): They lie and do not practice the truth. Here is *The Character of Those Walking in Light* (v 7): They have fellowship with one another and the blood of Jesus Christ cleanses them from all sin!

My dear friend, there are clear implications for the message Jesus declared to John, i.e., "that God is light and in Him is no darkness at all." Some of these implications relate to the professing believers assurance or false assurance. John mentions two ways to walk—two roads. One is the road that is dark. There is no light to guide those walking on the road of darkness. As Jesus said, that road is wide and broad, but it leads to destruction. Those who lie and do not practice the truth travel that road. The other road John mentions is the road that is light. Jesus calls it the narrow road, the narrow gate, but it leads to life. John says that those who walk down this road of light have continued fellowship with other believers and the privilege of having their sins cleansed. Which road are you traveling down—the dark, broad road which leads to destruction, or the narrow road of light which leads to life eternal? If it's not the narrow road you are traveling this day, why not make a u-turn away from the broad road to the narrow road which leads to life everlasting?

Questions to Consider

Are You Walking in the Light?

1 John 1:5-7

1. Read 1 John 1:5-7 and John 1:1-14. (a) What word does John use in both of these passages to describe God? (b) According to these two passages, what are the results of knowing the Light? (c) What does the statement "God is light" tell you about God?

2. Memorize 1 John 1:7.

3. John says in 1 John 1:5 that "God is light." (a) Because God is light, what benefits are there for those who know Him? See Psalm 27:1; Psalm 36:9; Psalm 84:11; Isaiah 60:19; John 1:9; John 8:12; John 12:35, 36; Revelation 22:5. (b) What is your response to this?

4. (a) According to Matthew 7:21-23, who claims to have fellowship with God but actually walks in darkness? (b) What happened to these people? (c) How do Jesus (Matthew passage) and John (1 John passage) describe those who claim to have a relationship with God but in fact do not? (d) Do you claim to know God? (e) Does your life measure up to that claim? (These last two questions are for you to answer in the privacy of your heart.)

5. (a) What contrasts do you see in the following passages between those who are in darkness and those who are in light? Luke 11:33-36; John 3:19-21; Acts 26:18; Romans 13:12-14; Ephesians 5:8-17; Colossians 1:12-14; 1 Thessalonians 5:1-8; 1 John 2:8-11. (b) How could you use Acts 26:18 as prayer for those you know who are in darkness?

6. (a) Besides light, what else do the Scriptures say about God? See Psalm 99:9; Psalm 116:5; John 3:33; John 4:24; 1 Corinthians 1:9; Hebrews 12:29; 1 John 4:8. (b) What does this tell you about God?

7. (Private question to consider.) Is there someone you know who claims to have fellowship with God and yet you know they are walking in darkness? Will you plead with them this week to consider the truths of 1 John, to consider that they are in darkness, that they lie, and that they are not of the truth?

8. Come with a prayer of thanksgiving to God for the cleansing of *all* your sins.

Chapter 3

What is Your Attitude toward Sin?

1 John 1:8-2:2

The late Dr. Wilbur Chapman often told the story of a Methodist preacher who regularly spoke on the subject of sin. The preacher minced no words, but defined sin as "that abominable thing that God hates." One day a leader in his congregation came to him and urged him to quit using the ugly word "sin." His reasoning was that the youth would be more likely to indulge in sin because the pastor was speaking so plainly about it. The leader suggested to the pastor that he use the words "inhibition," "error," "mistake," or even "a twist in our nature," in place of the word "sin." "I understand what you mean," the preacher said, and going to his desk he took out a bottle. "This bottle," he said, "contains strychnine. You will see the red label here reads 'poison.' Would you suggest that I change the label, and paste one on that says 'wintergreen'? The more harmless the name, the more dangerous the dose will be."

Sin. We don't like to talk much about it, do we? Perhaps some of us would like it re-labeled as an error or mistake, just like the man in that church. But, as children of God, what should be our attitude toward sin? Should we deny it, ignore it, justify it? John gives us two attitudes toward sin in the text we are going to study. And may I say that you either have one or you have the other, and that you cannot have both? Remember that the main idea mentioned in 1 John 1:5, the central theme of John's gospel or message, is the revelation of God's absolute holiness as manifested through the ministry of Jesus Christ's incarnation. God "is light" (vs. 5) and dwells "in the light" (vs. 7), without any hint of darkness at all, "and in Him is no darkness at all" (an emphatic negative in Greek). God does not remove Himself from that sphere of holiness to partnership with man—ever. Man must adjust to the nature of God, through the provision made by Jesus Christ's death, present ministry, and the empowering of the Spirit. Here is where our assurance of eternal life is anchored; and here is where our false assurance is unmasked, so we must keep this main idea in mind during this coming chapter also.[8] As you read the text, notice how many times John mentions the word sin:

1 John 1:8-2:2

> If we say that we have no sin, we deceive ourselves, and the truth is not in us. [9]If we confess our sins, He is faithful and just to forgive us our sins and to cleanse us from all unrighteousness. [10]If we say that we have not sinned, we make Him a liar, and His word is not in us. [2:1]My little children, these things I write to you, so that you may not sin. And if anyone sins, we have an Advocate with the Father, Jesus Christ the righteous. [2]And He Himself is the propitiation for our sins, and not for ours only but also for the whole world (1 John 1:8-2:2).

In the last chapter we learned about *The Character of God* (v 5): He is light! *The Character of Those Walking in Darkness* (v 6): They lie and do not practice the truth. *The Character of Those Walking in Light* (vv 6, 7): They have fellowship with one another and the blood of Jesus Christ cleanses them from all sin!

In this chapter, we'll see that the Apostle John continues reflecting on those who walk in the light and those who walk in darkness. As you read the passage above, did you notice that John mentions the word *sin* seven times in this text? (For some

[8] Obviously, in the forefront of the Apostle John's burden is the false assurance given by the heretical Gnostic teachers. Two Gnostic denials have been covered by the Apostle John so far: the denial of the true humanity of Jesus Christ, which was answered by the incarnation (1:1-4) that could be verified by empirical evidence, and the denial that sin breaks one's partnership with the Father (vs.6-7), which was answered by the revealed holiness of God as manifested in Jesus Christ. This second denial is answered by the foundational truth of verse 5. The fact that God's very nature is revealed holiness also answers the next Gnostic claim of verse 8: "If we say that we have no sin." This is a basic denial that sin exists in our nature.

translations it may be eight times.) Those who walk in the light will have a proper attitude toward sin; those who are not walking in the light will have an improper attitude toward sin. Our outline in this lesson will include those two attitudes toward sin:

The Wrong Attitude toward Sin (1:8 and 1:10)
The Right Attitude toward Sin (1:9 and 2:1-2)

Let's begin by looking at the wrong attitude toward sin. Notice what John says in verse 8.

The Wrong Attitude toward Sin
1 John 1:8

> If we say that we have no sin, we deceive ourselves, and the truth is not in us (1 John 1:8).

Once again John is referring to those who are claiming something verbally—we might call them the "if-we-sayers"—and this time he's referring to their claim to have no sin. In fact, they were boasting about it.[9] The Gnostics claimed to have no sin, because they believed they weren't responsible for the deeds done in the body. The phrase *have no sin* is different than what John will say in verse 10, *have not sinned.* Here in verse 8 the phrase indicates that the Gnostics were denying the whole principle of sin. They denied that sin was a part of their nature. In verse 10 John is referring to their denial of the acts of sin. John includes himself in this by the words *if we say*. He realizes that he too would be in grave danger if

[9] Curiously, Zane Hodges suggests that those making this false claim are genuine Christians: "But when a believer is experiencing true fellowship with God he may then be tempted to think or say that he is, at that moment at least, free from sin" cf. John Walvoord and Roy Zuck, *The Bible Knowledge Commentary* (Wheaton, IL: Victor, 1983), p 885. Yet Hodges is implying that *fellowship* (Greek, koinonia, or partnership in a common interest) is a subjective state that may change or effect the emotional feelings of a believer. When he "feels in fellowship" the temptation to deny sin may come or go. This is not the essence of koinonia. A believer cannot be "in fellowship" one day and "out of fellowship" the next. The word is not limited to active communion between two individuals, but indicates shared partnership in a common concern.

he were to say he had no sin. John says that if we say we have no sin, then two things are true about us. First, we deceive ourselves, and second, the truth is not in us. This is almost identical to what we saw in verse 6 in our last lesson.

If we have the attitude that we do not have sin, John says *we deceive ourselves*, which means literally, "we lead ourselves astray." In this we not only err, but we are responsible for it as well. This is not the person who is deceived without being aware he is deceived, but one who has led himself astray. It is interesting to note here that John does not say we deceive others, or deceive God, but we deceive ourselves. Those who know us well are not deceived by our hypocrisy. And of course we know that with God "all things are naked and open to the eyes of Him to whom we must give account" (Hebrews 4:13).

The second thing that is true about those who say they have no sin is that the truth is not in them. Now, what does John mean by saying that *the truth is not in us*? It means we have misled ourselves concerning the truth of the Gospel or Christ Himself. Jesus Christ is the way, *the truth*, and the life, according to John 14:6. A person can't deny their sin and still believe in the absolute holiness of God as essential to partnership with Him. The Gnostics claimed some special relationship with God, some superior knowledge, and John says, no, in fact, you are proving by your claim to not have sin that you are false and not true believers. The opposite of saying we have no sin is to realize that we do sin and to confess our sins. And this, my friend, is the attitude of those walking in the Light. This is the proper attitude toward sin; this is evidence that you are walking in the light. Look at verse 9.

The Right Attitude toward Sin
1 John 1:9

> If we confess our sins, He is faithful and just to forgive us our sins and to cleanse us from all unrighteousness (1 John 1:9).

The proper attitude toward sin is to admit we do sin and to confess it. What does it mean to *confess our sins*? It means to say the same thing as another; to admit the truth of an accusation. This is a woman who is conscious that she has done wrong; she is convicted that she has sinned, and she admits it. For example, "Lord, I know that my temper today with my child or my husband was sin, as Your Word says I am to put away all anger," or "Lord, I know that my jealousy over this friend is sin, as Your Word says love is not jealous," or "Lord, my frustration today with interruptions by circumstances or people You have allowed is sin, as Your Word says all things work together for my good, even these interruptions You have allowed." A woman who is walking in the Light will be conscious of those things and she will not try to excuse her sin away, but will admit it, confess it, and endeavor to forsake it. The tense here for *confess* is in the present tense and indicates that we keep on confessing. A believer in Jesus Christ is always in the habit of confessing their sins. That is a mark of genuine faith.[10] They have the attitude of the Psalmist in Psalm 32:5, who said: "I acknowledged my sin to You, and my iniquity I have not hidden. I said, 'I will confess my transgressions to the LORD,' and You forgave the iniquity of my sin."

Perhaps we should define what sin is here since John mentions it so much. *Sin* is lawlessness or transgression of God's will, either by failing to do what God's law requires or by doing what it forbids. For example, in this epistle John will tell us to that we are to love the brethren—that is something the law requires of us. But he will also tell us we are not to hate our brother—that is something that the law forbids. The transgression can occur in thought, word, or deed. The sins here that John mentions refer to are definite, specific acts of sin. To *confess our sins* is to name the specific sins, as I have just given examples. Now John is talking about confessing our sins to God, because the context says *He* is faithful to forgive and *He* is faithful to cleanse us from all unrighteousness. But may I also say that we should be confessing our sins to others when we need to? James says, in James 5:16, "Confess your trespasses to one another, and

[10] See Appendix A: Two Major Interpretations of 1 John 1:9.

pray for one another, that you may be healed. The effective, fervent prayer of a righteous man avails much." In other words, if I have lied to you, or have become angry with you, then I need to seek your forgiveness for those specific sins and turn away from such evil.

John now gives the first benefit of confessing our sins. Isn't it interesting that just as there are two consequences of saying we have no sin, there are two consequences for those who admit their sin and confess it? The first consequence is that God will be *faithful and just to forgive us our sins*. What does it mean that He is *faithful*? It means that He is dependable; we can count on Him to forgive us. He is faithful to forgive us. He is faithful to the covenant which He made. Psalm 103:12 states, "As far as the east is from the west, so far has He removed our transgressions from us." He is not only faithful, but John says He is *just*, which means that God cannot overlook our sin; He cannot let us get away with it. He also is just in the sense that it would be wrong—it would be unjust—if He withheld His forgiveness of our sins. His faithfulness and justice are not dependent on our confession, but rather when we do confess we will find Him to be faithful and just. And what is He faithful and just to do? He is faithful and just *to forgive us our sins. Forgive* means to send away; it is a cancellation of debts, or a dismissal of charges. The Greek term often refers to releasing a person from a legal obligation such as a debt (see Matthew 18:23-35).

The second benefit of confessing our sins is that He will *cleanse us from all unrighteousness*. To *cleanse* means to make holy or purify. Notice that the cleansing here is from *all* unrighteousness, just as in verse 7 the cleansing is from *all* sin. Amazing! And this cleansing is applied by the blood of Jesus Christ, as we also saw in verse 7. We might ask the question, "So, how is it that Christians are cleansed from sin, if they still sin? How are they saved from sin, if they still sin?" The answer is that we are saved from the power and influence of sin. Sin has no more mastery over us or power over us, as Paul says in Romans 6:6, 7: "knowing this, that our old man was crucified with Him, that the body of sin might be done away with, that we should no longer be slaves of sin. For he who has died has been freed from sin." What is the proper attitude toward sin? It is to admit it and confess it.[11]

John now goes back to mention those who will continue to say they have not sinned, in verse 10, and adds two more consequences of that improper attitude.

The Wrong Attitude toward Sin
1 John 1:10

> If we say that we have not sinned, we make Him a liar, and His word is not in us (1 John 1:10).

Here again we have the "if-we-sayers." This time John is referring to their claim that they have not sinned. While verse 8 describes those who deny that sin is even a part of their nature, verse 10 is focused on those who deny that they have ever committed a single act of sin. This Gnostic claim is the most radical of all, because it not only contradicts universal experience but it also rejects the clear testimony of Scripture, which teaches the universality of sin[12] (e.g., 1 Kings 8:46; Job 4:17; 15:14-16; Psalm 14:3; Proverbs 20:9;

[11] To summarize thus far, a true believers "walks in light" and cannot "walk in darkness." For this view, fellowship cannot be lost by the believer. The biblical position is that John is describing a characteristic of a false professor, i.e., denial of sin, with self-deception, and a characteristic of a genuine possessor, i.e., confession of sin, with forgiveness and cleansing. God's forgiveness and cleansing of the believer's sins are not dependent on their confession of specific sins on a sin-by-sin basis. The condition is that they are, as believers sharing in the New Covenant promise, characterized by continually confessing their sins as they grow in an intimate relationship with God, who has revealed Himself as holy!

[12] Strong gives a biblical and good theological definition of sin: "Sin is lack of conformity to the moral law of God, either in act, disposition or state" cf. Augustus Hopkins Strong, *Systematic* Theology (Old Tappan, NJ: Fleming H. Revell, 1976) p 549; or as the Westminster Shorter Catechism states, "sin is any want of conformity unto or transgression of, the Law of God" cf. Philip Schaff, ed., *Westminster Shorter Catechism: The Creeds of Christendom* (Grand Rapids, MI: Baker, 1919), p 678; cf. 1 John 3:4; 5:17 with Matthew 5:27-28; Jeremiah 17:9 James 4:17; Leviticus 5:17-19). To be sinless would necessitate total conformity to the moral law of God in act, disposition and state, in all behavior, in all thoughts and in the total person.

Ecclesiastes 7:20; Isaiah 53:6; 64:6; Romans 3:10-14, 23, etc.). The verb translated *have not sinned* (Greek, ouch hemartekamen) is in the perfect tense, suggesting that this refers to a past act with present results, meaning that they were denying past acts of sin and present responsibility or guilt. This is not only the claim that they were not sinning in the present, but that they were in the state of never having committed sin! I have met people like this and, let me tell you, they are difficult to be around. Now I would trust that most of us would say, "I know I sin." Though many of us would say we do sin, many of us are also pretty good about justifying our sin or blaming someone else for our sin. We add excuses like, "If only *they* hadn't done . . ." or "I was tired," or "I was lonely," or "I was hungry," or "I was fearful," "I was menopausal," "It was that time of the month," or "I'm pregnant." And when we do so, we still are not coming clean with ourselves or with God by admitting we have sinned.

So if we say we have never committed an act of sin, what does this say about us? Well, John says *we make Him a liar*. What does it mean that we make God a *liar*? How can we make God a liar when we know God cannot lie? What John is saying here is that we *accuse* God of lying. Think with me for a minute: God says very clearly that all have sinned and come short of the glory of God; there is not a just man upon the earth who does good and sins not; all we like sheep have gone astray, we have turned everyone to his own way. And on and on God says in His Word that we are all sinners and we all sin. So to say we have not sinned is to deny the principle of sin and to make God a liar. And, ladies, that is a serious accusation against a perfect, holy God! Again, let me bring out this truth: God does not lie! Numbers 23:19 states, "God is not a man, that He should lie." If we have no sin, then there is no need for a Savior, no need for Him to be our atoning sacrifice, as John will say in chapter 2, verse 2.

The second thing it says about us if we claim we have no sin is that *His word is not in us*. John said in verse 8 that the truth is not in us, and now he says that God's *word* is not in us. What is the difference? The truth is embodied in a Person, Jesus Christ; it is personal. His *word* is the idea of the Word of God or what He has said. And John says His word is no way in us! John is saying that if Jesus Christ is in us, if we have the truth, then we will love His Word, we will love what He says. But if He is not in us, then His Word is not in us, and we will have no regard for it or place for it in our lives.

In verses 1 and 2 of chapter 2, John continues on with the proper attitude toward sin. (This is one of those unfortunate chapter divisions. Remember, the translators came in and divided up the chapters and verses—they are not inspired!) And as he continues his thoughts regarding sin, John also includes another of his purposes for writing this epistle.

The Right Attitude toward Sin 1 John 2:1-2

> My little children, these things I write to you, so that you may not sin. And if anyone sins, we have an Advocate with the Father, Jesus Christ the righteous (1 John 2:1-2).

Why does John call them little children? *Little children* is a term of affection from this aged old apostle. It literally means "little born ones," and is a term he uses for them numerous times (2:12, 13, 18, 28; 3:7, 18; 4:4; 5:21). He also gives a second purpose for writing this epistle. In chapter 1, verse 4, we saw that one of his purposes for writing was in order that they would have joy, and here we see that his second purpose for writing is that they may not sin. What does John mean when he says *that you may not sin*? It means that he desires that they will avoid sin, refuse sin, and run from sin. Simply put, John did not want them to sin! The Apostle Paul felt the same way, as he told the church at Corinth that He was jealous over them with godly jealousy; he feared for them, to the point that he encouraged them to examine themselves to see if they were in the faith. The church at Corinth was involved in strife and backbiting and the like. The apostles knew there would be an accounting day and, because of that, they did not want their spiritual children to sin.

Many of us have felt the same way about children we have brought up to fear and to love God and women we have poured our lives into and mentored. Some perhaps get involved in sin and we grieve for them. We desire that they would not sin in the same way we desire that for ourselves. Do you know that should be the goal of all who believe in Jesus Christ? I fear many of us love sin, and I say that because many times we choose to sin instead of avoiding it. Jesus said in the Sermon on the Mount, "Therefore you shall be perfect, just as your Father in heaven is perfect." Peter tells us in 1 Peter 1:15-16, "but as He who called you is holy, you also be holy in all your conduct, because it is written, 'Be holy, for I am holy.'" Or again Paul says in Romans 6:1, "What shall we say then? Shall we continue in sin that grace may abound?" Even John will address this here in 1 John 3:1-3: "Behold what manner of love the Father has bestowed on us, that we should be called children of God! Therefore the world does not know us, because it did not know Him. Beloved, now we are children of God; and it has not yet been revealed what we shall be, but we know that when He is revealed, we shall be like Him, for we shall see Him as He is. And everyone who has this hope in Him purifies himself, just as He is pure." This is yet another proper attitude for those who walk in the light—they hate sin, they run from it, they avoid it.

John doesn't want them to sin, and yet he realizes that they will sin—he knows that perfection won't happen until glory—and so he says that *if anyone sins we have an Advocate with the Father, Jesus Christ the righteous*. Even though the goal for all believers is holiness and perfection, we will still sin (hopefully less and less every day!). But when we do sin, we have an advocate with the Father, Jesus Christ the righteous. We don't have to confess to a priest but can go straight to our advocate. What is an *advocate*? The Greek word, parakletos, means an intercessor or consoler. So it would be one who is called to stand by us or defend us. An advocate in a courtroom would be the one who defends their client. Christ defends us as not being guilty because of His shed blood. This is a blessed truth, my dear friend, because it tells me that my Lord not only loved me so much that He came to earth to die for me, but He continues to love me as evidenced by His continually pleading on my behalf before the Father. Why does John say He is *with the Father*? This speaks of the intimate relationship between the Son and the Father; Jesus is face to face with His Father. As He put it well in John 10:30, "I and My Father are one."

Why does John call him *Jesus Christ the righteous*? Because in the Greek there is no article, the phrase simply reads, "Jesus Christ righteous." Acting as defense attorney Jesus doesn't use tricks to get his client off; there is no plea-bargaining; He admits the guilt of the client and pleads on our behalf because He Himself has paid the penalty for our sin. The debt for our sin has been paid and He bears the wounds to prove it.[13] As 1 John 1:9 explains, Jesus Christ, being righteous, is the only one who can cleanse us from all unrighteousness. And not only is He our advocate, but John also tells us another wonderful truth about our Savior in verse 2.

> And He Himself is the propitiation for our sins, and not for ours only but also for the whole world (1 John 2:2).

What does it mean that He is *the propitiation for our sins*? It means that He, Himself, is the atonement for our sins; He is the atoning sacrifice for our sins. The word *propitiation* was used in secular writing for a sacrifice that would appease the wrath of an angry god. This would seem to suggest that God is justifiably angry at sin.

---

[13] The context undoubtedly is a legal one. The next verse refers to the Day of Atonement, when, according to Jewish interpretive translation of Leviticus 16, Satan was deprived of his power. The ancient role of Satan in relation to sinning believers is one of legal accuser (cf. Job 1:6-2:7; Zechariah 3:1-3). And here, Jesus Christ the Righteous One is seen as challenging Satan's role (cf. 1 John 3:8) by pleading the Christian's cause before God. The sense of the paragraph is: although false professors (i.e., the Gnostic secessionists) claim they have never sinned, genuine believers are characterized by confessing their sin, with the provision of the advocacy ministry of Jesus Christ.

Psalm 7:11 tells us that God is angry with the wicked every day. His Son, Jesus Christ, being the atoning sacrifice, the propitiation, made it possible to appease the wrath of God upon man's sin. We do sin, and therefore we are in need of someone to be the propitiation, the atoning sacrifice, for our sins, and that someone is Jesus Christ the righteous. And John says that not only is He the propitiation for our sins but also *for the sins of the whole world.* You might ask, is John a universalist? Does he think the whole world is going to be saved? No, John is not a universalist. More than likely, because John was a Jew, he was writing to a Jewish audience. When he is referring to the *whole world*, he means the Gentiles nations as well as the Jews. In Romans 11 we have the passage which deals with Israel's rejection of Christ. Because of Israel's rejection of Christ, Paul mentions the blessed privilege of the Gentiles being grafted into the olive tree. In other words, salvation is being offered to the Gentiles. John is referring to the Gentile nations as *the world* in verses 12 and 15.

It also could be a reference to what most of us have learned as a child, and that is from John 3:16, "For God so loved the world that He gave His only begotten Son, that whoever believes in Him should not perish but have everlasting life." The sense being that Christ loved the whole world and that He died for the whole world—but only those who believe and truly repent of their sins have the wonderful blessing of having their sins atoned for (see Appendix A). How can we continue to live in sin when Jesus Christ the righteous has sacrificed so much to atone for our sins?

Summary

In this chapter, we have seen *The Wrong Attitude toward Sin* (1:8 and 10): What is the wrong attitude toward sin? It is to deny the fact that we have a sin nature and to deny personal acts of sin. And we have seen *The Right Attitude toward Sin* (1:9 and 2:1-2): What is the right attitude toward sin? It is to admit it, confess it, hate it, run from it, and avoid it.

What is your attitude toward sin this day? Do you deny sin is a part of your nature? Do you deny specific acts of sin? Do you say that you have no sin? Do you justify your sin or minimize it? Do you call your sin a mistake? If so, then, my friend, you have deceived yourself, the truth is not in you, you have made God a liar, and His Word is not in you. Or, do you confess your sins? Do you run from sin, avoid it, and hate it? If so, then He is faithful and just to forgive your sins, to cleanse you, to plead with the Father on your behalf. What great promises for those who walk in the light!

Perhaps you are walking in the light this day, but you are struggling with an area of sin. May I lovingly suggest to you to not only kill sin in your members but find a person who will hold you accountable and pray for you? God never meant for us to go alone in our walk. Titus 2:1-5 is very clear about our responsibility to one another! Don't ever let pride keep you from getting help and from asking others to pray for you as you struggle with sin. I would echo the aged old apostle, who appealed to these believers to sin not! May we all have the attitude of the evangelist Billy Sunday, who said,

> "I'm against sin. I'll kick it as long as I've got a foot, and I'll fight it as long as I've got a fist. I'll butt it as long as I've got a head. I'll bite it as long as I've got a tooth. When I'm old and fistless and footless and toothless, I'll gum it till I go home to Glory and it goes home to perdition!"

Questions to Consider

What is Your Attitude toward Sin?

1 John 1:8-2:2

1. Read 1 John 1:1-2:2. (a) What repeated themes or words does John use in this passage? (b) Why do you think John repeats himself? (c) What do you think it means "to deceive ourselves," as it says in verse 8?

2. Memorize 1 John 2:1.

3. John says, "If we say that we have no sin, we deceive ourselves" (1 John 1:8) (a) List the other things that we can be deceived about, according to the following verses: Matthew 24:1-13; 1 Corinthians 3:18-23; 1 Corinthians 6:9, 10; 1 Corinthians 15:33; Galatians 6:3, 7, 8; James 1:22; James 1:26 (b) Looking back at these verses in their context, what is the remedy for self-deception?

4. (a) How could you use the following verses to confront the error of those who say that they have no sin? Ecclesiastes 7:20; Isaiah 53:6; 64:6; Romans 3:10-23. (b) What is the solution to the error of their way? See Psalm 32:5.

5. (a) What roles do Jesus Christ our Advocate and the Holy Spirit our Advocate play? See John 14:16, 26; 15:26; 16:7-15; Romans 8:26; Romans 8:34; Hebrews 4:14-16. (b) How do these verses encourage you as you walk through this life?

6. (a) What does Proverbs 28:13 say? (b) Are you in the habit of confessing your sins before God and others?

7. (a) Take some time this week to read and pray through Psalms 6, 32, 38, and 51. These are Penitential Psalms (Psalms of Repentance). (b) Do your attitudes toward sin match those of the Psalmist?

8. (a) Do you justify your sin or blame others for your sin? (b) After studying this passage, what do you believe the proper attitude toward sin should be? (c) What changes will *you* now make?

9. What sins in your life need to be eradicated? Write a prayer request addressed to your Advocate, Jesus Christ the Righteous!

Chapter 4

Does Your Talk Match Your Walk?

1 John 2:3-6

A question I often hear from believers is, "How can I know for certain that I am a Christian?" Many believers struggle with assurance and wonder if they really have made Christ Lord of their life. So, how does one know for sure that they are among the redeemed, and that they will for sure enter into the Kingdom of Heaven? Isn't it wonderful that God does not play "hide and seek" with us when it comes to our assurance? There are certain tests that He has left for us in His Word which validate whether or not we are His children. John gives us two of those evidences in this lesson that reveal if in fact we are truly born again. It is not in what we say, but it is in what we do. It is not in how we talk, but in how we walk. Let's look at this together and read 1 John 2:3-6.

1 John 2:3-6

> Now by this we know that we know Him, if we keep His commandments. 4He who says, "I know Him," and does not keep His commandments, is a liar, and the truth is not in him. 5But whoever keeps His word, truly the love of God is perfected in him. By this we know that we are in Him. 6He who says he abides in Him ought himself also to walk just as He walked (1 John 2:3-6).

We learned in our last lesson that there are two attitudes towards sin: *The Right Attitude toward Sin* (1:8 and 10), and *The Wrong Attitude toward Sin* (1:9 and 2:1-2). The wrong attitude, found in verses 8 and 10, is to make some denial of the fact that we have a sin nature and to deny personal acts of sin. The right attitude, found in chapter 1, verse 9, and in chapter 2, verses 1 and 2, is to admit it, confess it, hate it, run from it, and avoid it.[14] In this lesson, we'll see:

The Test of Obeying His Word (vv 3-5)
The Test of Walking His Walk (v 6)

Since John is on the topic of sin it only makes sense that he now writes regarding the importance of keeping God's commandments, since we know that sin is anything which is a violation of what God has commanded us to do in His Word. And so we come to a valid proof that we are His children, and that is the test of obeying His Word, in verses 3-5.

The Test of Obeying His Word
1 John 2:3-5

> Now by this we know that we know Him, if we keep His commandments (1 John 2:3).

Did you notice John did not say, we know we know Him if we walked down an aisle at a revival; we know Him if we said a prayer and asked Him into our hearts; we know Him if we have some fuzzy feeling at church; or that we know Him if we made some decision at church camp? John said none of that, did he? There is a valid test to make certain one is a believer in Jesus Christ, and it has nothing to do with the past but everything to do with the present. It has to do with keeping His commandments. John says we can know—we can be sure—that we know Him. How can I know for certain that I am a Christian? John says, "Here it is, the answer

---

14 Thus far John has confronted four heretical Gnostic claims: the claim that Jesus Christ was not really incarnated (1:1-4); the claim that they could partnership with God and walk in darkness (1:6-7); the claim that sin did not exist in their nature (1:8-9); and the claim that they had never sinned (1:10-2:2). He has also clearly stated the main idea of his gospel message, i.e., that God has revealed Himself as holy, through the Person of Jesus Christ and there is no hint of darkness in Him (1:5). First John 2:3 begins the body of the epistle, by surfacing one of the great questions of both ancient and modern man, i.e., "How can I know for certain that I know Jesus Christ?"

you've been waiting for: You can be sure you know Him if you keep His commandments."

What does it mean to *know Him*? To know Him expresses absolute, immediate knowledge of a fact, once for all. It does not mean that we have come to know about Him, but that we have come to know Him. It is the Greek word which means to know experientially, in contrast to knowing by intuition. The present tense of *knowing* (Greek, ginoskomen) brings out the day-by-day knowledge which is constantly being confirmed; the perfect tense of the term (Greek, egnokamen) speaks of the past act which has present results. A literal translation may be, "Now, by this we are knowing that we have come to know Him." But what is this knowing? The Greek word is not oida, which refers to knowing by reflection, making reference to intuition or information. Instead, the word is ginosko, which is knowledge by observation and experience. John selects this word to contrast with the Gnostic secessionists, who believed that their special revelation knowledge gave them special insight and information.[15] Because it is in the perfect tense, it speaks of a past experience with continuing effects. It could be rendered, "know we that we have come to know and still know him."[16] Our redemption is continuously manifested by our sanctification, by our conformity

---

[15] Recent scholarship challenges the sharp distinction between the Greek terms ginosko and oida. Burdick summarizes the positions: "Many have assumed that this kind of distinction consistently governs all New Testament occurrences of the two verbs. Among those who have held to this view are Lightfoot, Godet, H. Cremer, Westcott, Law, Plummer, Brooke, Robertson, Vincent, Lenski, and Hendriksen. Others such as Dodd, J. H. Bernard, H. Seesemann, Barrett, Nigel Turner, and Morris, have concluded that the distinction between the two verbs no longer existed in Hellenistic Greek. As with many things, the truth seems to lie between the two extremes … each occurrence must be examined independently and interpreted in the light of its own context" (cf. Donald W. Burdick, *The Letters of John the Apostle: An In-depth Commentary* (Chicago, IL: Moody Press, 1985), p 133; Richard N. Longnecker and Merrill C. Tenney, editors. *New Dimensions in the New Testament Study*, "Oida and Ginosko in the Pauline Epistles" by Donald W. Burdick, p 354). Burdick states on p 133 of his commentary, however, that in 1 John 2:3 and 2:29 the classical meaning of ginosko, "knowledge gained by experience," is used.

[16] *Robertson's Word Pictures in the New Testament*, Electronic Database (Biblesoft, 1997), and *Robertson's Word Pictures in the New Testament* (Broadman Press, 1985).

to the person of Jesus Christ. So to know Christ means that we have a personal relationship with Him, and it is a relationship that will continue to the end.

Some people will tell you that they know about Christ or they believe in God. They might even believe in His works, His death, His burial, and His resurrection, but does that equate with a personal relationship with Him? I can know facts about Christ and yet not know Him personally in the sense that John is saying here. For example, I may say to you, "I know President Obama." But what I mean is that I know facts about him. He is the president; he has two daughters; his wife is Michelle. There are other things that I know about him because I read the newspaper or watch the news on television. But do I know him? Do I have a personal relationship with Him? No I don't, as I have never even met the man! We must be so careful in assuming that others are believers because they say they know Christ. They may read about Him in the Bible, they may hear about Him at church or from the lips of others, but does that equate a personal relationship with Him? No! In fact, recorded for us in the High Priestly Prayer in John 17, Jesus prays concerning this truth in verse 3, where He says, "And this is eternal life, that they may know You, the only true God, and Jesus Christ whom You have sent." Jesus knew that knowing God in the true sense was equated with life eternal. James even tells us in his epistle that the demons believe and yet they tremble (James 2:19). The demons do not know God in the true sense.

The Gnostics boasted of their superior knowledge of Christ, and John challenges them and the readers of this epistle by saying that knowing God is not just possessing some superior knowledge. Instead, it is a knowledge that leads to action, and that action is keeping His commandments. The Gnostics professed superior knowledge about God, but it did not lead them to be holy in any sense. So John says, you can know for sure that you know Him, if you keep His commandments. What does it mean to *keep His commandments*? *Keep* here has the idea of a spirit of obedience. It means to guard and keep safe as a precious thing. By the way, this guarding and keeping is not done because we have to, but because we want to. John will tell us later on in his letter, in 1 John 5:3, "For this is the love of God, that we keep His commandments. And His commandments are not burdensome." The keeping of God's commands is not burdensome—they aren't irksome, they aren't weighty, and they aren't heavy. What did Jesus say in Matthew 11:28-30? "Come to Me, all you who labor and are heavy laden, and I will give you rest. Take My yoke upon you and learn from Me, for I am gentle and lowly in heart, and you will find rest for your souls. For My yoke is easy and My burden is light." Obeying God is not a burden; it is a joy, and it is freeing. Sin is heavy; sin is a burden.

I know people who claim to know Christ and yet they refuse to follow the Lord in baptism. They don't think it's necessary, or they're uncomfortable getting up in front of people, so they disregard His commandment to be baptized. It is a burden to them. Or, another person will say, "I am a Christian, but I don't need to go to church. I can worship God here at home. I can watch sermons on television or listen to sermons online." They neglect to obey Hebrews 10:25, "not forsaking the assembling of ourselves together, as is the manner of some, but exhorting one another, and so much the more as you see the Day approaching," which, by the way, is a command. They think it is a burden. It disrupts their Sunday and the things they want to do with their time. It is a burden to them to get up, and get the kids dressed and go to church. It is a burden to miss their sporting events or other things they want to do. That type of thinking is foreign to New Testament Christianity. It should be a joy and delight to obey the Lord. We do not have the option of only keeping the commandments that we find convenient. The Christian life is not a spiritual smorgasbord where I can pick and choose what I want to obey or not obey. Some of us love buffets, don't we? (My husband loves the Golden Corral.) Some of us like buffets because we can pick and choose what we want to eat, and I confess to you I usually pick and choose the things that are probably not too good for me, and I eat way too much. But we cannot treat God's Word like a spiritual buffet, picking and choosing what we want to obey or not obey.

For example, you may have awakened this morning and said, "Self, I don't feel like being submissive to my husband today, so I don't think I will," or "I don't feel like being kind to that picky neighbor, so I won't," or "I think I will tell my friend that juicy piece of gossip." We don't have that option. How do you feel when your children deliberately disobey you? It grieves you, doesn't it? And yet I fear we greatly grieve the Lord when we deliberately choose not to obey what He has commanded us to do in His Word.

By the way, the Greek tense here of the word *keep* means to keep on keeping. It describes one who goes on and on and on keeping God's commandments. Hebrews 3:6 and 14 and 6:11 all describe the genuine believer who goes on to the end. Now since John says we are to keep His commandments, we might stop and define a commandment. What is a *commandment*? The Greek word here is entole, which refers to the precepts of Christ. It would entail anything that is a revelation of God's will. The word commandment also is mentioned 14 times in 1 John, which is more than any other New Testament book. Jesus made it clear that this is something we are to teach when we go and make converts as mentioned in Matthew 28:19-20 where He says, "Go therefore and make disciples of all the nations, baptizing them in the name of the Father and of the Son and of the Holy Spirit, teaching them to observe *all things that I have commanded you;* and lo, I am with you always, even to the end of the age," (emphasis mine). It is unfortunate that when some share the gospel of Jesus Christ they fail to mention that being a Christian is more than coming to Christ as you are and enjoying the abundant life. They fail to compel others to consider the cost of the cross, and that one's life must be surrendered to another Master and to His Lordship.

You might say, "Susan, you're making this really hard. There is no way I can keep all of His commandments." You're right,

without Him and without the enabling of His Spirit you can't. The good news about keeping His commandments is what Jesus just said in Matthew 28, "I am with you always," or as he said in John 15:5, "without Me you can do nothing." On our own we cannot, but with Christ and with the power of the Holy Spirit we can keep His commandments. I once read about a man who was so disturbed about the fact that His fellowship with God was not right, that he stayed up reading the Word of God until he found which commandment he was disobeying. Are you that serious about obeying the Word of God? What did Jesus say in Luke 6:46? "But why do you call Me 'Lord, Lord,' and do not do the things which I say?" Jesus knew that a claim to His Lordship without obeying His Lordship was no Lordship! John goes on to write concerning the danger we are in if we claim Him as our Lord but do not conform to His Lordship.

> He who says, "I know Him," and does not keep His commandments, is a liar, and the truth is not in him (1 John 2:4).

In verse 4, we have the "if-we-sayers" again. (See verse 6, 8, 10.) It is a heartache to hear people say, "I know Him," but yet do not obey Him. The keeping of His commandments here is the same idea as seen in the previous verse. It is a constant, continuous watching over His commandments, not an occasional, whenever-I-feel-like-it kind of keeping His commandments. How can a person claim to know God, and yet not obey His laws? John says, if you say that you know Him and yet do not keep his commandments, then there are two things that are true about you. Number one—you are a liar. Number two—the truth is not in you. These people, John says, are liars and the truth is not in them. (See 1:6, 1:8 and 1:10 for similar ideas.) What does it mean to be *a liar*? It means that the whole character is false. Albert Barnes says it is one who "makes a false profession; professes to have that which he really has not. Such a profession is a falsehood, because there can be no true religion where one does not obey the law of God."[17]

---

[17] From *Barnes' Notes*, Electronic Database (Biblesoft, 1997).

If you have ever been around a person who lies you know that you cannot trust anything they say. And it is not only the things that they say that you cannot trust, but the whole of their life is false. Their principles, their lifestyle, their conduct, their goals in life—everything about them is a sham. So John says, not only are these people liars, but the truth is not in them. What does it mean that *the truth is not in him*? This is emphatic in the Greek and it literally means, "in this one the truth is not." Simply put, it means that there is no eternal life. Jesus, who is the way and the truth and the life, is not dwelling within this individual. Listen to what A.T. Robertson said about this verse:

> This is one of the pious platitudes, cheap claptrap of the Gnostics, who would bob up in meetings with such explosions. (I know him, I know him.) John punctures such bubbles with the sharp addition "and keepeth not" "The one who keeps on saying: 'I have come to know him,' and keeps on not keeping his commandments is a liar," just like Satan. There is a whip-cracker effect in John's words.[18]

John now contrasts the one who doesn't keep God's Word with the one who does, in verse 5.

> But whoever keeps His word, truly the love of God is perfected in him. By this we know that we are in Him (1 John 1:5)

The word *but* indicates a contrast between those who say they know God and yet don't keep His commandments, and those who say they know God and do keep His commandments. *Whoever* is also a very important term that we would do well to consider. Remember, the Gnostics claimed that a relationship with God was just for the elite, for those in the know. But John says no, whoever keeps His word, in him is the love of God perfected! It is not just for the elite; it is for anyone who will obey God!

[18] From *Robertson's Word Pictures in the New Testament*, Electronic Database (Biblesoft, 1997), and *Robertson's Word Pictures in the New Testament* (Broadman Press, 1985).

What does it mean to *keep His Word*? It means to guard or to keep an eye on. The tense indicates that it is to keep on keeping. It is a continual guarding of the Word, not just a sporadic guarding or whenever I feel like it. What is the *Word*? It includes all He has made known to us. John says whoever keeps His Word *truly the love of God is perfected in him*. Now the word *truly* is another word that is important in this verse; it means verily, or of a truth. John once again is stating that this prize is truly opened to all, not just confined to a few initiated Gnostics.

What does John mean when He says that if we keep His Word, *the love of God is perfected* in us? Well, the Greek word *love* is agape. The word *perfected* means complete. In other words, we prove our love for God, and our love for God is perfected or made complete, by our obedience. Look over at our Lord's words in John 14:15, 21-24; 15:10-14 for a further understanding of what John is saying. Jesus, in the Upper Room, relays to his disciples that if they really love God it will manifest itself in their obedience. Ladies, our love for God should be a motivation for obedience.

Then John repeats what he has already said in verse 3, *by this we know that we are in Him*. Or as he said in verse 3, *by this we know that we know Him*. By this, by keeping His Word, this is how we know that we are in Him—not by mouth confession, but by obedience. This is how we know that we know Him. John now turns from the test of obedience to the test of walking His walk.

The Test of Walking His Walk
1 John 2:6

> He who says he abides in Him ought himself also to walk just as He walked (1 John 2:6).

John now turns from those who claim they know Him to those who also claim they abide in Him. John says if you are going to make the claim that you abide in Him, then you must walk just like

He did. What does it mean to *abide in Him*? It means to remain in Him. This abiding is a lasting condition, without intermission. Jesus makes it very clear in John 15 (see the "Questions to Consider" at the end of this chapter) that those who claim attachment to the vine will indeed abide in the vine. In John 15:4-7, Jesus says,

> Abide in Me, and I in you. As the branch cannot bear fruit of itself, unless it abides in the vine, neither can you, unless you abide in Me. I am the vine, you are the branches. He who abides in Me, and I in him, bears much fruit; for without Me you can do nothing. If anyone does not abide in Me, he is cast out as a branch and is withered; and they gather them and throw them into the fire, and they are burned. If you abide in Me, and My words abide in you, you will ask what you desire, and it shall be done for you.

Judas had just gone out to betray our Lord when Jesus spoke these words to the eleven remaining disciples, and it is as if He is pleading with them that unless they remain attached to Him, they too could prove to be false like Judas. Remember, John, the one who was leaning on Jesus' breast, was there when Christ said these words recorded in John 15 and he knew that the branches could only draw life from the True Vine. We receive life and nourishment and everything we have from the Vine. As Jesus said, "Without me you can do nothing." John perhaps is reflecting on these words of Jesus as he writes this letter to his little children. And so to those who say they abide in Christ, John says, you ought *to walk just as He walked.* The word *ought* expresses a special, personal obligation. For example, if I borrow money from you, I ought to pay it back. It is my moral obligation to you. John is saying, you owe this to God after all He has done for you. He has sent His son to be the propitiation for your sins, as we saw in our last lesson. It is your moral obligation to walk as He walked.

What does it mean to *walk*? It comes from a word which means to walk about or around, as well as to walk in an orderly manner following a prescribed pattern. So we might say that walking means to follow a pattern or a rule. When I was in school I took a sewing class. I remember we had to trace the pattern on the material so that we knew where to cut and sew. We had to follow the pattern exactly or our garment would not turn out. (Mine were interesting indeed!) That is the idea here. We follow His footsteps; we trace the pattern He has set for us; and we walk the way He walked. It is like the idea that was popularized several years ago even to the point that people were wearing bracelets with the letters "WWJD"—What Would Jesus Do? We should ask, "What would Jesus do?" "What would Jesus say?" "Where would Jesus go?" In this way, walking would also indicate progress. When you walk, you don't just stand still in one place, you move forward, you move on, you progress. So it would indicate that we are growing as we walk; we are making progress.

John already mentioned in 1:7 that we are to walk in the light as He is in the light. We saw then that walking in the Light means we are to reflect that Light. In fact, the word *Christian* means a follower of Christ. By the way, this again is a continuous performance, not a spasmodic spurt. One man has said, "The test of our religious experience is whether it produces a reflection of the life of Jesus in our daily life; if it fails this elementary test, it is false."[19] Our actions should be consistent with our words, should they not? I have had conversations with well meaning Christians, and you probably have too, who desperately hope their loved one is a believer in Jesus Christ based on some past decision. And yet when you probe you find out that loved one does not abide in Christ. There is no hunger for the Word; there is no desire for obedience; there is no desire to be with God's people or to be in God's house. In fact, some have not entered into a church door for years. That type of Christianity is foreign to New Testament Christianity and what Christ and the apostles taught.

---

19 I. Howard Marshall, *The New International Commentary on the New Testament: The Epistles of John* (Grand Rapids, MI: Eerdmans, 1978), p 128.

Summary

So let's summarize the two tests John mentions: *The Test of Obeying His Word* (vv 3-5), and *The Test of Walking His Walk* (v 6). If you are struggling with your assurance today, it may be that you are not a believer, or it may be due to the fact that you are not keeping some of His commandments. Is there some known sin in your life? Are you keeping His commandments? Are you keeping all of them? I would encourage you to be diligent to seek the face of the Lord and ask Him to show you if you are just an "if-we-sayer," or if there perhaps is some sin that is causing you to doubt your relationship with Him. Secondly, are you walking His walk? Does your life reflect the life of the Savior? Are you doing as He would do? Are you saying what He would say? Are you going where He would go? There is a rather sobering thought found in the cathedral at Lubek, Germany, which perhaps is a good summary of what John is saying in these few verses we have covered.

> You call me Master, and obey Me not; You call me Light, and seek Me not; You call me Way, and Walk Me not; You call me Wise, and follow Me not; You call me Fair, and love Me not; You call me Rich and ask Me not; You call me Eternal, and seek me not; You call me Gracious, and trust me not; You call me Noble, and serve Me not; You call me Mighty, and honor me not; You call me Just, and fear me not; If I condemn you, blame me not.

Questions to Consider

Does Your Talk Match Your Walk?

1 John 2:3-6

1. Read 1 John 2:3-6. (a) What things do you see in these verses that are similar to what John has already said in 1 John 1:1-2:2? (b) Why are these repeated things important?

2. Memorize 1 John 2:4.

3. John says that one of the ways we can be certain that we know God is by our obedience to His commandments (2:3). (a) What other ways can we be certain that we know God, according to the following passages in 1 John? 1:3; 1:7; 1:9; 2:15; 3:3; 3:9; 3:13; 3:14; 3:18, 19; 3:22; 4:13; 5:18, 19. (b) Would you say you know God after looking at these verses? (c) What are some other evidences by which one can know for sure he/she is a believer? (Use Scripture other than 1 John to back up your answer.)

4. (a) What are some of the benefits of keeping God's commandments? See Psalm 119:6, 9; Ecclesiastes 8:5; John 14:21-24; John 15:10, 14; Hebrews 5:9; 1 John 3:22-24; Revelation 22:14. (b) What are the dangers of not keeping His commandments? See Deuteronomy 11:26-28; 1 Samuel 12:15; Proverbs 19:16; Luke 6:47-49; Romans 2:8, 9; 2 Thessalonians 1:7-10; James 1:22; 1 John 2:4.

5. (a) What do you think John means in 1 John 2:6 by "abiding" in Him? (b) According to Jesus' words in John 15:1-14, what are the evidences of those who abide in Him? Also, see 1 John 3:6 for another evidence. (c) What does Jesus say (in John 15:1-14) will happen to those who do not abide in Him?

6. John says that if we abide in Christ then we should walk as He walked (2:6). (a) According to the following passages, what are some of the ways that Christ walked while He was here on earth? Matthew 9:36; 20:27, 28; John 6:38; 8:29; 13:4, 5; Ephesians

5:2; Hebrews 5:8; 1 Peter 2:21-23; 1 John 3:16. (b) Would you say these things are evident in your life, since we are "to walk just as He walked"? (c) What changes do you need to make to conform to what Christ would have you to do?

7. (a) How are you keeping His commandments? (b) How are you abiding in Him? (c) How are you walking as He walked? (d) How can we pray for you?

Chapter 5

Do You Love Your Brother?

1 John 2:7-11

The story is told of a young girl who, after undergoing an operation, needed a blood transfusion. Her 14-year-old brother volunteered. While sitting by the bedside of his sister, the vein in his arm was opened so that the blood might flow from his body to that of his sister. When it was over, the doctor told the young man how brave he had been. The boy did not understand the nature of a blood transfusion and so, after a moment, he looked up at the doctor and said, "Doc, how long will it be before I croak?" As far as the boy was concerned, he had been dying slowly and willingly. He thought his sister's life would mean his own death.

This story illustrates the highest degree of human love. It certainly illustrates what Jesus said in John 15:13, "Greater love has no one than this, than to lay down one's life for his friends." In this chapter, John explains what Jesus says regarding loving the brethren in our text and reiterates also what was written in the Old Testament. Let's read together what John has written for us.

1 John 2:7-11

> Brethren, I write no new commandment to you, but an old commandment which you have had from the beginning. The old commandment is the word which you heard from the
> beginning. [8]Again, a new commandment I write to you, which thing is true in Him and in you, because the darkness is passing
> away, and the true light is already shining. [9]He who says he is in the light, and hates his brother, is in darkness until now.
> [10]He who loves his brother abides in the light, and there is no
> cause for stumbling in him. [11]But he who hates his brother is in darkness and walks in darkness, and does not know where he is going, because the darkness has blinded his eyes (1 John 2:7-11).

Now this is not the only time that the Apostle John writes of the importance of loving our brethren, as he will mention it several times throughout his epistle. The question we must come to grips with is this: Is it possible for you and me to not love our brother and at the same time have genuine saving faith?

We saw in our last lesson two tests of a genuine believer: *The Test of Obeying His Word* (vv 3-5), and *The Test of Walking His Walk* (v 6). And we saw that one of those tests concerns our obedience to God's commandments. John now speaks of one of the commandments that we must obey—that of loving our brother! In this lesson, we'll learn:

The Nature of the Old Commandment (v 7)
The Nature of the New Commandment (v 8)
The Nature of Those Who Hate Their Brother (vv 9, 11)
The Nature of Those Who Love Their Brother (v 10)

The Nature of the Old Commandment
1 John 2:7

> Brethren, I write no new commandment to you, but an old commandment which you have had from the beginning. The old commandment is the word which you heard from the beginning (1 John 2:7).

The New King James translation starts out with saying *brethren*. However, the correct translation of the term is *beloved*.[20] This is the first time in this epistle that John calls them beloved, a term which means dear. (See 3:2, 21; 4:1, 7, and 11, for other usages of this term.) And it is appropriate that John calls them beloved or dear,

[20] The KJV, following the *Textus Receptus*, has "brethren" (Greek, adelphoi). Bruce M. Metzger suggests, "The latter word [adelphoi], which the author of 1 John almost never uses in the vocative (only in 3:13), crept into the Byzantine text of the present passage because of its customary usage as the introductory word in lectionary pericopes derived from the apsotolos." In other words, the *Textus Receptus* and KJV have been influenced by later commentary insertions to change agapetoi to adelphoi. The correct reading is "beloved," as is reflected in the NASB and NIV.

as he is going to deal with the importance of loving one another. It is also important at this point in his letter because he is admonishing them strongly and the term beloved serves as a confirmation of his love to them. John is lovingly admonishing them.

What does John mean by saying, *I write no new commandment to you, but an old commandment which you have had from the beginning*? *New* means new in kind or new in quality. "I am not writing a new kind of commandment here," John is saying, "I am not telling you something that you have never heard before. I am writing you a commandment that is old." *Old* means antique or not recent. The commandment is here called old in the sense that they had heard it before. Now, what commandment is John talking about? It is defined in the context in verses 9-11, the command of loving the brethren.

Now, you might be wondering, when had they heard this? Where is this old commandment mentioned? Way back in the beginning in Leviticus 19:18, God said, "You shall not take vengeance, nor bear any grudge against the children of your people, but you shall love your neighbor as yourself: I am the LORD." John is saying you have heard this from the beginning of your Christian faith, and therefore it is an old commandment. They knew this commandment to love one another!

The emphasis that John places on it not being new or novel is important, because the Gnostics were introducing new and novel ideas. They thrived on novelty. John says there is nothing new or novel about this commandment. Christendom seems to be always seeking for new and novel ideas, things that will tickle the ears and warm the hearts. That always baffles me, because I feel there is so much in the 66 books that we have in the Scriptures, to learn, study and obey, that who has time for such novelties? (We could spend all our time on trying to perfect this commandment alone, couldn't we?)

The Nature of the New Commandment
1 John 2:8

> Again, a new commandment I write to you, which thing is true in Him and in you, because the darkness is passing away, and the true light is already shining (1 John 2:8).

John has just said in verse 7 that he is not writing a new commandment to them and now he says he is writing a new commandment. That may seem like a contradiction, but it is not. We can better understand what John is saying when we look at John 13:34, 35: "A new commandment I give to you, that you love one another; as I have loved you, that you also love one another. By this all will know that you are My disciples, if you have love for one another." Loving one another is not new in the sense that it was a commandment given, as we just saw, in Leviticus 19:18. But Leviticus 19:18 just said love your neighbor as yourself. Jesus says we are to love one another and adds, "as I have loved you." This is the new and fresh commandment that was added because of the new meaning Christ gave it while on earth. Believers are now motivated to love others because Christ loved us first and modeled for us how we are to love one another. By the way, Jesus said these words immediately after washing the disciple's feet. John himself had just had his own feet washed by the Lord and heard these very words from His lips! Ladies, we should love others because of our love for Christ.

The new commandment is fresh because it is *true in Him*, John says. It is true in Jesus Christ. True means it is genuine or reliable. John is saying, "Hey guys, this commandment to love one another is true in Him; it is reliable. It's the real thing!" Jesus had washed the disciple's dirty feet, and by doing that act of servanthood He manifested to us one of the greatest ways to love the brethren while on earth. Later, in John 15:12, while they are still in the upper room, Jesus says it again, "This is My commandment, that you love one another as I have loved you."

So the commandment is true in Him *and in you*, John says. This is part of walking as He walked, as John just stated in 2:6. This means we are to love the brethren just as Jesus loved the brethren. And John says this love that was in Him is now in us also, *because the darkness is passing away, and the true light is already shining*. The *darkness* is what we were in before Christ.[21] But ladies, that is gone, and now in us shines the *true light*, which is Christ. Isn't that what Jesus said to Paul when sending him out to share the gospel with the Gentiles? In Acts 26:18 we read, "to open their eyes, in order to turn them from darkness to light, and from the power of Satan to God, that they may receive forgiveness of sins and an inheritance among those who are sanctified by faith in Me." Jesus Himself said, in John 8:12, "I am the light of the world. He who follows Me shall not walk in darkness, but have the light of life." He is the true light in contrast to the many false lights out there, including Gnostics. And by the way, all false lights belong to Satan. Remember what Paul said about Satan in 2 Corinthians 11:14? "For Satan himself transforms himself into an angel of light." But praise God that we as believers in Jesus Christ can claim 2 Corinthians 4:6, "For it is the God who commanded light to shine out of darkness, who has shone in our hearts to give the light of the knowledge of the glory of God in the face of Jesus Christ."

So what is the nature of the new commandment? It is to love the brethren as Christ did! John now continues by speaking of those who do not love their brother but, in fact, hate their brother.

---

[21] The *darkness* (Greek, skotia) is metaphorical and refers to moral evil and error, which is in the continual process of retreating (Greek, paragetai is present tense). Hence John refers to the *true light* (Greek, to phos to alethinon), which implies the existence of a spurious or counterfeit light. As noticed under 1:5, *light* metaphorically refers to holiness and truth. Holiness and truth are in the continual process of being revealed (Greek, ede phainnei is present tense). John's picture is of the overlapping of the two eras. As moral evil and error are retreating and holiness and truth are advancing, the commandment to love one another is not novel, as the Gnostic secessionists were claiming, but tried and tested with lasting value and at the same time fresh and vital, as exemplified through the example of Jesus Christ and lived out by true believers now!

The Nature of Those Who Hate Their Brother
1 John 2:9

> He who says he is in the light, and hates his brother, is in darkness until now (1 John 2:9).

Here are the "if-we-sayers" again! This time they are saying they are in the light, and yet they hate their brother. They have said they have fellowship, and yet walk in darkness (1:6); they have said they have no sin and yet they deceive themselves (1:8); they have said they know Him and yet do not keep His commandments (2:4) and they have said they abide in Him and yet do not walk as He walked (2:6). Now they are saying that they are in the light and yet they hate their brother—these things that they are saying are ludicrous! To walk in the light means that we reflect that light—Jesus Christ—that we claim to walk in. So John says if you claim that you are in that light, and yet you hate your brother, you are in darkness even until now.

What does it mean to *hate* my brother? The word hate means to detest or abhor. The present tense indicates a continuous attitude of hatred rather than a momentary hatred. This is important, as even John, the apostle of love, the author of this epistle, had not been perfect in this commandment. There was a time when he struggled with hatred that was temporary. In Luke 9:51-56, both John and James wanted to call fire down from heaven and blast a Samaritan village because they would not let Christ come into their village. Jesus told James and John that they did not know what manner of spirit they were of, and that the Son of Man did not come to destroy men's lives but to save them. We all have times in which we forget what manner of spirit we are of, that we are daughters of the King. But our lives should be characterized by loving others.

The Gnostics claimed to be in the light and yet they looked with disdain on those who did not have the same superior knowledge that they claimed to have. John says if you hate your brother, you are not in the light, my friends, but you are in the darkness. (John has already mentioned them being in darkness in 1:6.) John says you are in darkness *until now*. What does that mean? It means that you are in darkness up until this moment. The person who has an ongoing attitude of hatred toward others is in darkness right up to this moment, and he has never been in any other condition but darkness. In fact, John will say later on in his epistle, in 1 John 3:15, "Whoever hates his brother is a murderer, and you know that no murderer has eternal life abiding in him." There's not much wiggle room there, even though some of us are probably wiggling by now! Perhaps a good rule for all of us would be what Booker T. Washington once said: "I am determined to permit no man to narrow or degrade my soul by making me hate him."

The nature of those who hate their brother is that they are in darkness. In contrast to those who hate their brother, we have those who love their brother in verse 10.

The Nature of Those Who Love Their Brother
1 John 2:10

> He who loves his brother abides in the light, and there is no cause for stumbling in him (1 John 2:10).

Worthy of noting here is that John does not say *if we say*. He just says *he who loves his brother*. A genuine Christian may not necessarily say, "I love my brother," but he does show by his actions that he loves his brother. He loves in action, not with his mouth. He doesn't go around praising himself, but goes through life not letting his left hand know what his right hand is doing. He is not like the Gnostics who were the "if-we-sayers," nor like the hypocrites whom Jesus mentions in the Sermon on the Mount, who loved to let others know when they were doing good deeds to the point that they would sound a trumpet to do so.

Now to *love* our brother does not mean that we have to have some warm fuzzy affection for all believers. But it does mean that our attitude toward believers will be one of looking out for their interests above our own. We will not ignore them or despise them. The term that John uses for love is agape. This is a love that is not a feeling about another person, but it is a choice we make about another person. For an example of this, look at Luke 10:30-37.

> Then Jesus answered and said: "A certain man went down from Jerusalem to Jericho, and fell among thieves, who stripped him of his clothing, wounded him, and departed, leaving him half dead. Now by chance a certain priest came down that road. And when he saw him, he passed by on the other side. Likewise a Levite, when he arrived at the place, came and looked, and passed by on the other side. But a certain Samaritan, as he journeyed, came where he was. And when he saw him, he had compassion. So he went to him and bandaged his wounds, pouring on oil and wine; and he set him on his own animal, brought him to an inn, and took care of him. On the next day, when he departed, he took out two denarii, gave them to the innkeeper, and said to him, 'Take care of him; and whatever more you spend, when I come again, I will repay you.' So which of these three do you think was neighbor to him who fell among the thieves?" And he said, "He who showed mercy on him." Then Jesus said to him, "Go and do likewise" (Luke 10:30-37).

When you look at this story that Jesus told about the Good Samaritan you realize that this man did not have a warm fuzzy feeling about the guy that was injured—he didn't even know him. But he made a choice to show love and it cost him time and money. (By the way, he puts the religious guys, the priest and the Levite, to shame.) The Samaritan is a good example of what John will say later in his epistle in 1 John 3:17-18, "But whoever has this world's goods, and sees his brother in need, and shuts up his heart from him, how does the love of God abide in him? My little children let us not love in word or in tongue, but in deed and in truth."

John uses the present tense for love just as he did for hate. In other words, it is not a sporadic moment of love, but an ongoing reality of loving the brethren. We don't show acts of love one day and then take a break from showing love to others for a month or two. It is ongoing; we are always looking for ways to love the brethren. John says he who loves *abides in the light*, which means staying in a permanent residence rather than a temporary stay. It is in the presence tense, which puts the emphasis on the permanence of the relationship. John also states that the person who loves their brother not only abides in the light, but that *there is no cause for stumbling in him*. This does not mean he causes others to stumble, but that there is no occasion of stumbling in his own way. Stumble means anything against which one strikes or stumbles. It is the trigger in a trap which kills the one who stumbles into the trap or makes him a prisoner of the trap. It refers to a person being deceived into thinking that what he is about to do is beneficial. (Like an animal getting ready to fall into a trap thinking it's a good idea to partake of some of those vittles!) So a person may think he is doing well, and has deceived himself into thinking that what he is doing is beneficial, when it actuality it leads him to being trapped. Loving others frees us and enables us to make progress in our spiritual walk and keeps us from stumbling. When we have an attitude of hatred, unforgiveness and bitterness toward others, we cannot progress in our spiritual walk. We are like the animal in the trap. John Wesley says, "He that hates his brother is an occasion of stumbling to himself. He stumbles against himself, and against all things within and without; while he that loves his brother has a free disencumbered journey."[22] What is the nature of those who love their brother? They abide in the light and they don't stumble. John finishes his thoughts with going back now to those who hate their brother.

The Nature of Those Who Hate Their Brother 1 John 2:11

> But he who hates his brother is in darkness and walks in darkness, and does not know where he is going, because the darkness has blinded his eyes (1 John 2:11).

[22] John Wesley, *Explanatory Notes upon the New Testament* (Grand Rapids, MI: Baker, 1981), p 632.

But is a word of contrast. In contrast to the lover of the brethren in verse 10, we have the hater of the brethren in verse 11. John has already said the hater is in darkness, but now he adds that not only is he *in darkness*, but he also *walks in darkness*, and that darkness *has blinded his eyes*. The mention of him walking in darkness is an indication that this is a habit of his life to the point that he doesn't even know where he is going because the darkness has blinded his eyes. The verb form of *blinded* is the same as in 2 Corinthians 4:4, where we read, "whose minds the god of this age has *blinded,* who do not believe, lest the light of the gospel of the glory of Christ, who is the image of God, should shine on them" (emphasis mine). *Blinded* here in 1 John is in the aorist tense, which pictures the decisive moment when the darkness finally overtakes the sinner. This is a very sobering statement that John is making. This person fails to understand the destination they are headed for because darkness has blinded their eyes and they cannot see. We see a glimpse of this when Jesus pleads with an unbelieving crowd in John 12:35-36, "Then Jesus said to them, 'A little while longer the light is with you. Walk while you have the light, lest darkness overtake you; he who walks in darkness does not know where he is going. While you have the light, believe in the light, that you may become sons of light. These things Jesus spoke, and departed, and was hidden from them."

Ladies, walking in darkness is a sobering thought. Being blinded to the point that you cannot see is a sobering thought. Not only is the darkness for this life but also for the life to come, as Jude describes hell as "the blackness of darkness forever." There will never be a trace of light in hell.

Summary

The question asked by ancient man is also the question asked by modern man: "How can I know for certain that I really know Jesus Christ?" And in view of the clear revelation in the New

Testament concerning the multitudes that will discover, to their horror, that they never really knew Jesus Christ, this question must be answered by every thinking man or woman. John answers by two clear objective tests. First, we can know we know Jesus Christ by a life which is manifesting obedience (2:3-6). Obedience to His words is the maturing fruit of a genuine love for Jesus Christ, which motivates the believer to follow in His steps. Second, we can know for certain we really know Jesus Christ by a life manifesting love (2:7-11). The commandment to love one another is not novel, as the Gnostics were claiming, but tried and tested with lasting value. At the same time, it is also fresh and vital, as exemplified through the example of Jesus Christ and lived out by true believers now. The reason it is both "old" and "new" is because the age of darkness (i.e., evil and error) has begun to pass away and the age of light (i.e., holiness and truth) has begun to shine.

The Nature of the Old Commandment (v 7) is to love the brethren. *The Nature of the New Commandment* (v 8) is to love the brethren as Christ did. *The Nature of Those Who Hate Their Brother* (vv 9, 11) is that they are in darkness, they walk in darkness, and they don't know where they are going because the darkness has blinded their eyes. *The Nature of Those Who Love Their Brother* (v 10) is that they abide in the light and do not stumble.

Do you love the brethren? Do you really love the brethren? Are you patient with people, especially your husband and your children and those in your family? Love is very patient. Are you kind to others? Does it show in your tone of voice and in your body language? Love is kind. Are you jealous of other people, wanting what they have? Do you envy their position, their looks, or their material possessions? Love is never jealous or envious. Do you boast around others about how great you are or what you have accomplished? Do you secretly think you are better than others and judge others in your heart? Love is never boastful, proud, or haughty. Do you always insist on your own way? Do you pout when you don't get your own way? Do you resent the time or energy that you give to others? Love is not selfish, nor does it demand its own way. Do you cut people off in traffic? Do you treat your children or husband as second-class citizens? Are you abrupt on the phone with others? Love is not rude. Are you agitated and frustrated with others or with circumstances that God allows? Do others know it is that "time of the month" by your behavior? Love is not irritable or touchy. When someone hurts your feelings, do you bring it up to them? Do you remember all the mistakes your husband has made? Love does not hold grudges and will hardly even notice when others do you wrong. Do you secretly or even openly gloat when an enemy of yours gets their due? Do you rejoice when others excel, especially in the things of Christ? Love is never glad about injustice, but rejoices whenever truth wins out. Are you loyal to your marriage, to your children, to your friendships, to the leaders in your church? If you love someone, you will be loyal to them no matter what the cost. You will always believe in them, always expect the best of them, and always stand your ground in defending them.

Tradition tells us that the aged old apostle, in bidding farewell to his congregation before he died, admonished them to love one another, love one another, love one another. "But we want something new," they said, "Give us a new commandment!" John replied, "Brethren, I write no new commandment to you, but an old commandment which you have had from the beginning … that you should love one another."

Questions to Consider

Do You Love Your Brother?

1 John 2:7-11

1. In 1 John 2:7, 8, John mentions an old commandment that they had heard from the beginning. (a) Read Leviticus 19:18 to discover what this old commandment was. (b) So then, what does John mean in verse 8 by a new commandment? See John 13:34. (c) What makes this commandment different from the old commandment? (d) Do you think verses 7 and 8 are contradictory? (e) Why or why not?

2. Memorize 1 John 2:9.

3. (a) According to 1 John 2:9, 10, how does one know for sure if he is a believer? (b) How does John describe loving one's brother later on in this epistle? See 1 John 3:17, 18. (c) List some ways that we can "measure up" to John's description of loving our brother.

4. Read Matthew 25:31-46 and answer the following questions (a) What animals does Jesus use to describe those who love the brethren and those who hate the brethren? (b) Why do you think He uses these different animals? (c) What deeds characterize those who love the brethren and those who hate the brethren? (d) What are the destinations of those who love the brethren and of those who hate the brethren? (e) Do you think the goats knew they were lost? Why or why not?

5. (a) Why is loving the brethren so imperative? See John 13:35; Romans 13:8; 1 Corinthians 13, and 1 John 4:11. (b) Rewrite the qualities of love from 1 Corinthians in your own words. (c) What changes do you need to make so that you will love others in the way described in 1 Corinthians 13?

6. (a) Do you love the brethren? (b) What proof is there in your life that you love the brethren? (For the brave, ask those closest to you, "Does my life manifest that I indeed love the brethren?")

7. (a) Is there someone you need to love more actively? (b) What will you do about it?

8. In what areas has the Lord convicted you through the study of this lesson? Write out a prayer request to share with others.

Chapter 6

John's Encouraging Words to the Family of God

1 John 2:12-14

In his classic book, *Knowing God*, J. I. Packer asks and answers some very interesting questions. "What were we made for? To know God. What aim should we set ourselves in life? To know God. What is the best thing in life, bringing more joy, delight and contentment than anything else? Knowledge of God. What, of all the states God ever sees man in, gives God most pleasure? Knowledge of Himself."[23] Knowing God is what the Christian life is all about, is it not? Jesus, Himself, in the High Priestly prayer, prayed, "And this is eternal life, that they may know You, the only true God, and Jesus Christ whom You have sent" (John 17:3). The wonderful thing about being a believer in Jesus Christ, whether we're babes in Christ or aged saints, is that we know God. John clarifies this concept in the few short verses in our lesson. In contrast to the Gnostics who claimed knowledge of God was only for a select few, John says no, all Christians know God, whether they are little children in the faith or fathers in the faith. Let's read the text together.

1 John 2:12-14

> I write to you, little children, because your sins are forgiven you
> for His name's sake. [13]I write to you, fathers, because you have
> known Him who is from the beginning. I write to you, young
> men, because you have overcome the wicked one. I write to
> you, little children, because you have known the Father. [14]I have
> written to you, fathers, because you have known Him who is
> from the beginning. I have written to you, young men, because
> you are strong, and the word of God abides in you, And you
> have overcome the wicked one. (1 John 2:12-14)

[23] J. I. Packer, *Knowing God* (Downer's Grove, IL: InterVarsity Press, 1973), p 29.

In our last lesson we learned: *The Nature of the Old Commandment* (v 7) is to love the brethren. *The Nature of the New Commandment* (v 8) is to love the brethren as Christ did. *The Nature of Those Who Hate Their Brother* (vv 9, 11) is that they are in darkness, they walk in darkness, and they do not know where they are going because the darkness has blinded their eyes. *The Nature of Those Who Love Their Brother* (v 10) is that they abide in the light and they don't stumble. As we look at John's encouraging words to the family of God in this lesson, we'll see the three different age groups of the family of God to whom John writes.

The Message to All the Children (v 12)
The Message to the Fathers (vv 13a, 14a)
The Message to the Young Men (vv 13b, 14b)
The Message to the Little Children (v 13c)

Let's look first at the message to all the children.

The Message to All the Children
1 John 2:12

> I write to you, little children, because your sins are forgiven you for His name's sake (1 John 2:12).

In contrast to those in verse 11 who are blind and walking in darkness are the little children, the little born ones of God, in verse 12. John gives them an assurance in verse 12 that they are not in darkness but that they are in the light. Walking in the light brings many blessings. One of those blessings is that we no longer have the black, heavy load of sin to carry around day in and day out, but instead have the privilege of having our sins forgiven.

John first addresses the *little children*. So we must ask the question, what does John mean by little children? The Greek word here is different than the one John uses in verse 13. The term here is teknia, which refers to all people who are born of God. This would

include all believers in Jesus Christ. John addresses them as little children throughout this letter (2:1, 12, 18, 28; 3:7, 18; 4:4; 5:21; a total of 8 times). (The aged old apostle is about 100 years old at this point, so he considers them all his little children, no matter what age group they are in.) It's as if John is saying, "Dear sons and daughters," or "Dear Christian converts." John perhaps remembered this term being used by his Lord when He addressed the disciples in John 13:33, "Little children, I shall be with you a little while longer. You will seek Me; and as I said to the Jews, 'Where I am going, you cannot come,' so now I say to you."

So John writes to all the little children, all the believers in Jesus, for a reason, and the reason is because their *sins are forgiven.* What does it mean that their sins are forgiven? The word *forgiven* means sent away. This is one of the blessings that all of God's children have, no matter what age they are. John has already mentioned this wonderful privilege in 1 John 1:9.[24] So, John reminds them again that their sins have been forgiven; they were forgiven at the time of their conversion, and they are still being forgiven. What does John mean that our sins are forgiven *for His name's sake*? John is saying that, because of the name of Christ and because of what He has done for us in saving us and bringing us to Himself, it is for His own name's sake! Some of us, bless our hearts, think that our salvation is all about us, but it is not; it is all about Him and for His glory! So what is the message to all the children? Your sins are forgiven!

---

[24] Once again, remember that a central purpose of John's epistle or sermon is to correct the Gnostic errors. Gnosticism held to a caste system of those who were really in the know, those who were only partially in the know and those who were totally ignorant. "Gnostics are those set within a world where they are *spiritual persons* (pneumatikoi) who possess the light particles and need only to be awakened in order to inherit their destinies. In the world there are also said to be *psychic persons* (psychikoi), who are a grade lower and need to work for whatever salvation they may be able to attain. The Gnostics often identified such psychics with [normal] Christians and understandably irritated the Christian heresiologists…The third division of this view of humanity is composed of *material persons* (hylikoi or sarkikoi), who have no chance to inherit any form of salvation but are destined for destruction" cf. Walter A. Elwell, *Evangelical Dictionary of Theology* (Grand Rapids, MI: Baker, 1984), p 446. And yet, biblical Christianity majored on what we all share in common, i.e., the forgiveness of sins and the knowledge of the Father.

We could end our lesson now on this encouraging note, but John has more to say to the children of God. He continues writing in the next two verses to the three categories within the family of God: the fathers, the young men, and the little children. First of all he addresses the fathers.

The Message to the Fathers
1 John 2:13

> I write to you, fathers, because you have known Him who is from the beginning (1 John 2:13a).

Now the question might come to mind, "Who are the fathers?" The *fathers* would be those who are mature in the faith. We might say they are the "seasoned saints." When we think of an earthly father, we usually think of someone who is older and who has authority. John tells these fathers that they *have known Him* from the beginning. The words known Him mean come to know and still know. Knowledge is one of the characteristics of a father. They should be wiser and more knowledgeable than a child, and have the maturity and experience of life to back up the knowledge they possess. Spiritual fathers not only know doctrine, but they know the God behind the doctrine. They walk with God and delight in communing with Him.

What does John mean when he says they have known him *from the beginning*? It is possible that because these men were older in age they had actually seen Christ, and so from the beginning could be referring to the beginning of Jesus' ministry with the disciples. It would have been 40 years since Paul had first proclaimed the gospel in Ephesus, as mentioned in Acts 18:19. So, many of the readers that John is writing to would have been believers for a while. It also could mean that the fathers had known Him from the beginning of their conversion. By the way, may I say that the spiritual fathers and spiritual mothers—the spiritually mature—are believers you want to spend a lot of time with? You can learn so much from watching their faith, from seeing their example, from observing their wisdom and their relationship with God. God made this clear in Titus 2 that this is what He desires for us.

> But as for you, speak the things which are proper for sound doctrine: that the older men be sober, reverent, temperate, sound in faith, in love, in patience; the older women likewise, that they be reverent in behavior, not slanderers, not given to much wine, teachers of good things—that they admonish the young women to love their husbands, to love their children, to be discreet, chaste, homemakers, good, obedient to their own husbands, that the word of God may not be blasphemed. Likewise exhort the young men to be sober-minded, in all things showing yourself to be a pattern of good works; in doctrine showing integrity, reverence, incorruptibility, sound speech that cannot be condemned, that one who is an opponent may be ashamed, having nothing evil to say of you (Titus 2:1-8).

So what is the message to the fathers? John encourages them that they have known God from the beginning.

The Message to the Young Men 1 John 2:13b

> I write to you, young men, because you have overcome the wicked one (1 John 2:13b).

John then addresses the young men. John says *I write to you, young men, because you have overcome the wicked one*. Who are the *young men*? Physically speaking, a young man in Biblical times would have been between the ages of 24-40. They would be midway in life, as they would not be children, but they would not be aged fathers either. Spiritually speaking, young men would be men who are well-grounded in the truth, men who have been through spiritual warfare, who are no longer agitated by doubts and fears, and who have an abiding testimony in Christ. Young men can discern between good and evil and usually have a pretty good grasp on the doctrines of the faith. Sometimes I think back to my youth and some of the dumb things I did and the foolish choices I made based on my emotions and not my mind. Young men are not like that; they are stable, and they have put away childish and foolish things. Paul puts it well in 1 Corinthians 13:11 when he says, "When I was a child, I spoke as a child, I understood as a child, I thought as a child; but when I became a man, I put away childish things."

Being a young man in the faith can also be a dangerous time, as young men in the faith often think they have all the answers and know everything. They can at times think they have arrived, which can lead to pride and spiritual apathy. That is the way it sometimes is in the physical realm, isn't it? Some young men think they have all the answers, and their pride can get them into trouble if they are not careful. John says these young men in the faith *have overcome the wicked one*. To overcome means to subdue or to get the victory. The tense in the Greek indicates that this is a permanent victory after conflict. This does not mean that the wicked one, Satan, never tempts them, but that young men know what they believe and have the Word of God grounded in their heart and mind and Satan does not have the advantage over them. They are more aware and less vulnerable to his tactics than the babes in Christ. So how does John encourage the young men? He does so by reminding them of the fact that they have overcome the wicked one.

The Message to the Little Children
1 John 2:13c

> I write to you, little children, because you have known the Father (1 John 2:13c)

Next John addresses the *little children*. The Greek word for little children is different than the term used verse 12. Here in verse 13 the Greek word is <u>paidia</u>, which refers to infants. These are spiritual babes who have limited spiritual understanding and who are in need of a lot of instruction. They are just learning to walk and talk. They need wisdom to overcome foolishness. This can be a very wonderful stage in the believer's life, but it can also be a very vulnerable stage. It is such a joy to see people embrace Christ and begin their pilgrim walk. Everything is new and wonderful to them. They have such zeal and passion that many older saints seem to lose. They remind me of my children, and now my grandchildren, when they were babies and young toddlers. Everything to a little child is new and the simplest things bring excitement and joy. This was evidenced to me one night when my 7 week old grandson, Ethan, was at my home. I was holding him and he spent a long time watching the clock in my kitchen tick-tock, tick-tock. He was fascinated! Spiritually speaking, if we are not careful as we mature in Christ, we can come to take for granted those simple things that used to be so exciting—things like the cross, the Holy Spirit, the Word of God, the fellowship of the saints. We should never "get over" those simple things that are amazing when we start our new life in Christ.

Being a babe in Christ can also be a very dangerous time in that without the help and care of the Father, the child is vulnerable to dangers. Just as a newborn baby will starve if it is not fed, so a newborn babe in Christ will starve spiritually if they are not feeding on the Word of God. As babies becomes toddlers they can get themselves into all kinds of dangerous situations such as burning their hand on the stove or fireplace, running out into the street, sticking their fingers in the electrical sockets and drinking poisonous liquids. Parents are there to guide, direct and discipline the child. The same is true in the spiritual realm. It can be a dangerous time because babes in Christ do not have the discernment and knowledge to combat false teaching and the devices that Satan might use to lure them away from Christ. Babes in Christ need the guidance, direction and discipline of their Heavenly Father as they grow into being young men and women in the faith and then on to being aged fathers in the faith. For those who are older in the faith, we need to remember to exercise great patience with new believers. We must remember that they don't know the entire Bible yet; they don't know yet what they are supposed to do; nor do they understand many of the doctrines of the faith like justification, sanctification, and glorification. They are in the infant stage, and we must exercise great patience as they grow. But John says he is writing to them because they *have known the Father*. They know the Father—they can say "Dada!" They call him, "Papa, Father," just as the aged old saints do. In fact, in the physical realm what are the first words a baby usually says? Dada, mama. Why? Because they know the mama and the dada. They are the people they're most familiar with. This is an important statement that John makes here, that the children know the Father too, just as the fathers know the Father. Remember, the Gnostics claimed that it was only the fathers, the spiritual giants, the ones in the know, who could know God. But John says no, all believers know the Father, whether they are old in the faith or young in the faith!

Interesting to note here is that John says to the little children that they have known Him, but leaves out the words from the beginning, as he wrote to the fathers in verse 13. This perhaps is another indicator that the aged men had actually seen Christ from the beginning of His ministry. So what is the encouraging message to the little children? They also know the Father! Speaking of knowing him from the beginning, John now repeats this same phrase to the fathers in verse 14.

The Message to the Fathers 1 John 2:14a

> I have written to you, fathers, because you have known Him who is from the beginning (1 John 2:14a).

John repeats the phrase to the fathers that he has already said in verse 13. Why John repeats this phrase is a mystery to me. Anytime something is repeated it is usually done for emphasis, and why the emphasis is given here I am not sure. Two interesting things to note are that John has now said some form of I have written or I write six times in these three verses. And he has changed the form from the present tense, I write to you, to the past tense, I have written to you.

And so of course, I asked why? Why the change from the present tense to the past tense? Some think that this refers to a former epistle which was lost, but there is no evidence of a former epistle. Others say that the first two verses are written from John's point of view, while the later verse, verse 14, is written from the reader's point of view. And yet another thought is that John got interrupted after he wrote verses 12 and 13, and that when he resumed his writing in verse 14, he said I have written. It is interesting to note that from here on in this epistle John uses the past tense. (See 1:4; 2:1, 7, 8, 12, 13, 14, 21, 26; 5:13.) So it does make me wonder if John did get interrupted. I know I get interrupted many times while I'm writing, so it makes sense to me! I don't know which interpretation is correct, but one thing I know for sure is that John wrote this epistle. The message to the fathers in verse 14 is the same as in verse 13—you have known Him from the beginning.

The Message to the Young Men
1 John 2:14b

> I have written to you, young men, because you are strong, and the word of God abides in you, and you have overcome the wicked one (1 John 2:14b).

John now addresses the young men one more time. John has already mentioned in verse 13 that the young men have overcome the wicked one, but now he adds that *you are strong and the word of God abides in you*. What does it mean that they are *strong*? It means they are forcible, which speaks of ability and power; it speaks of moral character and not of accomplishment. When you think of young men, usually you think of strength, and generally speaking it is a characteristic of that age. As Proverbs 20:29 says, "The glory of young men is their strength, And the splendor of old men is their gray head." (Amen to that latter part!) Where does this strength come from? Paul tells young Timothy, in 2 Timothy 2:1, where that strength comes from: "You therefore, my son, be strong in the grace that is in Christ Jesus." Our strength can only come from the Lord.

Not only are young men strong, but John says to them that *the word of God abides in you*. This means that the truth of God abides in them; it remains in them and does not leave them. And that is a promise of the New Covenant, according to Hebrews 8:10: "For this is the covenant that I will make with the house of Israel after those days, says the LORD: I will put My laws in their mind and write them on their hearts; and I will be their God, and they shall be My people."

John then repeats that the young men have overcome the wicked one, as he has already said in verse 13. It is worthy of noting here that as the young men are strong, and as they abide in the Word of God, they overcome the wicked one. It is only as we are strong and are abiding in the Word that we can quench the fiery darts of the devil. (See Ephesians 6:10-17.) Isn't that what you see when you look at the temptation of Christ? How is it that He overcame Satan? It was by the strength of His relationship with His Heavenly Father—which, by the way, may have been made stronger by the fact that He had just fasted 40 days and 40 nights. You can look at the instances in the Word of God when men and women fasted and prayed (See *With the Master On Our Knees*[25]) and note that God intervened in miraculous ways when His people humbled themselves by fasting and praying. So what is the encouragement to the young men? They are strong, the Word abides in them, and they have overcome the wicked one.

Summary

So what is *The Message to All the Children of God* (v 12)? Your sins are forgiven! What is *The Message to the Fathers* (vv 13a, 14a)? They have known Him from the beginning! What is *The Message to the Young Men* (vv 13b, 14b)? They have overcome the wicked one, they are strong, and the Word of God abides in them.

[25] Susan J. Heck, *With The Master On Our Knees* (Bemidji, MN: Focus Publishing, 2009), chapters 11 and 12.

What is *The Message to the Little Children* (v 13c)? They have known the Father!

As we come to the end of this lesson, it is important to bring out the fact that John is writing to these three groups of individuals, the fathers, the young men, and the children. You might wonder why this is important. It is important because the Gnostics divided people into three groups, and to them it was only the fathers, the elite group, who knew God. But John says no! All Christians know God, whether they are children, young men or fathers. Secondly, it is important to say that all of these characteristics should be true of all of God's children, no matter what stage they are at in the faith. Even though these specific truths are especially true of the ages John mentions, all of these truths should be true of all ages. All of us should know the Father. All of us have the joy of having our sins forgiven. All of us should be strong and be actively overcoming the wicked one. All of us should be abiding in the Word of God.

In closing, I would ask you, do you know the Father? J.I. Packer says that knowing God does not mean you have a shiver down your back, or a dreamy, off the ground, floating feeling, or tingling thrills and exhilaration, or even an intellectual experience. Knowing God, he says, will manifest itself in four ways.

1. People who know God will have great energy for God.
2. People who know God will have great thoughts of God.
3. People who know God will have great boldness for God.
4. People who know God will have great contentment in God.[26]

Do you know God? Do you have a personal relationship with Him? Do you have great energy for God, great thoughts of God, great boldness for God, and great contentment in God? If you do know God, then some questions to consider are these: Where are you in your walk with the Lord? Are you a babe in Christ, a

[26] J. I. Packer, *Knowing God* (Downer's Grove, IL: Intervarsity Press, 1973), p 27.

young man (or woman) or a father (or mother)? Another question to consider is this: Should you be further along in your growth than you are? For example, if you have been in the faith 30 years, and are still acting like a babe in Christ, why is that? Why aren't you growing? Howard Hendricks made the comment once that many of us are walking around in our spiritual diapers when we should not be. The writer to the Hebrews writes in chapter 5, verses 12-14, that some of his readers were dull of hearing and they should be teachers but they needed to be taught all over again. He says, hey you guys, you should be digesting meat, but you are in need of milk. They had not grown as they should have. If you are not where you should be in your spiritual journey, if you have not grown as you should, and you are truly in the faith, then may I suggest to you that perhaps you have not appropriated the means of grace that God has provided for your growth? You need to grow. I want to challenge you as we close this chapter, and we will do it in the form of an acrostic: GROW.

***G**et in church:* God did not mean for you and me to go the Christian life alone. You look around at the Christians you know who are mature in the faith, and I could almost guarantee they are the ones that are in the house of the Lord consistently. They are not just Sunday morning pew warmers, but they are an active part of the body of Christ, and they do not forsake the assembly, as Hebrews 10:25 mentions.

***R**ead your Bible:* If you are not in the habit of being in the Word consistently, you are stunting your growth. What does Peter say in 1 Peter 2:2? "As newborn babes, desire the pure milk of the word, that you may *grow* thereby." I would encourage you to spend some time in Psalm 119 and see the attitudes that we should have towards the Word of God and the benefits we will gain from knowing the Word of God. I would encourage you to read it, meditate on it, study it and memorize it. Knowing God's Word is one of the greatest means of your spiritual growth. Without it your spiritual life will wither.

O*pen communication with God:* Ladies, you need to be praying and communicating with your Father, if you are going to grow from a babe to an adult in Christ. How did you get to know your husband before you married him? Not by osmosis, but by spending time with him and lots of it. You were able to know him by being with him, talking to him. Paul tells us in 1 Thessalonians 5:16 that we are to "Pray without ceasing."

And lastly, ***W****oman to Woman:* If you do not have accountability in your life from an older woman you are missing out on the most exciting way that I believe God grows us as women. Titus 2:4, 5 says, "the older women likewise, that they be reverent in behavior, not slanderers, not given to much wine, teachers of good things—that they admonish the young women to love their husbands, to love their children, to be discreet, chaste, homemakers, good, obedient to their own husbands, that the word of God may not be blasphemed." This is a command of God and it will be used by God to grow you into His image.

My dear sisters, I would ask you, do you know God? Do have a personal relationship with Him? Are you growing? If not, why not? Every one who is called a child of God should be growing, whether they are a babe in the faith, a young woman in the faith, or an aged mother in the faith. My prayer for all of you is from 2 Peter 3:18: "But grow in the grace and knowledge of our Lord and Savior Jesus Christ. To Him be the glory both now and forever. Amen."

Questions to Consider

John's Encouraging Words to the Family of God

1 John 2:12-14

1. (a) What phrase does John repeat several times in 1 John 2:12-14? (b) Why do you think he repeats this phrase so much? (c) What do you think is meant by the terms children, young men, and fathers? (d) In what ways do these few verses encourage you in your walk with Christ?

2. Memorize 1 John 2:13.

3. John writes to the young men because they have overcome the wicked one. (a) How is it possible for us to overcome the wicked one? See 1 John 4:4, and 5:4, 5. (b) Read the account of Christ and Satan in the wilderness in Matthew 4:1-11, and make note of all the ways that Christ overcame the wicked one. (c) How does Christ's example encourage and equip you as you resist the wicked one?

4. John writes to the little children in 1 John 2:12 because their sins are forgiven them for His name's sake. Read Leviticus 16:20-22 and answer the following questions. (a) What animal was used to bear the sins of the Israelites? (b) What happened to that animal? (c) Was it seen again? (d) How does this help you to understand what "forgiveness of sins" means? (e) In contrast, as New Testament saints, what was the sacrifice that was made for the forgiveness of our sins? See Hebrews 9:11-22 and 10:4-18. (f) What does having your sins forgiven mean to you?

5. (a) Why is it imperative that the Word of God abide in us, according to Joshua 1:7, 8; Psalm 1:1-3; Psalm 19:7-11; 119:11; 119:97-105; John 15:3; 2 Timothy 3:15-17 and James 1:21-25? (b) What is your relationship to the Word of God? In other words, how much time do you spend reading it, studying it, memorizing it, meditating on it, and obeying it? (c) How has the Word made a difference in your life this week?

6. (a) What are some physical, emotional and mental characteristics of little children (babies), young men and fathers? (b) What are some of the strengths and weaknesses of each category? (c) How do these characteristics help you to understand the spiritual characteristics that each category has?

7. (a) How long have you been a Christian? (b) Would you classify yourself as a babe in Christ, a young man (woman) or a spiritual father (mother)? (c) What is keeping you from maturing in Christ as you should?

8. After contemplating your answer from 5b and/or 7c, write down a prayer request that relates to these questions.

Chapter 7

Three Deadly Sins!

1 John 2:15-17

Several years ago my niece and her three children came to visit my husband and me. The day they arrived, I had been preparing and studying for this lesson in 1 John, and so loving the world and what that meant were on my mind. At dinnertime, I decided to ask her three children what they thought loving the world meant. The two younger ones said that they didn't know, but the older one, who was 10 at the time, said he wanted some time to think about it. Later on in the evening, he came up to me and said, "Aunt Suzie, I have an answer for your question. I think loving the world means that you take care of it, and help it grow by feeding it nutrition and stuff." Of course, I had to chuckle inside, and I thanked him for his answer. If I were to ask you the same question I asked my great nieces and nephew, what would be your answer? Just what does loving the world mean? When the aged old Apostle John wrote that we are not to love the world, he had something a little different in mind than my great nephew did. Let's read verses 15-17 and discover just what it means to love the world.

1 John 2:15-17

> Do not love the world or the things in the world. If anyone loves
> the world, the love of the Father is not in him. 16For all that is
> in the world—the lust of the flesh, the lust of the eyes, and the
> pride of life—is not of the Father but is of the world. 17And the
> world is passing away, and the lust of it; but he who does the
> will of God abides forever (1 John 2:15-17).

John has just written to three categories of believers in the previous verses: the little children, the young men, and the fathers. We learned of John's *Message to All the Children of God* (v 12): that

their sins are forgiven! John's *Message to the Fathers* (vv 13a, 14a): that they have known Him from the beginning! John's *Message to the Young Men* (vv 13b, 14b): that they have overcome the wicked one; they are strong; and the Word of God abides in them. And lastly, John's *Message to the Little Children* (v 13c): that they have known the Father!

We saw that each age group has characteristics unique to it, even though those characteristics should be true of all believers. We also saw that John's division of Christians into three age categories is important because the Gnostics were also divided into three categories, claiming that only the fathers, the elite, knew God. John says no, all children of God know the Father, from the little children to the young men to the aged old saints.

John ends verse 14 with writing about the wicked one that the young men have overcome. The wicked one, Satan, is the prince of this world, as he is called four times in Scripture. The transition is easy to see as John continues to write. Those who are in Christ should not be lovers of the world, which is governed by Satan, the prince of the world. It is also interesting that this admonition to not love the world comes after his address to young men in verse 14. The reason is that a characteristic of youth is the false perception of immortality, as young people seem to think they are immune to physical dangers. John's unstated analogy is similar, as he warns the spiritually young men of a danger that could detour them away from the source of victory. This does not mean little children and fathers don't have a temptation to love the world, but it would appear that young men have a distinct danger in that area. John writes to all the "little children" that they cannot be considered children of God and be lovers of the world. In this lesson we'll see:

The Command to Not Love the World (v 15a)
The Reasons to Not Love the World (vv 15b-17a)
The Reason to Love God (v 17b)

Let's begin by looking at the command to not love the world in verse 15.

The Command to Not Love the World 1 John 2:15a

Do not love the world or the things in the world (1 John 2:15a).

Because John speaks so much about loving the world in these few verses, we need to ask ourselves what this means. The word for *love* that John uses here is agape, and it is used in a moral sense. It is a love that is supreme, that is due God. The word for *world*, kosmon, is a word which has a general meaning of an orderly arrangement, a word Peter uses in 1 Peter 3:3, which speaks of a woman's adornment, which is an orderly arrangement. Here, in 1 John, it also has an evil connotation, which describes the world system which opposes and is hostile toward God.[27] In fact, John mentions the world 6 times in these few verses. One commentator has described the world as "the life of human society as organized

[27] In the New Testament, the word kosmos is found 187 times, translated "world" in each case with the exception of 1 Peter 3:3. Of those 186 times, John 3:16 uses kosmos in a uniquely restricted sense in reference to the humanity of the world system, apart from the evil institutions and practices. Lewis S. Chafer helps, with a good general description of the world: "The cosmos is a vast order or system that Satan has promoted, which conforms to his ideals, aims, and methods. It is civilization now functioning apart from God—a civilization in which none of its promoters really expect God to share, who assign to God no consideration in respect to their projects; nor do they ascribe any causativity to Him … Satan does incorporate into his vast system certain things which are good in themselves. Many humanitarian ideals, morals, and aspects of culture are consonant with spiritual realities, though resident in the cosmos. The root evil in the cosmos is that in it there is an all-comprehensive order or system which is methodized on a basis of complete independence of God. It is a manifestation of all that Satan can produce as a complete exhibition of that which enters into the original lie. It is the consummating display of that which the creature—both angelic and human—can produce, having embarked on an autonomous career. The cosmos is not a battleground whereon God is contending with Satan for supremacy; it is a thing which God has permitted, that the lie may have its fullest unveiling" cf. Lewis S. Chafer, *Systematic Theology: Angelology, Anthropology and Hamartiology,* Vol. II (Dallas, TX: Dallas Seminary Press, 1947), pp 79, 84.

under the power of evil."[28] So, loving the world includes loving anything that is in opposition to God. It would include thoughts that are opposed to God, habits that are opposed to God, actions that are opposed to God, words that are opposed to God, and relationships that are opposed to God.

The tense in which the command *do not love the world* is given is the present active imperative, so with the negative it means, "stop loving the world!" *Love* is also in the present tense, which means that we are to be constantly not in love with the world. It is an absolute denial. God forbid! Why would we love the world when we consider what is in it the world—the lust of the flesh, the lust of the eyes and the pride of life—and the fact that the "whole world lies under the sway of the wicked one" (1 John 5:19)?

Now you might be saying, so am I to hate the world? No! Christians do not hate the world in the sense that they hate creation or any of God's created beings. God Himself loved the world He made. In fact, it says in Genesis 1:31, "Then God saw everything that He had made, and indeed it was *very good.* So the evening and the morning were the sixth day" (emphasis mine). And we know from John 3:16 that Jesus says, "For God so loved the world that He gave His only begotten Son, that whoever believes in Him should not perish but have everlasting life." So we can conclude that John is saying that we should hate the world in a moral sense, the world that is apart from God. This would include wrong principles, wrong desires, wrong values and such. You don't have to be around people in the world long before you realize what those principles, desires, and values are. I am not around unbelievers that much, but when I am, I am always surprised at how they think; it seems very bizarre to me. They think and act in a way that is very contrary to the Word of God and contrary to how a believer should conduct herself.

John goes on with his command to say that we are not only to not love the world, but we are also not to love *the things in the*

[28] John R. W. Stott, *Tyndale New Testament Commentary: The Letters of John* (Grand Rapids, MI: Eerdmans, 1988), p 103.

world. What are the things in the world? John is not saying that we're not to love what is in the world, like flowers, birds, trees, and such. We should admire their beauty and we should admire the Creator of them. In the next verse John will describe the things that are in the world, and they are a far cry from flowers and trees. He describes them as the lust of the flesh, the lust of the eyes, and the pride of life. John now moves from the command to not love the world to give the reasons why we should not love the world. And there are five of them.

The Reasons to Not Love the World
1 John 2:15b-17a

> If anyone loves the world, the love of the Father is not in him. For all that is in the world—the lust of the flesh, the lust of the eyes, and the pride of life—is not of the Father but is of the world. And the world is passing away, and the lust of it (1 John 2:15b-17a).

So what happens if you and I love the world? What happens if we have values and principles, speech and goals like the world? John says *if anyone loves the world, the love of the Father is not in him*. This is the first reason to not love the world—*the love of the Father is not in him*. The tense gives it this meaning: If anyone has a continual practice of loving the world, the love of the Father is not in him. And notice that there is no exception here; John says if *anyone* loves the world. You can be a pastor, a pastor's wife, a Sunday school teacher, you can sing in the choir, you can be actively involved in ministry, but, if you love the world, John says the love of the Father is not in you. What does John mean by saying that *the love of the Father is not in him*? It means that his love is not toward the Father. The love of the Father is not in him means more than that he does not love God; it means that not loving the Father is the governing principle of his life. It is as Jesus said very plainly in the Sermon on the Mount in Matthew 6:24: "No one can serve two masters; for either he will hate the one and love the other, or else he will be loyal to the one and despise the other. You cannot serve God and mammon." Jesus very plainly is saying that we cannot love God and love the world at the same time. You either hate God and love the world, or else you love God and hate the world. That is pretty simple, isn't it?

John goes on to describe the things in the world—three deadly sins—that every believer must avoid at all costs. These things are also three more reasons John gives as to why we should not love the world: *all that is in the world—the lust of the flesh, the lust of the eyes, and the pride of life—is not of the Father but is of the world.* The second reason we should not love the world is because *the lust of the flesh* is in the world. Now what is the lust of the flesh? *Lust* is a longing for what is forbidden. It is the desires of our flesh that want immediate gratification. *Flesh* is the sensual appetite. It would be any craving one has to satisfy their physical desires. This is not the posture of a believer in Jesus Christ. Consider what Paul says in Titus 2:11-12: "For the grace of God that brings salvation has appeared to all men, teaching us that, denying ungodliness and worldly lusts, we should live soberly, righteously, and godly in the present age." Peter echoes this in 1 Peter 2:11, "Beloved, I beg you as sojourners and pilgrims, abstain from fleshly lusts which war against the soul." Some will say, well, I just can't help myself! Oh? James says something different in James 1:13-15: "Let no one say when he is tempted, 'I am tempted by God'; for God cannot be tempted by evil, nor does He Himself tempt anyone. But each one is tempted when he is drawn away by his own desires and enticed."

You might say, so I see how serious the lust of the flesh is and that I am to avoid it, but what specifically is the lust of the flesh? Paul gives a pretty extensive list in Galatians 5:19-21: "Now the works of the flesh are evident, which are: adultery, fornication, uncleanness, lewdness, idolatry, sorcery, hatred, contentions, jealousies, outbursts of wrath, selfish ambitions, dissensions, heresies, envy, murders, drunkenness, revelries, and the like; of which I tell you beforehand, just as I also told you in time past, that those who practice such things will not inherit the kingdom of God." I would encourage you to look up these words and study what they mean; it would be a great study as well as an eye opener. But for now let me provide some examples of the lust of the flesh so that perhaps its meaning will be clearer. For instance, being hungry for food or having an appetite is not sinful. God made our bodies to feel hunger and to eat. But when that appetite becomes out of control and we gorge, then we have fallen prey to the lust of the flesh. Or if you starve that appetite because you have some sinful desire to be ridiculously thin, you have fallen prey to the lust of the flesh.

Let's take another example of the lust of the flesh: our sexual appetite. There is nothing wrong with that; God made our bodies to enjoy sexual relationship. Paul even says in 1 Corinthians 7:9 that it is better to marry than to burn with lust. But when that sexual appetite becomes out of control, to the point that we give way to sexual perversions such as fornication, adultery, homosexuality, bestiality and the like, then we have fallen prey to the lust of the flesh. By the way, the readers of this epistle would understand this, as the city of Ephesus was rampant with pagan religions which glorified sex. Sex had become perverted in John's day just as it has in our day. And of course, the readers of this epistle did not have the ready availability of pornography as we do today.

Let's also take the desire of having material things, like a home or a car or even furniture. There is nothing wrong with that. But if that desire becomes an idol to the point where you have to have more and more material things, or you always have to have the latest stuff and your lust is never satisfied, you have fallen prey to the lust of the flesh. Paul gives the remedy for the lust of the flesh in Romans 13:14, where he says, "But put on the Lord Jesus Christ, and make no provision for the flesh, to fulfill its lusts."

John now gives a third reason to not love the world and that is because *the lust of the eyes* is in the world. What is the lust of the eyes? The lust of the eyes is the seeking of mental pleasures, whereas the other, the lust of the flesh, is the seeking of physical gratification. This is a greedy craving that wants whatever it sees. There are some good examples of this in the Word of God. In Genesis 3:6 it states, "So when the woman saw that the tree was good for food, that it was pleasant to the eyes, and a tree desirable to make one wise, she took of its fruit and ate. She also gave to her husband with her, and he ate." Of course we know that this is the account of Eve and her transgression. But notice it says she saw and it was pleasant to the eyes. It was a high price she paid, as it is for the rest of us as well!

Another good example is found in Joshua 7:20-21, "And Achan answered Joshua and said, 'Indeed I have sinned against the LORD God of Israel, and this is what I have done: When I saw among the spoils a beautiful Babylonian garment, two hundred shekels of silver, and a wedge of gold weighing fifty shekels, I coveted them and took them. And there they are, hidden in the earth in the midst of my tent, with the silver under it.'" In this account, Achan relates how he took what God had forbidden the Israelites to take when He told them to destroy everything in Jericho. Achan confessed that he saw what God had forbidden and coveted it. He paid a high price, as well, for the lust of his eyes, as he was later stoned for his disobedience.

Another account that we are all probably familiar with is found in 2 Samuel 11:2-3: "Then it happened one evening that David arose from his bed and walked on the roof of the king's house. And from the roof he saw a woman bathing, and the woman was very beautiful to behold." We know this is the account of David and Bathsheba. But notice that he saw her and took her. And the price David paid for his lust was the death of his child when it was only seven days old.

Now all these are examples of the lust of the eyes which resulted in the carrying out of the lust of the flesh. Some perhaps think they can get away with the lust of the eyes because they think that's where it ends. Jesus, however, says something very different in Matthew 5:27-30,

> You have heard that it was said to those of old, 'You shall not commit adultery.' But I say to you that whoever looks at a woman to lust for her has already committed adultery with her in his heart. If your right eye causes you to sin, pluck it out and cast it from you; for it is more profitable for you that one of your members perish, than for your whole body to be cast into hell. And if your right hand causes you to sin, cut it off and cast it from you; for it is more profitable for you that one of your members perish, than for your whole body to be cast into hell (Matthew 5:27-30).

Jesus says lusting with the eyes is a sin worthy of damnation. Job said he made a covenant with his eyes that he would not look lustfully upon a woman (Job 31:1). In our day and age, lusting with the eyes becomes difficult to avoid because of so much media that former generations did not have to deal with. The internet, television, movies, commercials, magazines, billboards, and the like have been used to arouse the lust to have things to the point that many spend the bulk of their time shopping for things that they don't need and cannot afford. In addition to this, the media has created a gross lust for sex. The internet has made pornography so easy to come by, and we are seeing little children exploited and abused and some even murdered. Manufacturers don't sell products, but they sure sell sex. If the lust of the eyes is a problem for you I would encourage you to limit your exposure to media.

John goes on to mention the third deadly sin that is in the world and the fourth reason we should not love the world, and that is *the pride of life*. What is the pride of life? The pride of life is a boasting of one's own resources or in the stability of earthly things. It is the Greek word alazon, which means braggert. A great Greek scholar who did a character study on the word alazon said, "he stands in the harbor and boasts of the ships that he has at sea; he ostentatiously sends a messenger to the bank when he has a shilling to his credit; he talks of his friends among the mighty and of the letters he receives from the famous. He details at length his charitable benefactions and his services to the state. All that he occupies is a hired lodging, but he talks of buying a bigger house to match his lavish entertaining. His conversation is a continual boasting about things which he does not possess and all his life is spent in an attempt to impress everyone he meets with his own importance"[29] I have met people like that and, quite frankly, they are boring! Another man says this pride of life manifests itself as "a conceited pretentious humbug, who seeks to impress everyone he meets with his own non-existent importance"[30] He boasts about what he has done and what he will do. This is the person who thinks he is the Master of his own destiny, since he thinks he has all under control and is in control. The pride of life would certainly be a rebuke to the Gnostics who were claiming and boasting about some superior knowledge they claimed to have. This is not of God, John is saying. It is as old as Satan himself, as you can see in Genesis 3 in the "Questions to Consider" at the end of this chapter. An article in the Wall Street Journal recently caught my eye—*Technology, Good or Bad?*[31] It went along with many articles which have dealt with social networking venues and the pros and cons of them. Many people (non-believers, I might add) have come to realize that Facebook and other social networking have made us more engrossed in ourselves to the point that we have become consumed with not only sharing our own business with everyone but also with wanting to know everyone else's business. The Pride of Life! I was shocked when the writer of this particular article stated that "12% of people check their emails in their place of worship." I was sick at heart to think that we can no longer go to church to worship without checking our email! The pride of life has swallowed us up! What is so important in our email that it demands our attention and must interrupt our worship?

---

[29] William Barclay, *The Letters of John and Jude* (Louisville, KY: Westminster John Knox Press, 1960), p 58.

[30] John R. W. Stott, *Tyndale New Testament Commentary: The Letters of John* (Grand Rapids, MI: Eerdmans, 1988), p 105.

[31] L. Gordon Crovitz, *Wall Street Journal* (August 23rd, 2010).

John goes on to say these things—these 3 deadly sins—are *not of the Father*, but are *of the world.* Can you imagine our Lord ever being involved in such heinous sins? Jesus Himself was in the world, but you can read the pages of the New Testament and you will not find Him delighting in the world or involved in lust of any kind or in prideful boasting. When He was tempted with those things in the wilderness He never once succumbed to them. He has set the example for us and we should follow it. John will write later that this is possible, in 1 John 5:4-5, "For whatever is born of God overcomes the world. And this is the victory that has overcome the world—our faith. Who is he who overcomes the world, but he who believes that Jesus is the Son of God?"

John continues on with the fifth and final reason why we should not love the world in verse 17. He says, *the world is passing away, and the lust of it; but he who does the will of God abides forever*. The fifth reason we should not love the world is that it *is passing away*. These things on which the world spends money, time and energy are passing away. We rush and fret over these things and yet they are passing away. What did Paul say in 2 Corinthians 4:18? "While we do not look at the things which are seen, but at the things which are not seen. For the things which are seen are temporary, but the things which are not seen are eternal." Do we give thought to the fact that what we spend so much time on is temporary? As one man said, "The workaholic will die unfulfilled. The greedy politician will die in despair. The pleasure-mad partygoers will find their lives ruined by drugs or alcohol. Indulgence never satisfies; it only whets the appetite for more."[32] Many years ago I was helping my daughter Cindi plan her wedding. We were speaking to the photographer who was going to do the pictures at her wedding. He asked her what she and David (her fiancé) enjoyed doing together. She answered, "talking, watching the sunset, and doing things outdoors." He looked rather surprised and commented that the number one answer he gets from young couples about to be married is "watching TV

32 Bruce B. Barton, *Life Bible Application Commentary: 1, 2, and 3 John* (Carol Stream, IL: Tyndale House Publishers, 1998), pp 46-47.

and going to movies." I quickly commented that if that was what those relationships were based upon they would not last. How sad to think of couples in love and their one common enjoyment is entertainment. You cannot build relationships on entertainment. Ladies, these things are fleeting—they will not last.

Now what does John mean when he says the world is *passing away*? He means that it is departing. This word is in the present tense, which means that the world system has already begun the process of decaying and it will eventually be gone. Paul says in 1 Corinthians 7:31, "and those who use this world as not misusing it. For the form of this world is passing away." In fact, Peter says in his epistle (2 Peter 3:10), "But the day of the Lord will come as a thief in the night, in which the heavens will pass away with a great noise, and the elements will melt with fervent heat; both the earth and the works that are in it will be burned up." Why spend so much time on things that are going to burn up?

Not only is the world passing away, John says, but also *the lust of it*. What does that mean? It means that the urgent desires, the evil passions that we see and struggle with now, are going to pass away. There isn't going to be any lust of the flesh, lust of the eyes or pride of life in heaven. John makes this clear in another book he wrote, the Book of the Revelation: "But there shall by no means enter it anything that defiles, or causes an abomination or a lie, but only those who are written in the Lamb's Book of Life" (Revelation 21:27).

The Reason to Love God
1 John 2:17b

but he who does the will of God abides forever (1 John 2:17b).

John has given us five reasons why we should not love the world, and now as he ends this portion on loving the world he gives one grand reason why we should love God! In contrast to the lovers of the world, John says *but he who does the will of God abides forever*. In contrast to the world which is passing away we have God who is forever! What a great reason to love God—we will abide forever! John says those who do His will abide forever. What does it mean to do *the will of God*? Or perhaps we should ask: What is the will of God? The word for *will* is thelema—it is what He wants accomplished. That is the will of God. What did Jesus say in Mark 3:35? "For whoever does the will of God is My brother and My sister and mother."

John says, if you do the will of God you abide forever. What does it mean to *abide forever*? It means this person remains forever. In John 6:51, Jesus says "I am the living bread which came down from heaven. If anyone eats of this bread, he will live forever; and the bread that I shall give is My flesh, which I shall give for the life of the world." The person who abides in Him will also delight to do His will in this age and in the age to come. What bliss! What joy!

With the help of the Apostle John, we have seen: *The Command to Not Love the World* (v 15a): Don't love the world. *The Reasons to Not Love the World* (vv 15b-17a): 1. It proves that the love of the Father is not in you. 2. The lust of the flesh is in the world. 3. The lust of eyes is in the world. 4. The pride of life is in the world. 5. The world is passing away. *The Reason to Love God* (v 17b): You will abide forever!

Summary

Are you a world lover? Do you prefer the world to the Lord? Paul says in 2 Timothy 4:10 that Demas forsook him because he loved the present world. And yet Demas had helped Paul in the ministry, according to Colossians 4:14 and Philemon 24. But something happened to Demas; he loved the world. We aren't told exactly what tempted Demas to forsake Paul and the ministry and fall in love with the world, but something did. Perhaps it was the lust of the eyes, the lust of the flesh or the pride of life. You might be asking, well Susan, how would I know if I am a world lover? I think the answer lies in looking at the three areas John mentions in the text, the lust of the eyes, the lust of the flesh and the pride of life, and being willing to ask yourself some hard questions. You might start with the "Questions to Consider" at the end of this chapter. From there you might keep a schedule for a week of all the things you do. At the end of the week, ask yourself, what am I doing with my time? Am I involved in things that will last and will count for eternity, or am I spending the bulk of my time on things that are going to burn up in the end? As Paul would tell Timothy, his son in the faith, "You therefore must endure hardship as a good soldier of Jesus Christ. No one engaged in warfare entangles himself with the affairs of this life, that he may please him who enlisted him as a soldier" (2 Timothy 2:3, 4).

Ladies, if we love the Lord we will want to spend our days pleasing Him, doing His will, and not involved in things that are in opposition to Him and to His Kingdom. There is no way that we can be doing the will of God and at the same time be loving the world. There is no way we can be doing the will of God and at the same time be lusting with our flesh. There is no way that we can be doing the will of God and at the same time be lusting with our eyes. There is no way that we can be doing the will of God and at the same time be boasting of this life and all we have done. As C.S. Lewis once said "If we insist on keeping hell, or even earth, we shall not see heaven. If we accept Heaven we shall not be able to retain even the smallest and most intimate souvenirs of hell."[33]

[33] C. S. Lewis, *The Complete C. S. Lewis Signature Classics* (San Fransisco, CA: HarperOne, 2001), p 466.

Questions to Consider

Three Deadly Sins!

1 John 2:15-17

1. Read 1 John 2:15-17. (a) What is the main command in these verses? (b) Why do you think John transitions into this subject after verses 12-14?

2. Memorize 1 John 2:15.

3. (a) Read the accounts in Genesis 3:1-6 and Matthew 4:1-11, and note the ways in which Eve and the Lord were both tempted by the lust of the flesh, the lust of the eyes and the pride of life. (b) How did Christ withstand the temptation? (c) Why did Eve not withstand the temptation? (d) What do you learn from both examples?

4. (a) How does James describe worldliness in James chapter 4? (b) What words does James use to describe those who love the world? (c) What is the remedy for worldliness according to James?

5. (a) What does John 3:16 say? (b) What does 1 John 2:15 say? How do you reconcile these verses?

6. (a) Why is it imperative according to 1 John that believers not love the world? 1 John 2:16-17; 1 John 5:19. (b) What other passages come to mind that warn us of the dangers of loving the world?

7. (a) What did Jesus pray in John 17:11, 14-15? (b) How can a believer be in the world but not of the world? Support your answer with Scripture.

8. (a) What do *you* think worldliness is? (b) What are some common forms of worldliness? (c) What are some forms of worldliness that you personally are drawn to? (d) How do you resist those temptations?

9. Honestly evaluate your life in light of the following questions. (a) Am I in love with this world? (b) How am I enticed by the lust of the flesh, the lust of the eyes, or the pride of life? (For example: Do I concentrate on satisfying the lusts of my flesh? What attracts the attention of my eyes? Am I proud about my accomplishments or myself?) (c) Am I doing the will of the Father?

10. Please write down a prayer request after contemplating question 9.

Chapter 8

The Character of Antichrist

1 John 2:18-22

Several years ago my daughter and I were having a conversation about the things of the Lord. We were discussing sin and its monstrous effect in our lives, and she said, "Mom, one of the greatest fears Gunner (David) and I have is that we would one day prove to be among the false believers. We fear apostasy." You might be saying, isn't that kind of extreme? Two graduates of The Master's College fearing apostasy from the faith? What are they, nuts? Did you know the Apostle Paul feared the same thing? In 1 Corinthians 9, Paul writes about the Christian life and he compares it to running in a race. He speaks of this race as agonizing, running, fighting and beating the air. And then in verse 27, he says, "But I discipline my body and bring it into subjection, lest, when I have preached to others, I myself should become disqualified." (Some translations say castaway.) Paul is saying that he was afraid that he might be rejected or cast off in the end. He had a holy fear which motivated him to beat his body into subjection and not allow his body, his flesh, to master him. Paul did not have a smug confidence in his flesh.

We have sobering examples in Scripture of those who apostatized from the faith. Judas, one of the Lord's disciples, betrayed the Lord and later went out and hanged himself. Jesus says about him, "It would have been good for that man if he had never been born" (Mark 14:21). Demas is another example of one who defected from the faith. Paul says in 2 Timothy 4:10 that Demas forsook him because he loved the present world. And still today we have men and women who deny the faith they once claimed to believe—they apostatize. They are, indeed, antichrists, as John will say in the passage we're getting ready to look at. This was happening in the Apostle John's day, and he writes to his little children to warn them of this danger. He warns them of not only the antichrists of their day, but also the fact that one day the Antichrist will come. Let's examine verses 18-22 of 1 John chapter 2.

1 John 2:18-22

> Little children, it is the last hour; and as you have heard that the Antichrist is coming, even now many antichrists have come, by which we know that it is the last hour. [19]They went out from us, but they were not of us; for if they had been of us, they would have continued with us; but they went out that they might be made manifest, that none of them were of us. [20]But you have an anointing from the Holy One, and you know all things. [21]I have not written to you because you do not know the truth, but because you know it, and that no lie is of the truth. [22]Who is a liar but he who denies that Jesus is the Christ? He is antichrist who denies the Father and the Son (1 John 2:18-22).

In our last lesson, we learned of *The Command to Not Love the World* (v 15a): Don't love the world. *The Reasons to Not Love the World* (vv 15b-17a): 1. It proves that the love of the Father is not in you. 2. The lust of the flesh is in the world. 3. The lust of eyes is in the world. 4. The pride of life is in the world. 5. The world is passing away. *The Reason to Love God* (v 17b): You will abide forever! In this lesson, we'll see,

The Characteristics of the Last Hour (v 18)
The Characteristics of Antichrists (vv 19, 22)
The Characteristics of the Lovers of God (vv 20-21)

We ended our last lesson by contrasting the lovers of the world and the lovers of God. The lovers of the world are involved in three deadly sins—the lust of the flesh, the lust of the eyes and the pride of life. They are devoted to things that are going to pass away and burn up. In contrast to them, we saw the lovers of God, who do the will of God. They are involved in things that will not burn up but will last forever. They, too, as John said, will abide or live forever.

John has just mentioned in verse 17 that the world is passing away, and the lust of it. He is writing of the world which is passing away, which is a reminder that there is a last hour soon to come. And so he warns the little children, "Little children, the world is passing away; it is the last hour; beware of antichrists!" And so John begins this passage with the characteristics that mark the last hour.

The Characteristics of the Last Hour
1 John 2:18

> Little children, it is the last hour; and as you have heard that the Antichrist is coming, even now many antichrists have come, by which we know that it is the last hour (1 John 2:18).

As we begin this verse, we might ask, "Who are the *little children*?" The Greek word for children in this verse is paidia and is different than teknia. (We had this term before, in verses 12-14.) Teknia refers to all those who are born of God. Paidia, on the other hand, refers to the little babes, the new converts with limited spiritual understanding. Young men have the special temptation of the things of the world, but little children are vulnerable to deception.[34] As little children, they would be especially vulnerable to the false teachers, the antichrists of the day. New in the faith, they would be more likely to not be discerning, just as babies or little children, who have no idea that they should not walk out in the street or that putting their finger in the electrical socket is dangerous. They do not yet have that discernment. Paul gives us an indication of the danger little children are in when he admonished the church at Ephesus, the same church John is writing to, in Ephesians 4:14-15, "that we should no longer be children, tossed to and fro and carried about with every wind of doctrine, by the trickery of men, in the cunning craftiness of deceitful plotting, but, speaking the truth in love, may grow up in all things into Him who is the head—Christ." The young men and fathers in the faith would have more spiritual discernment,

[34] The Greek word paidia, translated *children*, is related to paideuo, meaning "to train." This suggests that the spiritual "little children" are subordinate and under discipline during this stage of their spiritual maturity; they are in training for maturity.

and would more likely recognize truth from error, but not these little children. So, John warns them, it is the *last hour* or the last time. The last hour, or the last time, began with the first coming of Christ and will end with His second coming. When John wrote this epistle, they were already in the last hour. And yet, right now, you and I are also living in the last hour. When you think about it, every hour is the last hour, and one of these days will be the final hour!

John goes on to say, *and as you have heard that the Antichrist is coming.*[35] Now you might be asking, "When did they hear that antichrist would come?" They heard this from the apostles. Consider these passages: Acts 20:29, 30, "For I know this, that after my departure savage wolves will come in among you, not sparing the flock. Also from among yourselves men will rise up, speaking perverse things, to draw away the disciples after themselves." Also, in 1 Timothy 4:1, "Now the Spirit expressly says that in latter times some will depart from the faith, giving heed to deceiving spirits and doctrines of demons." And still yet another, 2 Thessalonians 2:3-10,

> Let no one deceive you by any means; for that Day will not come unless the falling away comes first, and the man of sin is revealed, the son of perdition, who opposes and exalts himself above all that is called God or that is worshiped, so that he sits as God in the temple of God, showing himself that he is God. Do you not remember that when I was still with you I told you these things? And now you know what is restraining, that he may be revealed in his own time. For the mystery of lawlessness is already at work; only He who now restrains will do so until He is taken out of the way. And then the lawless one

[35] The universal testimony of the church fathers viewed the antichrist as a person yet to come, not a system: Justin Martyr (A.D. 103), Irenaeus (A.D. 140), Tertullian (A.D. 150), Origen (A.D. 184), Cyprian (A.D. 250), Jerome (A.D. 330), Chrysostem (A.D. 347), and Augustine (A.D. 384). Later views saw the antichrist as having already come: Mariana sees antichrist as Nero; Bossuet in Diocletian and in Julian; Grotious in Caligula; Wetstein in Titus; Hammond in Simon Magus; Whitby in the Jews; Schottgen in the Pharisees; Jarduin in the high-priest Ananias (cf. John McClintock and James Strong, *Cyclopedia of Biblical, Theological, and Ecclesiastical Literature, Vol. 1* (Grand Rapids, MI: Baker Book House, 1981), p 259.). Evidently, the first to recommend the near historical fulfillment of antichrist (i. e., coming in the first century at the destruction of Jerusalem under Titus or through the Roman Empire in the person of Nero or Diocletian) was Alcasar, a Spanish Jesuit in A.D. 1604.

> will be revealed, whom the Lord will consume with the breath of His mouth and destroy with the brightness of His coming. The coming of the lawless one is according to the working of Satan, with all power, signs, and lying wonders, and with all unrighteous deception among those who perish, because they did not receive the love of the truth, that they might be saved (2 Thessalonians 2:3-10).

John is writing 1 John several years after these other books were written and so his readers would have known of the warning of antichrist and the fact that he would come. So John says you have heard that antichrist *is coming*, or literally he is coming and is about to come. What is John talking about? More than likely John is referring to the passage in 2 Thessalonians 2:3, 4, where Paul speaks of the man of sin who exalts himself above all that is called God. There is coming a day when antichrist will come. The word *antichrist* occurs in the New Testament and only in these epistles of John—1 John 2:18, 22; 4:3; 2 John 7. So what does *antichrist* mean? *Anti-* means against or instead of. So an *antichrist* is one who is against Christ or one who tries to take the place of Christ or one who opposes Christ. In fact, any person, thing, doctrine, or system of religion which is opposed to Christ is antichrist.

John says not only will antichrist come, and you have heard that he is coming, but also *even now many antichrists have come.* Now what does John mean by this? Remember, John is combating Gnosticism in this epistle, and the Gnostics certainly belonged to a system of religion that was opposed to Christ. They denied that Jesus was the Christ! The Gnostics teachers, and all their followers, were definitely included in these many antichrists. And John says *by this we know it is the last hour*. How does the fact that there are many antichrists point to the fact that it is the last hour? The fact that antichrists will multiply is a sign for us to know that it is the last time; Jesus said that we would know by this that it is the last time. Consider Matthew 24:1-28, especially noting verses 5 and 24. Jesus says, in Matthew 24:5, "For many will come in My name, saying, 'I am the Christ,' and will deceive many," and in verse 24, "For false christs and false prophets will rise and show great signs and wonders to deceive, if possible, even the elect." And may I say that there are many antichrists today? You don't have to watch television or read the newspaper or magazines for long before you come to the conclusion that this world we live in is opposed to God. Many have tried to take the place of God, setting themselves up as their own gods to rule and govern their own lives. As the end of the age draws to its final chapter, I believe we will see more and more false teachers and those who oppose God. So what are the characteristics of the last hour? Antichrist and many antichrists will arise on the scene. These antichrists that John speaks of did not necessarily stand out as those who were opposed to Christ at the first! They were, in fact, at one time in the church, as John mentions in verse 19. And, ladies, this is a frightening warning to us all! Yes, the particular warning is to the little children who would be the most vulnerable being theologically naïve but the danger extends to all of us. And so we turn from the characteristics of the last hour to the characteristics of antichrists.

The Characteristics of Antichrists
1 John 2:19

> They went out from us, but they were not of us; for if they had been of us, they would have continued with us; but they went out that they might be made manifest, that none of them were of us (1 John 2:19).

Now who are *they* that John mentions? Since John is talking about the antichrists, the Gnostic teachers along with those who followed their teachings, this is the group he's referring to. Evidently, some had gone out from the church who had once been present in the church. The Greek phrase *went out* is speaking of a physical location. They went out from the church. This is not talking about church discipline or excommunication, as mentioned in Matthew 18, but a voluntary going out of their own free will. The Greek tense indicates that it means they left of their own accord. They left the church of Jesus Christ. These were religious people, but not Christ's children. They had attached themselves to the church, but they themselves were not an actual part of the church of Jesus Christ. This is a sobering warning of apostasy. John says they physically went out from us, but listen little children, the fact is *they were not of us, for if they had been of us, they would have continued with us; but they went out that they might be made manifest, that none of them were of us*! John says these guys proved by their going out that they were never in the faith. This happens today as well. People leave the church and never return. Why? They do so because they were never really in the church of Jesus Christ. But may I say that true believers in Jesus Christ do not fall away from the faith? They do not apostatize.

Consider the following passages: Matthew 24:13; Hebrews 3:14; 6:11, 12; 10:38, 39. Ladies, if we persevere to the end, it proves the sincerity of the commitment we have made. If we fall away, it proves the fact that we were never sincere or regenerated in the first place.[36] This may not be manifested until judgment day when God will separate the wheat from the tares and the sheep from the goats, according to Matthew chapters 13 and 25. Many people get involved in the body life of a church, they play the game and they do the

[36] The perseverance of the saints is, for the Apostle John, a test of genuine faith. As F. F. Bruce states, "Continuance is the test of reality." cf. *The Epistles of John* (Old Tappan, NJ: Revell Publishing Company, 1970), p 69. Zane Hodges dulls the sharp edge of this passage by suggesting that the pronoun "us" (Greek, hamon) refers to the Apostles instead of the Christian congregation of John's readership. Because he rejects the doctrine that genuine believers will indeed continue in the faith to the end, the pronoun provides a way to escape the simple meaning of the passage (cf. John F. Walvoord and Roy B. Zuck, *The Bible Knowledge Commentary: New Testament* (Wheaton, IL: Victor Books, 1983), p 891). The doctrine of perseverance, simply stated, is: "That continuous operation of the Holy Spirit in the believer, by which the work of divine grace that is begun in the heart, is continued and brought to completion." cf. Louis Berkhof, *Systematic Theology* (Grand Rapids, MI: Eerdmans Publishing House, 1986), p 46; cf. Romans 8:29-39; John 10:27-30; Hebrews 7:25; Philippians 1:6; 2 Timothy 1:12; 1 Peter 1:5; Jude 24, etc. Berkhof answers the central objection to the doctrine, that the warnings against apostasy would be uncalled for, if the believer could not fall away (cf Matthew 24:12; Colossians 1:23; Hebrews 2:1; 3:14; 6; 11; 1 John 2:6), stating: "They do not prove that any of those addressed will apostatize, but simply that the use of means is necessary to prevent them from committing this sin. Compare Acts 27:22-25 with verse 31 for an illustration of this principle" (Ibid. p 548).

religious thing, and often no one will know they are tares or goats until the end of the age. But these people that John mentions in verse 19 had already gone out and proved themselves to be antichrists. So one of the characteristics of antichrists is that they do not continue in the faith. In contrast to those who had gone out, we have those who have remained. And here we find the characteristics of those who are lovers of God.

The Characteristics of the Lovers of God
1 John 2:20-21

> But you have an anointing from the Holy One, and you know all things. I have not written to you because you do not know the truth, but because you know it, and that no lie is of the truth (1 John 2:20-21)

John says, *but*, in contrast to those who went out from us because they were never of us, in contrast to those who are apostate are you, the true, the genuine believers, *you have an anointing from the Holy One, and you know all things*. The word *anointing* means a smearing or something that is rubbed in. It refers to the sacred oil used in the Old Testament as a symbol of the receiving of the Spirit. They would also use this oil to anoint kings and priests and prophets for service. We see examples of this in 1 Samuel 10:1; 15:1 and 16:13. When Samuel anointed Saul he poured the oil upon his head. This anointing would have been a special ceremony which would indicate a setting aside for service. In the New Testament oil is used as a symbol of the Holy Spirit who anoints us. We also have an anointing from the Holy One and we also are set apart for service just like Saul was set apart for the service of king in the Old Testament. We have the example of Jesus at His baptism in Matthew 3:16, where it states that the Spirit of God descended like a dove and alighted upon Him. This was a sign of Christ being set apart for the office of Messiah, the Anointed One. So when we become children of God, we are the anointed ones. In contrast to those who are antichrist in verse 19, we are the anointed ones. John is saying, you have an anointing from the Holy One and you as believers are set apart for service for Christ. John will speak about this again in verse 27, "But the anointing which you have received from Him abides in you, and you do not need that anyone teach you; but as the same anointing teaches you concerning all things, and is true, and is not a lie, and just as it has taught you, you will abide in Him."

John then adds a phrase that has been misused much in our day: *and you know all things*. What does John mean by this? In contrast to the Gnostics, who claimed that only a few were in the know, John says no, you all know. Fathers in the faith know, young men in the faith know, and even little children are in the know, contrasted to the Gnostic idea that only some are in the know.[37] This is one aspect of the New Covenant where the "law of God is written on the heart and mind."[38] Believers all have this knowing. Remember the promise Jesus made to the disciples in John 14:26? "But the Helper, the Holy Spirit, whom the Father will send in My name, He will teach you all things, and bring to your remembrance all things that I said to you." Paul also helps us here with what he says in 1 Corinthians 2:14-16, "But the natural man does not receive the things of the Spirit of God, for they are foolishness to him; nor can he know them, because they are spiritually discerned. But he who is spiritual judges all things, yet he himself is rightly judged by no one. For 'who has known the mind of the LORD that he may

[37] The KJV holds to manuscript evidence of panta ("ye know all things"); the NASB and NIV hold to manuscript evidence of pantes ("you all know" and "all of you know"). Bruce Metzger points out that the reading of panta is perhaps a correction introduced by copyists who felt the need of an object after oidate ("ye know"). Hence, the more difficult reading would be pantes, leaving oidate without an object. A basic rule of textual criticism opts for the more difficult reading of the text (cf. *A Textual Commentary on the Greek New Testament* (New York, NY: United Bible Society, 1975), p 709). Also, the KJV translation of panta leaves the wrong impression, i.e., that even the *little children* of John's congregation know everything. This runs counter to the immediate context where the Apostle is warning them about their immature understanding.

[38] The New Covenant promise that the Word of God would be written on the hearts and minds of believers does not exclude the need for human teachers or effort in study (e.g., 2 Timothy 2:15). The New Testament gives special emphasis on the imperative ministry of human teachers, who explain the Word of God (cf. Ephesians 4:11-16; 1 Corinthians 12:28, 29; 1 Timothy 3:1, 2; 4:12-16; 5:17; 2 Timothy 2:1-7, 23-26; 3:14; 4:4; Hebrews 5:11-14; 2 Peter 3:17, 18; 1 John 2:24-27; 4:5, 6, etc.).

instruct Him?' But we have the mind of Christ." John says, you guys possess all you need to know regarding the truth, even though the Gnostics claimed that they were the only ones who possessed knowledge. Beware of any system of religion that teaches that only a few in the hierarchy are in the know. William Tyndale helps us here: "We are not anointed with oil in your bodies, but with the Spirit of Christ in your souls: which Spirit teacheth you all truth in Christ, and maketh you to judge what is a lie, and what truth, and to know Christ from antichrist."[39]

John goes on to mention more facts regarding those who love Christ. He says, *I have not written to you because you do not know the truth, but because you do know it*. What is *the truth*? It is the truth that Jesus is the Christ and the truth which affected their daily lives and the way they lived. John says *no lie is of the truth*. John says you guys are not ignorant of the truth. You are able to judge false teachers who are liars. You know that no lie is of the truth. What *lie* specifically is he speaking of? Well, he defines it in verse 22. And so we turn from the characteristics of those who love Christ—they have an anointing from the Holy One; they know all things; and they know the truth—back to the characteristics of those who are antichrist.

The Characteristics of Antichrists
1 John 2:22

> Who is a liar but he who denies that Jesus is the Christ? He is antichrist who denies the Father and the Son (1 John 2:22).

John says *who is a liar*? Who is false? Who is an imposter? *He who denies that Jesus is the Christ*. What lie is he referring to? He is referring to the lie that Christ is not who He claimed to be. Those who are liars are those who deny that Jesus is the Christ. What does it mean to deny that Jesus is the Christ? It means to reject, and it is an attitude of continual denial and rejection. This was the heresy of

[39] William Tyndale, *The Works of the English Reformers* (Whitefish, MT: Kessinger, 2009), p 435.

Gnostism. They denied that Jesus was the Christ. They divided the two. They denied the revelation of God in His Son Jesus Christ. The Gnostics rejected the incarnation of Christ. They claimed that Jesus could not be the Christ. The Gnostics taught that Christ descended upon Jesus when he was baptized, but that Christ left Jesus before He was crucified. Therefore, Jesus could not be the Christ. The Gnostics were liars. They separated Jesus from the Christ. John goes on to say: He is antichrist who denies the Father and the Son. This is not a reference to a person, but to a principle. If you deny that Jesus is the Christ, then you have the spirit of antichrist. You have placed yourself against God and in His stead. (There are other important verses to consider here: 1 John 4:1-3; 2 John 7). So an antichrist is one who denies the Father and the Son. Why does John say the Father and the Son? To deny one is to deny the other, as the Father and the Son are one. In John 10:30, Jesus says, "I and my Father are one." And in John 5:23, He also says, "that all should honor the Son just as they honor the Father. He who does not honor the Son does not honor the Father who sent Him."

Many people will tell you that they believe in God. I even had one person tell me once that they believed in a god, whatever that meant. But to believe in God without believing in His Son Jesus Christ does not equate to Christianity. And we must never assume that believers in God are believers in Jesus Christ. As Jesus Himself said in John 14:6, "I am the way, the truth, and the life. No one comes to the Father except through Me." To deny the Father is to deny the Son. To deny the Son is to deny the father. And to deny that Jesus is the Christ is the master of all lies. Paul tells us in 2 Thessalonians 2:9 that when antichrist comes he will deceive many with his signs and power and lying wonders. And then Paul says something very interesting in the next two verses, verses 10 and 11: "and with all unrighteous deception among those who perish, because they did not receive the love of the truth, that they might be saved. And for this reason God will send them strong delusion, that they should believe the *lie*" (emphasis mine). Antichrist, that great liar, who is against God and sets himself up as a god, will deceive many with his lying wonders, and Paul says God will give them over to such strong delusion that they will believe the lie. They will prefer antichrist and his lies in comparison to the pure truth of the gospel. The good news is that one day the Antichrist who opposes God and exalts himself will be thrown into the lake of fire to deceive no more (Revelation 19:20). But what a sad, sad day for those who, along with the Antichrist, have denied that Jesus is the Christ. What are the other characteristics of antichrists? They deny that Jesus is the Christ; and they deny the Father and the Son.

Summary

So what are *The Characteristics of the Last Hour* (v 18)? Antichrist and many antichrists will arise on the scene, giving special risk to immature little children in the faith. What are *The Characteristics of Antichrists* (vv 19, 22)? They do not continue in the faith; they deny that Jesus is the Christ; and they deny the Father and the Son. What are *The Characteristics of the Lovers of God* (vv 20-21)? They have an anointing from the Holy One; they know all things; and they know the truth.

In closing let me ask you: Do you believe that Jesus is the Christ? Do you really? How has it affected the way you have lived this week? Do you have a spirit of antichrist? Do you set yourself up against God in any form? Loving the world as we saw in our last lesson would be a form of setting yourself against God. Are you against any of the things He has laid forth for you in His Word? Do you place yourself in His stead? Do you think you have a better idea? Another question to ponder is this: Are you in a church where the leaders are discerning and can discern false doctrine and teachers? Is false teaching being tolerated in your church? Are false teachers allowed to remain in your fellowship? If so, why are you worshiping there and what are you doing about it? We must guard our hearts and our minds against anything that is opposed to Christ and we must make sure that we as individuals are not setting ourselves up against Christ in any form, whether it is in our attitudes or our actions. How terrible and dreadful it would be to be among those who went out from us, because they were never of us!

Questions to Consider

The Character of Antichrist

1 John 2:18-22

1. Read 1 John 2:18-22. (a) What are the characteristics of antichrists according to this passage? (b) What are some modern day cults or religions that fall under this category?

2. Memorize 1 John 2:19.

3. (a) John says in 1 John 2:18 that one way we know that it is the last time is that there are many antichrists. According to the following passages, what are some other signs of the last time? 1 Timothy 4:1-3; 2 Timothy 3:1-5; 2 Peter 3:3-7; Jude 18, 19. (b) Do you think we are in the last times? Why or why not?

4. (a) Can a genuine believer lose their salvation? (b) What does Scripture teach on this? See John 10:27-29; Hebrews 3:12-14; 10:38, 39; 1 John 2:19. (c) How can these verses be used as a warning but also a comfort? (d) What do you think John means by the phrase "they went out from us" (1 John 2:19)?

5. (a) What does John mean by the statement in 1 John 2:20, "and you know all things"? (The following verses may be helpful in answering this question: Proverbs 28:5; John 10:4, 5, 14; John 14:26; John 16:13; 1 Corinthians 2:13-16; Hebrews 8:11.) (b) In what ways could 1 John 2:20 be taken out of context and used incorrectly?

6. (a) Why is it imperative that we, as believers, be discerning about false teaching and antichrists? Back up your answer with Scripture. (b) Do you think you can discern truth from error? (Can you recognize a false teacher?) (c) How will you better equip yourself?

7. (a) Do you believe that Jesus is the Christ? (b) How has it affected the way you have lived your life this week?

8. (a) Do you know someone who has apostatized (gone out from the faith)? (b) What will you do about it? (Please be discreet in sharing.)

9. What do you think you should do to make sure you are not among those John mentions in 1 John 2:19? Please put your answer in the form of a prayer request.

Chapter 9

Confess, Continue, and Continually Live with the Son and the Father

1 John 2:23-27

In the past few years there has been an alarming increase in the number of people who say they believe there is no God. These people claim to be atheists. This new "religion" is taking over the country. And along with the increase in atheism we are seeing an increase in what is called Universalism, the belief that all people will eventually be saved. According to this way of thinking, you do not have to believe in Jesus—in fact, you don't have to believe in anything really—to have everlasting life. Even in our city, Tulsa, Oklahoma, one of the largest churches went defunct several years ago when its pastor, Carlton Pearson, claimed his new found revelation that one does not have to believe in Jesus to enter into eternal life. He proclaimed himself a Universalist and lost his pastorate over the change in his doctrinal beliefs. He later wrote a book called *The Gospel of Inclusion*, in which he spells out his religious heresy.

Can a person really not believe in Jesus and yet be a Christian and expect to go to Heaven? To answer this question, we must not go to some human author of a book, but we must go to the Divine Author of the Divine Book; we must go to The Authority, and that is the Word of God. What does The Authority have to say? Well, let's see as we read 1 John 2:23-27 together.

1 John 2:23-27

Whoever denies the Son does not have the Father either; he who
acknowledges the Son has the Father also. [24]Therefore let that
abide in you which you heard from the beginning. If what you

> heard from the beginning abides in you, you also will abide in the Son and in the Father. [25]And this is the promise that He has promised us—eternal life. [26]These things I have written to you concerning those who try to deceive you. [27]But the anointing which you have received from Him abides in you, and you do not need that anyone teach you; but as the same anointing teaches you concerning all things, and is true, and is not a lie, and just as it has taught you, you will abide in Him (1 John 2:23-27).

In our last lesson we saw *The Characteristics of the Last Hour* (v 18), which were that Antichrist and many antichrists will arise on the scene putting spiritual little children at risk. We then looked at *The Characteristics of Antichrists* (vv 19, 22), which were that they do not continue in the faith; they deny that Jesus is the Christ; and they deny the Father and the Son. Lastly, we saw *The Characteristics of the Lovers of Christ* (vv 20-21), which were that they have an anointing from the Holy One; they know all things; and they know the truth. In this lesson, we'll see that John writes to his children concerning:

Confessing the Son and the Father (v 23)
Continuing with the Son and the Father (v 24)
Continually Living with the Son and the Father (v 25)
Concerns about False Teachers (v 26)
Comforter, the Holy Spirit (v 27)

John is still expressing his concern about these antichrists who claim to have religion and yet reject the Son and the Father. And as he does so, he writes to his children about the importance of confessing the Son and the Father in verse 23.

Confessing the Son and the Father
1 John 2:23

> Whoever denies the Son does not have the Father either; he who acknowledges the Son has the Father also (1 John 2:23).

Notice that John begins with a word he has used before in his epistle: *whoever*. John is once again combating Gnostism, whose adherents claimed to have a relationship with God and yet denied the Son. John says no, there is no exception here. If you deny the Son you do not have the Father. What does John mean when he says *denies the Son*? The phrase means to disavow or reject, and the tense indicates it is a continual denial. This is not a denial like Peter when he denied our Lord three times. Yes, Peter did deny the Lord, but he did not continually deny Him. Peter repented from his evil act; in fact, he went out and wept bitterly. You can read 1 and 2 Peter and see a Peter who no longer denies his Lord. So if one denies the Son, John says that one *does not have the Father either*. Literally it means "not even does he have the Father." The Son and the Father are one, just as you can see in the Questions to Consider following this chapter. Jesus Himself said in John 15:23, "He who hates Me hates My Father also." Also, remember Jesus' words to the Jews in John 8:42? "Jesus said to them, 'If God were your Father, you would love Me, for I proceeded forth and came from God; nor have I come of Myself, but He sent Me.'"

In contrast to those who would deny the Son, we have those who confess the Son. John says he who *acknowledges the Son has the Father also*. What does it mean to *acknowledge* or confess the Son? To confess means to make a public proclamation that expresses a commitment, a covenant, and an obligation. It is an open confession. That's why in the New Testament you see conversion and baptism happen simultaneously. They believed and were baptized. When the New Testament saints were born again they made a public, open confession of their faith and commitment to Christ at their baptism. To further illustrate this practice, consider the following passages: Acts 2:37-41; 8:12, 13; 8:36-38; 10:47-48; 16:30-33. It is unfortunate that we teach in our day that a believer can put baptism off. Such a concept would be foreign to a New Testament saint. Paul reminds us of the importance of our confession of Christ in Romans 10:9-10: "That if you confess with your mouth the Lord Jesus and believe in your heart that God has raised Him from the dead, you will be saved. For with the heart one believes unto righteousness, and with the mouth confession is made unto salvation."

The word here for acknowledge is also a continual practice just like the denial is. We continually confess publicly and openly our relationship and commitment to Christ. Matthew 10:32, 33 is a very sobering passage concerning this: "Therefore whoever confesses Me before men, him I will also confess before My Father who is in heaven. But whoever denies Me before men, him I will also deny before My Father who is in heaven."[40] It goes without saying what Jesus is warning of here. If we confess the Son, then John says we have *the Father also*. As important as it is to openly confess our relationship to Christ, we must be on the alert that we also continue that relationship with Christ. John continues on by mentioning the importance of continuing with the Father and the Son in verse 24.

Continuing with the Son and the Father
1 John 2:24

> Therefore let that abide in you which you heard from the beginning. If what you heard from the beginning abides in you, you also will abide in the Son and in the Father (1 John 2:24).

The *you* here is in the emphatic in the Greek, which is in contrast to the false teachers. "As for you," you can almost hear John appealing to his little children and urging them, "don't be lead astray by those false teachers, my little children. Continue in the Son and in the Father. This is the only way to eternal life." Nothing is new, of course, as today there are many false teachers and idolatrous leaders who are competing for your loyalty to Christ. Many of them sound good, and many are appealing to the flesh. But we must be on

[40] The doctrinal test of an orthodox belief in the incarnation of Jesus Christ, as essential for genuine faith, would exclude not only heretics like Cerinthus, but all other religions, e.g., Judaism, Islam, Hinduism, Buddhism, Unitarianism, etc. The present evangelical debate over the inclusion of sincere religious practitioners of other religions is answered in this passage. Here is the biblical rejection of the heresy of religious Pluralism (i.e, the belief that it does matter what a person believes about Jesus Christ)! Not only faith in His work but also in His Person is the essential tenant of Christianity!

guard and sober-minded, and we must be a discerning people. No wonder John says in 3 John 4, "I have no greater joy than to hear that my children walk in truth." Gnosticism was sweeping many away into dangerous heresy.

John says, "What we have heard from the beginning of our salvation, we must let it abide till the end." We must not allow ourselves to be lead astray. John says *let that abide in you which you heard from the beginning*. From the time you heard about Christ, from the time you received the gospel, let it abide, let it stay in a given place, let it remain in you. John is telling them that as they do this, they *will abide in the Son and with the Father*. We cannot just merely have said a prayer in the past or given some mental assent to the gospel and be saved. We must abide, stay, remain and continue.[41] And may I say this will flesh itself out in how you live your life? Christianity makes a radical change in the life of believer. Things should not continue as they always have been. Paul makes this clear in 2 Corinthians 5:17: "Therefore, if anyone is in Christ, he is a new creation; old things have passed away; behold, all things have become new."

[41] There is some debate concerning the tense of the verb in the last clause. Some suggest that it is a future tense (Greek, meneite), i.e., *"ye shall abide in Him"*(KJV), but superior manuscript evidence suggests it is a present tense (Greek, menete), i.e., *"abide in Him"* (NASV). However, the bigger question concerns the mood of the verb. 1.) Some suggest the mood is *indicative* or a statement, "you abide in Him," and John is expressing his confidence in his readers. They suggest this because the menei at the beginning of the verse is indicative and suggests the same here. 2.) Others suggest the mood is *imperative* or a command, i.e., "abide in Him," and John is exhorting his readers to do what Jesus earlier told the disciples to do (cf. John 15:4). They suggest this because in verse 28 the imperative verb is clearly used (Greek, menete). The *weakness* of this view is seen in the redundancy of John, if this were taken as an imperative command. John's intent is to state a point of fact, expressing his confidence in his readers. The mood is in the indicative of statement. Two safeguards assure the genuine believers that they will not become apostate, one commanding their steadfast determination, i.e., they are to abide in the Word of God and not depart from it, and one promising them God's determined promise, i.e., the Spirit of God will remain in them and continue to guide them into truth.

So, if what we have heard remains in us, then we shall continue or remain in the Son and in the Father.[42] What a wonderful promise. Jesus himself said in John 8:31, "If you abide in My word, you are My disciples indeed." A genuine believer remains, abides and continues in the Son and the Father. It doesn't mean we never have struggles or trials or temptations, but it does mean we persevere. What did Jesus say in Matthew 10:22? "He who endures to the end shall be saved." When we think of continuing in the Son and the Father, our minds naturally take us to eternity, where we will continue with our Lord and Savior forever. And that brings us to verse 25 where John now writes concerning continually living with the Son and the Father

Continually Living with the Son and the Father
1 John 2:25

> And this is the promise that He has promised us—eternal life (1 John 2:25).

At first glance, this may seem like a strange statement John puts here between the admonition to continue in the Son in verse 24 and then the warning about those who would seduce them in verse 26. But when you think about it is not so strange. It's as if John is reminding his readers that those who continue in the Son and the Father are promised eternal life. Those who are seduced by false teachers are guaranteed eternal damnation. John says *this is the*

[42] Within a few years of John writing his epistles and warning about false doctrine, he was exiled to the island of Patmos and received the Revelation. Within that revelation, Christ Himself addressed the contemporary (i.e., A.D. 95) church at Ephesus, which had evidently been faithful in theological battle: "I know thy works, and thy labor, and thy patience, and how thou canst not bear them which are evil: and thou hast tried them which say they are apostles, and are not, and hast found them liars: And hast borne, and hast patience, and for my name's sake hast laboured, and hast not fainted … this thou hast, that thou hatest the deeds of the Nicolaitans, which I also hate" (cf. Rev. 2:2-6, KJV). Unfortunately, some of the other local churches in the area had failed in their vigilance in doctrinal purity, i.e., the church at Pergamum (cf. Revelation 2:12-17), the church at Thyatira (cf. Revelation 2:18-29), the church at Sardis (cf. Rev. 3:1-6), and the church at Laodicea (cf. Revelation 3:14-19).

promise that he has promised us—eternal life. What is a *promise*? A promise is an assent or a pledge. So what has been promised to us? Eternal life! What is *eternal life*? Eternal life is perpetual life. It is duration of life. It is a quality of life which we possess now and in the future. A believer in Jesus Christ who does not enjoy life now, who does not enjoy the peace and joy of knowing God and having their sins forgiven is a mystery to me. But eternal life is not only a quality of life now, but also the life to come in which we will be with Him forever. Revelation 21:3-4 speaks of a quality of life in the future that is utterly amazing: "And I heard a loud voice from heaven saying, 'Behold, the tabernacle of God is with men, and He will dwell with them, and they shall be His people. God Himself will be with them and be their God. And God will wipe away every tear from their eyes; there shall be no more death, nor sorrow, nor crying. There shall be no more pain, for the former things have passed away.'" John's mind now turns to those who do not have the wonderful blessing of eternal life in this life or in the life to come—false teachers!

Concerns about False Teachers
1 John 2:26

> These things I have written to you concerning those who try to deceive you (1 John 2:26).

Here in verse 26 we find yet another purpose for which John writes 1 John. (See 1:4 and 2:1 for other purpose statements.) John is writing because he is concerned about the false teachers who are seducing them. What does it mean to seduce or *deceive*? It means to cause to roam, to lead astray. The present tense here in the Greek indicates that these false teachers never let up trying to deceive them. This was a constant, unyielding effort. Paul warns of this very thing in 1 Timothy 4:1, 2: "Now the Spirit expressly says that in latter times some will depart from the faith, giving heed to deceiving spirits and doctrines of demons, speaking lies in hypocrisy, having their own conscience seared with a hot iron."

There is a special warning to us as women regarding the seduction of false teachers and our propensity to be deceived, in 1 Timothy 2:14, "And Adam was not deceived, but the woman being deceived, fell into transgression." Paul also mentions women's tendency to be led astray by false teachers in 2 Timothy 3 where he speaks of the last days and false teachers. Consider what he says,

> But know this, that in the last days perilous times will come: For men will be lovers of themselves, lovers of money, boasters, proud, blasphemers, disobedient to parents, unthankful, unholy, unloving, unforgiving, slanderers, without self-control, brutal, despisers of good, traitors, headstrong, haughty, lovers of pleasure rather than lovers of God, having a form of godliness but denying its power. And from such people turn away! For of this sort are those who creep into households and make captives of gullible women loaded down with sins, led away by various lusts, always learning and never able to come to the knowledge of the truth. Now as Jannes and Jambres resisted Moses, so do these also resist the truth: men of corrupt minds, disapproved concerning the faith; but they will progress no further, for their folly will be manifest to all, as theirs also was. But you have carefully followed my doctrine, manner of life, purpose, faith, longsuffering, love, perseverance, persecutions, afflictions, which happened to me at Antioch, at Iconium, at Lystra—what persecutions I endured. And out of them all the Lord delivered me. Yes, and all who desire to live godly in Christ Jesus will suffer persecution. But evil men and impostors will grow worse and worse, deceiving and being deceived. But you must continue in the things which you have learned and been assured of, knowing from whom you have learned them, and that from childhood you have known the Holy Scriptures, which are able to make you wise for salvation through faith which is in Christ Jesus. All Scripture is given by inspiration of God, and is profitable for doctrine, for reproof, for correction, for instruction in righteousness, that the man of God may be complete, thoroughly equipped for every good work (2 Timothy 3:1-17).

Isn't it interesting that Paul makes the same appeal in 2 Timothy 3:14 as John makes in 1 John 2:24? And I would make the same appeal to you. Continue in the things which you have learned. My dear sisters, don't be lead away by new and novel ideas. Throughout the years as I have been ministering to women, I have been saddened by the lack of biblical discernment among women and by their ongoing naivety. I sometimes wonder if they think there is some spiritual merit in remaining naïve. We must beware, and we must be women of the Word.

Sobering words for all of us to consider, whether we are male or female, are Christ's own words in Mark 13:22: "For false christs and false prophets will rise and show signs and wonders to deceive, if possible, even the elect." That's a scary thought—that false teachers will try to deceive us. Jesus, however, gives us assurance here that it is not possible, as He says *if* it were possible. But the fact remains that some will try to deceive believers. The prophet Jeremiah wept over the false teachers in his day and wrote, "An astonishing and horrible thing has been committed in the land: The prophets prophesy falsely, and the priests rule by their own power; and My people love to have it so. But what will you do in the end?" (Jeremiah 5:30, 31). Are you prepared? Are you armed with the Word of God? Can you discern a false teacher? Perhaps we would do well to listen to James, who tells us to not to rush into the office of teacher (James 3:1), and Paul, who tells Timothy not to lay hands suddenly on any man (1 Timothy 5:22). Tyndale's Life Application Commentary provides some helpful ways in which we can discern and evaluate false teachers.

1. Use condemnation sparingly. First of all, we're warned not to cast off all teachers. Some are misguided and just need more instruction. Remember Apollos in Acts 18? He only knew the baptism of John and was speaking boldly in the synagogue of this. When Priscilla and Aquila heard him speak, Scripture says, they took him aside and expounded unto him the way of God more perfectly. Apollos was in need of a better understanding of the truths of God.

2. Pay attention to the teacher's ethical and moral behavior. The Bible makes clear that false teachers will have immoral lifestyles. 2 Peter and Jude have much to say about false teachers and their moral behavior. In 2 Peter 2:13-14, Peter says they "will receive the wages of unrighteousness, as those who count it pleasure to carouse in the daytime. They are spots and blemishes, carousing in their own deceptions while they feast with you, having eyes full of adultery and that cannot cease from sin, beguiling unstable souls. They have a heart trained in covetous practices, and are accursed children." And in Jude 1:16, "These are grumblers, complainers, walking according to their own lusts; and they mouth great swelling words, flattering people to gain advantage." And those are just a few lovely characteristics of these rascals! Read those passages in their contexts sometime if you want a clear picture of a false teacher's lifestyle. Watch how they treat people and money; don't excuse or cover up their bad behavior.

3. Choose your church carefully. Is Christ the center of the church? Do its leaders pray? Is the Bible honored and taught? Is God at work there? False churches may be very busy, but their teachings reveal the void when Christ and the Bible are pushed to the side. If that is the case, go somewhere else. Some of the modern day false teachers who deny that Jesus is the Christ are: Seventh Day Adventists, Jehovah's Witnesses, Mormons, Liberalism, New Age, and Christian Scientists, just to name a few. We also must beware because even some professing evangelicals are beginning to deny some essentials of Biblical doctrine, like the man I mentioned at the beginning of this chapter. [43]

John now shifts from the subject of false teachers to the blessed comforter our Holy Spirit. This is a wonderful way to end this lesson—with a look at the Spirit. So John writes regarding the Comforter, the Holy Spirit.

---

[43] Bruce B. Barton, *Life Bible Application Commentary: 1, 2, and 3 John* (Carol Stream, IL: Tyndale House: 1992), p 182.

Comforter, the Holy Spirit
1 John 2:27

> But the anointing which you have received from Him abides in you, and you do not need that anyone teach you; but as the same anointing teaches you concerning all things, and is true, and is not a lie, and just as it has taught you, you will abide in Him (1 John 2:27).

But is a contrast to the false teachers. John is saying, but as for you, in contrast to the seducers. What does John mean by *the anointing which you have received from Him*? What is *the anointing*? The anointing is the Holy Spirit which each believer has. We covered this in verse 20 as well. John says we received the Spirit *from Him*. And *Him* refers to the Father. Jesus makes this clear in John 14:26: "But the Helper, the Holy Spirit, whom the Father will send in My name, He will teach you all things, and bring to your remembrance all things that I said to you."

John says this anointing *abides in you*. In other words, the Holy Spirit remains in us. John is not commanding them to let the Holy Spirit dwell in them, but stating the fact that He does dwell in them. Paul says in Ephesians 1:13-14, "In Him you also trusted, after you heard the word of truth, the gospel of your salvation; in whom also, having believed, you were sealed with the Holy Spirit of promise, who is the guarantee of our inheritance until the redemption of the purchased possession, to the praise of His glory." The Holy Spirit doesn't come and go in the life of a New Testament saint. He indwells us, and we have been sealed by Him until the day of redemption. This is an important phrase here, as the Greek world also knew something of anointing. But it was not the anointing of the Holy Spirit. Anointing would take place as an initiation into the mystery religions, Gnostism being one of them. By this anointing it was claimed that one would gain special knowledge of God. In fact, it was said that these false teachers would say, "We alone of all men are Christians, who complete the mystery at the third portal and are anointed there with speechless anointing."[44] John says no, you have the true anointing which Christ gave, not which some false teacher has claimed. And then he makes a statement that has been used out of context by many: *and you do not need that anyone teach you.* (At a conference I was speaking at I actually had someone come to the book table and tell me that they did not need to buy any books because they did not need anyone to teach them!) This is similar to what we read in verse 20, where John states *and you know all things*. John is writing concerning the things of eternal life, the things of Christ, the things which you have heard from the beginning (verse 24). John is saying, you don't need these Gnostics giving you a bunch of error. Don't listen to their lies. You don't need them to teach you.

The Gnostics taught that they were the only ones who could teach others concerning the things of God because they were the only ones in the know. Again, this is a verse which is often taken out of context to teach that we don't need others to teach us and that the Holy Spirit does all the teaching. That is not what John is saying. If it was, then we would have to throw out verses like Titus 2:1-8, where it states that the older women are to teach the younger women and the older men are to teach the younger men. Paul also speaks of the gift of teaching in 1 Corinthians 12:28 and Ephesians 4:11. We also know the apostles went about teaching and preaching. Also, we would need to do away with the book we are studying, as the Apostle John is doing what? He is teaching as he writes this book! We must always be looking at context if we want to interpret the Bible correctly.

John goes on to say, *but as the same anointing teaches you concerning all things, and is true, and is not a lie*. John is saying what you are taught by the Holy Spirit is true and it is no lie. Of course, that makes sense because the Holy Spirit is part of the Trinity, and we know that God cannot lie. God is truth. But the Gnostics were

[44] William Barclay, *The Letters of Jude and John* (Louisville, KY: Westminster John Knox Press, 1960), p 78

claiming that Jesus was not the Christ. John says you know what is truth and what is a lie. The Gnostics are teaching you lies! And then John ends by saying *and just as it has taught you, you will abide in Him*. Just as the Holy Spirit has taught you, you will remain in Him. *In Him* refers to Christ. What is John saying here? He's saying you shall persevere in the faith. What a blessed promise to those of us who have confessed Jesus and continue to walk with Jesus. The best is yet to come, as we will continually live with Jesus forever in the Kingdom of God.

Summary

Let's wrap up what we've learned. John has written concerning *Confessing the Son and the Father* (v 23): Do you confess the Son and the Father? Have you made a public profession of that by being baptized since your conversion, and are you still publicly acknowledging the Son and the Father? John also writes of *Continuing with the Son and the Father* (v 24): Are you continuing with the Son and the Father? How has your life shown this week that you are remaining with the Son and the Father? Next, John writes about *Continually Living with the Son and the Father* (v 25): Are you enjoying a quality of life now that God has promised you? Are you looking forward to eternal life with the Father and the Son? From there John moves on to write about his *Concerns about False Teachers* (v 26): Are you discerning regarding the false teachers of our age? And lastly, John writes regarding the *Comforter, the Holy Spirit* (v 27): Are you thankful for the precious Holy Spirit whom God has given to you as the guarantee of your inheritance? What rich nuggets of truth John has written for those who believe and confess Jesus! We are blessed to have the wonderful gifts of His Spirit now and eternal life to come!

Questions to Consider

Confess, Continue, and Continually Live with the Son and the Father

1 John 2:23-27

1. Read 1 John 2:23-27. What characterizes a genuine believer according to these verses?

2. Memorize 1 John 2:25.

3. (a) Why does John say, in verses 23 and 24, that to deny, confess, or to continue with the Son is the same as to deny, confess, or to continue with the Father? See John 10:30, 38; 14:9-10; 17:21. (b) What do the following passages teach you regarding this union of the Father and the Son? 2 Corinthians 4:4; Colossians 1:15; Hebrews 1:1-3.

4. (a) Who is given eternal life? See Matthew 25:46; John 17:2; Romans 2:5-7; James 1:12. (b) What is eternal life? See John 14:3; 17:3; 2 Timothy 2:11, 12; Revelation 22:1-5. (c) According to Titus 1:2, when was eternal life first promised? (d) How did Jesus reiterate this promise while He was on earth? See John 3:15, 16, 36; 6:40, 47, 57.

5. 1 John 2:24 says that believers remain and continue in the Son. What do the following passages teach you about this marvelous truth and how this remaining and continuing is possible? John 10:27-30. Romans 8:38, 39; Philippians 1:6; 2 Timothy 1:12; 1 Peter 1:3-5.

6. (a) Do you think that John is teaching, in 1 John 2:27, that we do not need others to teach us? Support your answer with Scripture.

7. (a) Have you confessed the Father and the Son? (b) Are you continuing with the Father and the Son? If you answered yes to both of these questions, then rejoice, as you will continually live with the Father and the Son! If you answered no to either of these questions, then I would encourage you to repent and turn to Him!

8. How would you explain eternal life to someone who asked you what it meant?

9. Do you know anyone who is being seduced by false teachers? What will you do to warn them of the danger they are in? (Please be discreet).

10. Come with a prayer of thanksgiving to God for your eternal life!

Chapter 10

Living in Light of the Lord's Return

1 John 2:28-3:3

Around the end of each year, as the Christmas season approaches, most Christians are beginning to reflect on the first coming of Christ. We start to think about God in the flesh, about God as a baby coming to earth! We meditate on Christ's coming to save His people from their sins. We think of God who sent His son Jesus Christ to die in order that we might have life eternal. But as we reflect on His first coming during this time of the year, do we also reflect on His second coming? This same Savior who came the first time to die for our sins, is coming again the second time to judge the living and the dead for their sins. This same righteous Savior who came the first time is going to come the second time and take His righteous ones home with Him. The Apostle John puts it this way:

1 John 2:28-3:3

> And now, little children, abide in Him, that when He appears, we may have confidence and not be ashamed before Him at His coming. 29If you know that He is righteous, you know that everyone who practices righteousness is born of Him. 3:1Behold what manner of love the Father has bestowed on us, that we should be called children of God! Therefore the world does not know us, because it did not know Him. 2Beloved, now we are children of God; and it has not yet been revealed what we shall be, but we know that when He is revealed, we shall be like Him, for we shall see Him as He is. 3And everyone who has this hope in Him purifies himself, just as He is pure (1 John 2:28-3:3).

In our previous lesson, we learned that John wrote to his spiritual children concerning: *Confessing the Son and the Father* (v 23); *Continuing with the Son and the Father* (v 24); *Continually*

Living with the Son and the Father (v 25); *Concerns about False Teachers* (v 26); and the *Comforter, the Holy Spirit* (v 27). John has just written in verse 27 regarding the importance of abiding in Christ. It is imperative for believers to abide in Christ until the time comes for God to take us home either by death or by the return of His Son, Jesus Christ. And because of that, John now transitions to the theme of the Lord's return for those who are abiding in Him. In this lesson, we'll consider the following questions:

> *How Should We Live in Light of the Lord's Return?* (2:28a, 29, 3:3)
> *Why Should We Live this Way in Light of The Lord's Return?* (2:28b, 3:2)

How Should We Live in Light of the Lord's Return?
1 John 2:28a

> And now, little children, abide in Him, (1 John 2:28a).

The first two words John uses, *and now*, are used to describe a new section or a new thought. And indeed it is a new thought, even though John touched briefly on the fact that it is the last hour in 2:18, and the fact that believers abide in Him in 2:27. John says, *and now, little children, abide in Him. Little children* is a term we've had before. It is the Greek word teknion, which means all children of God or all born ones of God. The Apostle had addressed fathers (2:13, 14), young men (2:13, 14b-17) and little children (2:13, 18-27) and now returns to admonish all believers. John calls for all of God's children to abide in Him, which means to remain in Him. It refers to a permanent relationship between the believer and the Father which runs deep. The tense is such that it means "keep on abiding in Him." All believers are to abide in Christ. Specifically, what are we being called to do? As we discovered in 2:6, to *abide in Him* (Greek, en autoi menein) goes beyond being *in Him* (Greek, en autoi esmen), suggesting an intimate relationship of abiding or remaining. It involves personal determination and effort until the coming of Christ or the end of one's life. This is contrasted with those who were not abiding but departing (cf. 1 John 2:18-19).[45] This is the first way for all believers to live in light of our Lord's return—abide in Him.

Why Should We Live this Way in Light of the Lord's Return? 1 John 2:28b

> that when He appears, we may have confidence and not be ashamed before Him at His coming (1 John 2:28b)

John has already spoken of abiding in verse 24 and 27. You might say, "Why should I abide in Him? I mean, why not live it up before the Lord returns? I have my fire insurance!" Well, John now gives two reasons why we should abide in Him in view of His return. First of all, John says so that *when He appears, we may have confidence*. This is the first reason why we should abide in Him till He returns—so that we will have confidence when He comes. The word *appear* means to make manifest or visible. The word translated *when He appears* is better translated as "when He is manifested," because the Greek, phanerothei, is an aorist tense and passive voice, calling attention to the suddenness of the event, in which God the Father is the agent of the revelation of His Son.[46] Christ is one day going to appear. This was foretold right after Christ ascended into heaven. In Acts 1:9 we have recorded for us that the disciples saw a cloud take Christ out of their sight. Of course, the disciples were gazing up into heaven and wondering what was going on. And remember, two men standing by, probably angels, said, "Men of Galilee, why

---

[45] The Apostle John uses the term *abide* (Greek, meno) 20 times in First John and nine times in this chapter alone (cf. 2:6, 10, 14, 17, 18, 24, 27, 27, 28). Later in the epistle, John defines how to "abide in Him," i.e., by personal obedience (cf. 1 John 3:24).

[46] The term phaneroo is used of Christ for His incarnation (cf. 1 John 1:2; 3:5, 8; John 1:31; 3:11; 7:4; 1 Peter 1:20); His words and works (cf. John 2:11; 17:6); His appearances after the resurrection (cf. 1 John 3:2, 8; John 21:1, 14); and His second coming (cf. 1 John 2:28; 3:2; Colossians 3:4; 1 Timothy 3:16). The term phaneroo is never used to describe God the Father (cf. Robert L. Thomas, *Exegetical Digest of First John* (Copyright by Robert L. Thomas, 1984), p 221).

do you stand gazing up into heaven? This same Jesus, who was taken up from you into heaven, will so come in like manner as you saw Him go into heaven" (Acts 1:11). One day Christ will be made visible once again. He will appear. And John says abide in Him so that when He does come back *we may have confidence*. Notice that John includes himself in this, as evidenced by the pronoun *we*. John knew he must abide also. He was no different than you and me. What does it mean to have confidence? It means to have boldness in speaking. It was a word that had a range of meanings: speaking openly rather than secretly; speaking truth rather than lies; speaking courageously rather than keeping quiet out of fear or respect; and speaking plainly rather than obscurely. In fact, it was a word that described the martyrs in the early church as they faced their killers: they had confidence. It was also used to describe the free citizens of Athens who were allowed to freely speak their mind with boldness in the assembly.[47]

Ladies, as we abide in Christ we can be assured that we will have confidence or boldness when He comes. One man helps us with this by saying: "The thought here is of the confidence with which a person may enter into the royal presence and speak with

[47] This is the first instance of parresia, a word that occurs 9 times in the Gospel of John, and 4 times in 1 John, constituting 40% of total New Testament usage (31 times). Etymologically, it comes from pan-resia, meaning "saying all"; and its range of meaning includes: speaking openly rather than secretly; speaking truth rather than falsehood; speaking courageously rather than keeping quiet out of fear or respect; speaking plainly rather than obscurely … parresia was an important concept in Attic democracy, being more aggressive than "freedom" (elsutherostomia) in expressing the right to speak against a tyrant. Among friends it covered the right to correct moral faults, and it was used that way especially by the Cynics and Isocrates. Although relatively infrequent in the LXX, this noun in Judeo-Hellenistic literature (Philo, Josephus) took on a meaning not found elsewhere: the right to speak openly to God, e.g., of Moses as a friend of God. The New Testament usage seems to draw upon both backgrounds …. In all 4 uses in 1 John it refers to one's having confidence before God or His Son as one makes petitions (5:14) or faces judgment (2:28; 4:17), or both (3:21-22). This is the same meaning parresia has in Heb. 4:16; 10:19. In the early church, martyrs are said to have parresia both on earth against their opponents and in heaven toward God (for they are His friends). cf. Raymond E. Brown, *The Epistles of John, The Anchor Bible, Vol. 30* (Garden City, NY: Doubleday, 1982), pp 380-1.

the king without any fear."[48] John will speak of this fact again in 1 John 4:17, 18: "Love has been perfected among us in this: that we may have boldness in the day of judgment; because as He is, so are we in this world. There is no fear in love; but perfect love casts out fear, because fear involves torment. But he who fears has not been made perfect in love." If we are abiding in Him as John has just admonished us to do, then it is only natural that we will have boldness or confidence when our Lord returns. As Paul says in Romans 8:1, "There is therefore now no condemnation to those who are in Christ Jesus, who do not walk according to the flesh, but according to the Spirit."

John moves on to the second reason for abiding in Him until He comes: *so that we will not be ashamed before Him at His coming*. What does it mean to *be ashamed*? The thought is that of separation and shrinking from God through the shame of a guilty conscience. There will be shame for those who have lived unrighteously, but for those who have lived holy before God and others, for those who have been abiding in Him, there will be no shame. The Psalmist put it well in Psalm 119:6, when he said, "Then I would not be ashamed, when I look into all Your commandments." Or as the Apostle Peter penned it, "Therefore it is also contained in the Scripture, 'Behold, I lay in Zion a chief cornerstone, elect, precious, and he who believes on Him will by no means be put to shame'" (1 Peter 2:6). And even Paul states, "For the Scripture says, 'Whoever believes on Him will not be put to shame'" (Romans 10:11).

John says as you abide in Him you will have confidence and you will not be ashamed *at His coming*. When John says His coming, he means His presence. It is a word that was used to express the visit of a King or Emperor. It implies that our Lord's return will involve His personal presence. He is now absent, but will one day be seen. John tells us in the book of the Revelation, "Behold, He is coming with clouds, and every eye will see Him, even they who

48 I. Howard Marshall, *The Epistles of John* (Grand Rapids, MI: Eerdmans, 1978), p 166.

pierced Him. And all the tribes of the earth will mourn because of Him. Even so, Amen" (Revelation 1:7). And John goes on to give us the second way we should be living in light of His return in verse 29.

How Should We Live in Light of the Lord's Return? 1 John 2:29

> If you know that He is righteous, you know that everyone who practices righteousness is born of Him (1 John 2:29).

Perhaps a better rendering of this verse would be: "If you know as an assured fact that He is righteous, you will logically conclude that anyone who practices righteousness has been born of Him." This is the second way we should live in view of His return—practice righteousness. What does the word *righteous* mean? It means to do right. God is righteous; He does what is right. So the logical conclusion is that everyone who is born of God does right! The person who does righteousness is born of Him; they have been regenerated. The tense indicates that the new birth has not only taken place but is still effective. This person who is born of God continues to practice righteousness. Even the Old Testament saints understood this, as David makes clear in Psalm 15:1, 2: "LORD, who may abide in Your tabernacle? Who may dwell in Your holy hill? He who walks uprightly, and works righteousness, and speaks the truth in his heart." David is saying, "Lord, who is truly religious? Who is your friend? Who can dwell with you?" And then David follows those questions with a list of ten imperatives, and two of those mention practicing righteousness. And in the next three verses in 1 John, John continues on with this theme of living in view of the coming of Christ, though there is an unfortunate chapter division at this point. With the reminder that we are born of Him is also a reminder of the Father's love to us—the reminder that we are called His children! John says:

> Behold what manner of love the Father has bestowed on us, that we should be called children of God! Therefore the world does not know us, because it did not know Him (1 John 3:1).

John starts this verse with the word *behold*. This means listen up, pay attention! John says look at *what manner of love the Father has bestowed on us*! What does John mean by this? *Manner of love* means quality and quantity of love! It is a love beyond measure. It is a love that I think is described well in Romans 8:35-39:

> Who shall separate us from the love of Christ? Shall tribulation, or distress, or persecution, or famine, or nakedness, or peril, or sword? As it is written: 'For Your sake we are killed all day long; we are accounted as sheep for the slaughter.' Yet in all these things we are more than conquerors through Him who loved us. For I am persuaded that neither death nor life, nor angels nor principalities nor powers, nor things present nor things to come, nor height nor depth, nor any other created thing, shall be able to separate us from the love of God which is in Christ Jesus our Lord (Romans 8:35-39).

Now, ladies, that is an incredibly awesome and powerful love. The word *manner* is an interesting word in the Greek. It is used to describe something foreign, like a country or a race. John is saying, "What a foreign kind of love this is that the Father has bestowed on us, that we should be called the children of God." John once again includes himself by using the pronoun *we*. God's love is a kind of love that is certainly foreign to the world in which we live. It is a love which comes from another country indeed—a heavenly country! The word manner is also a word which is used to describe astonishment. We would say, "Wow!" *Love* here is agape love, which speaks of God's love to man. It is not emotional; it is a love which seeks the good of the other. John says this is amazing love, that we should be named the *children of God*. John is referring here not to the relationship between an adopted child and a father, but to the natural relationship between a child and a father. What kind of love is this that we depraved souls should identify with this Holy God? We who were once haters of God, we who were once proud and involved in all kinds of evil, should be children of God? As the songwriter put it so well, "What wondrous love is this, O my soul, O my soul, what wondrous love is this, O my soul. What wondrous love is this, that caused the Lord of bliss to bear the dreadful curse for my soul, for my soul, to bear the dreadful curse for my soul."[49] Ladies, the fact that God loves us and has called us and predestined us to salvation should not ever produce pride in us, but humility. It is not because of our good works, but according to His righteousness and great love that He saved us! This should also be a motivating factor in all of us to live holy lives!

John says, *therefore the world does not know us because it did not know Him*. The word *know* means to recognize, understand, appreciate and to be in a friendly relationship with. The world does not understand us. They don't understand our principles and our convictions. They don't know why we can have peace and joy in the midst of pain. They don't know or understand the hope we possess. They're not in a friendly relationship with us. So why does the world not understand or know us? John says, *because it did not know Him* either. They thought He was crazy! They thought He had a demon! Christ made it clear that the world would have the same response toward us as it does toward Him. In John 15:18-19, He says, "If the world hates you, you know that it hated Me before it hated you. If you were of the world, the world would love its own. Yet because you are not of the world, but I chose you out of the world, therefore the world hates you." Even later on John will mention this in 1 John 3:13 when he says, "Do not marvel, my brethren, if the world hates you." And in light of this, John goes on to mention two more reasons why we should live righteously while we wait for His return.

Why Should We Live this Way in Light of the Lord's Return? 1 John 3:2

> Beloved, now we are children of God; and it has not yet been revealed what we shall be, but we know that when He is revealed, we shall be like Him, for we shall see Him as He is (1 John 3:2).

[49] Alexander Means, *What Wondrous Love Is This*.

John uses the term *beloved*, agapatos, which means dear friends. It is a word used to describe those loved by the Father as well as those loved by the Apostle John. John says to his dear friends, *now we are the children of God*. We are children of God now and we will be in the life to come. We don't have to wait until we die or until the second coming of Christ to be called the children of God; we are children of God right now! And John goes on to say, *and it has not yet been revealed what we shall be*. What we are now is not what we will be, thanks be to God! Even though we are now His children, we are still growing in sanctification and looking more and more like Christ. And we will not be completely like Him until we are resurrected. John puts it like this: *when He is revealed, we shall be like Him*. The word *like* is a Greek word which means a qualitative comparison. We will never be equal to Christ, but we will be similar to him in holiness and in our resurrected bodies. We will be similar in appearance and in character. Paul put it well in Philippians 3:21: "who will transform our lowly body that it may be conformed to His glorious body, according to the working by which He is able even to subdue all things to Himself." We know from the Word of God that our body will have no more pain or sickness. We will have a new body! We will not decay. We will never die. What a deal!

This is the third wonderful reason to live righteously in light of His return—we will be like Him. In addition to this, John also says *we shall see Him as He is*. What does this mean? It means to gaze with wide open eyes. John speaks of this in Revelation: "Behold, He is coming with clouds, and every eye will see Him, even they who pierced Him. And all the tribes of the earth will mourn because of Him. Even so, Amen" (Revelation 1:7). Again, in another place in Revelation: "They shall see His face, and His name shall be on their foreheads" (Revelation 22:4). This is the fourth reason to live holy in view of His return—we will see Him. This is perhaps the most blessed reason to live a holy life till He returns. We will be forever with the one who died for us! It's interesting to note that Jesus says in Matthew 5:8: "Blessed are the pure in heart, for they shall see God." And Paul says in Hebrews 12:14, "Pursue peace with all people, and holiness, without which no one will see the Lord." Both Jesus and Paul are saying exactly what John is saying in this epistle: Without living a righteous life we will not see God. And with that, John concludes his thoughts on the return of our Lord and gives us the third way we should live in light of the Lord's return.

How Should We Live in Light of the Lord's Return? 1 John 3:3

> And everyone who has this hope in Him purifies himself, just as He is pure (1 John 3:3).

John says *everyone*—no exception—everyone *who has this hope in Him purifies himself. Hope in Him* is better rendered hope set on Him. The hope here is not an "I hope so" kind of hope, but it is an assured expectation. The coming of Christ should be the hope of all believers. It is as Paul says in Titus 2:13, "looking for the blessed hope and glorious appearing of our great God and Savior Jesus Christ." If we have the hope of one day seeing our Savior, then we will, as John says, *purify* ourselves. What does it mean to purify oneself? It means to make clean, to be free from moral stain. It is also interesting that right before Paul speaks of the blessed hope he also speaks of the importance of purity in Titus 2:12: "teaching us that, denying ungodliness and worldly lusts, we should live soberly, righteously, and godly in the present age." Peter tells us in 2 Peter 3:10-11, "But the day of the Lord will come as a thief in the night, in which the heavens will pass away with a great noise, and the elements will melt with fervent heat; both the earth and the works that are in it will be burned up. Therefore, since all these things will be dissolved, what manner of persons ought you to be in holy conduct and godliness." Peter echoes what Paul, Jesus and John are saying: God is coming; therefore live in purity! This is the third way John has mentioned that we should be living in light of our Lord's return—purify yourself.[50]

---

[50] Agnizei, "purifies," and agnos, "pure," are not to be restricted here to abstention from sexual immorality, as in 2 Corinthians 11:2. In comparison to agios, the term agnos came to refer to cleanness with regard to general morality. In the LXX, agnos often

This is an important statement John makes here because of the heresy of the Gnostics. They said that the body was evil and it therefore did not matter what one did in the body. In their minds, they could sin all they wanted and it wouldn't matter. John says, no, if we have this hope in us, then we will purify ourselves as He is pure. We will strive for perfection and we will live holy lives even in our physical bodies. I am not quite sure what the Gnostics would do with Paul's admonition in Romans 12:1: "I beseech you therefore, brethren, by the mercies of God, that you present your bodies a living sacrifice, holy, acceptable to God, which is your reasonable service." Peter even tells us how to be pure in 1 Peter 1:22: "Since you have purified your souls in obeying the truth through the Spirit in sincere love of the brethren, love one another fervently with a pure heart." Peter says the key to a purified soul, a purified heart, a purified life, is obedience. Many people will tell you that the key to a better you is to diet, exercise, attend self-esteem classes and support groups to get in touch with the inner you. But God tells us the key to purity is obedience to His Word. So John ends by saying purify yourselves, just as He is pure. In fact, Habakkuk tells us He is so pure that He cannot even look upon evil (Habakkuk 1:13).

Summary

Through the Apostle John we have addressed two important questions. First, we asked *How Should We Live in Light of the Lord's Return?* (2:28a, 29; 3:3) Three ways: 1. Abide in Him. Are you abiding in Him? 2. Practice righteousness. Are you doing what is right? 3. Purify yourself. How are you purifying yourself? Second, we asked *Why Should We Live this Way in Light of The Lord's Return?* (2:28; 3:2) Four reasons: 1. We will have confidence when

---

carries the connection of integrity. John's use of the present tense agnizei indicates that the hope of Christ's coming results in a continuing process of purification. That the cleansing is not automatic is apparent from the fact that the possessor of the hope purifies himself (cf. Donald W. Burdick, *The Letters of John the Apostle: An In-depth Commentary* (Chicago, IL: Moody Press, 1985), p 235).

He comes. Will you be bold at the Lord's return? 2. We will not be ashamed at His coming. Will you shrink in shame at His return? 3. We will be like Him. Are you excited at the prospect of a new body? 4. We will see Him. Is this your heart's cry—to see Him?

The fact of the Lord's coming should be a motivator for us to live in holiness. As we think about His first coming, let us also think about His second coming. Let us live in light of one day standing before Him and giving an account of our lives. What are the ways in which we should be living? They are: abiding in Him, practicing righteousness, and purifying ourselves. And the wonderful results will be confidence when He comes, not being ashamed when He comes, being like Him, and seeing Him! What great things await those who love God and who are called according to His purpose!

Questions to Consider

Living in Light of the Lord's Return

1 John 2:28-3:3

1. (a) Read 1 John 2:28-3:3. According to this passage, how should believers live in view of the Lord's return? (b) Is this how you are living? Memorize 1 John 3:1.

2. (a) Read Matthew 24:36-25:30, and note the ways that Christ tells us we should live in view of His return. (b) Again, is this how you are living?

3. (a) How does the Apostle Paul describe depraved man in Romans 3:9-20? (b) In what way(s) does this help you understand the depth of what John is saying in 1 John 3:1a? (c) What is your response to this?

4. John says that "when He is revealed, we will be like Him" (1 John 3:2). (a) What do you think this means? (b) How do the following verses help you to understand what John is saying? Luke 24:36-43; 1 Corinthians 15:35-55; Philippians 3:20, 21; Revelation 21:4.

5. (a) Why is it important that we purify ourselves as He is pure, according to Matthew 5:8 and Hebrews 12:14? (b) How does one purify himself? Support your answer with Scripture. (Some helpful ideas: Galatians 5, Ephesians 6, Colossians 3, to name a few.) (c) Can you purify yourself in your own strength? See John 15:5.

6. (a) Are you ready for the Lord's return? Why or why not? (b) How do you live in light of the Lord's return? (c) What changes do you need to make in your life so that you will not be ashamed at His coming?

7. After contemplating 6c, come with a prayer request to share.

Chapter 11

The Children of God Contrasted with the Children of Satan: Part 1

1 John 3:4-8

Over the past several years I have had an increased interest in nativity scenes and have even begun a collection of them. Many of my nativities are from different places around the world. Some are very unusual; some are elegant; some are cute; a few I think are actually downright ugly. I enjoy displaying them around my house at Christmastime and observing how each artist depicts that wondrous moment—how they depict baby Jesus, the wise men (if they were there), Mary and Joseph, the manger and even the lambs and camels. I really don't know why I began to like them so much or how I got started collecting them, but I do. But, as I think about how I have enjoyed those nativities over the years, and have observed the many interesting details, I realize that Christ is no longer in a manger, and I'm very grateful He isn't. If He were still in that manger bed, you and I would have no need to study His Word. Christ did not come as a baby in a manger to remain a baby in a manger. Rather, quite the opposite, He came as a baby so that He might grow up to be a man and eventually suffer and die on a cruel cross to take away our sins. Those who repent of their sins and turn to Him, committing their life to His Lordship, behave very differently from those who do not. John contrasts the two in our text and explains the reasons why Christ came—and it wasn't to remain in the manger! He puts it like this:

1 John 3:4-8

> Whoever commits sin also commits lawlessness, and sin is
> lawlessness. [5]And you know that He was manifested to take
> away our sins, and in Him there is no sin. [6]Whoever abides

> in Him does not sin. Whoever sins has neither seen Him nor known Him. [7]Little children, let no one deceive you. He who practices righteousness is righteous, just as He is righteous. [8]He who sins is of the devil, for the devil has sinned from the beginning. For this purpose the Son of God was manifested, that He might destroy the works of the devil (1 John 3:4-8).

In our last lesson we learned the answers to two important questions: First, *How Should We Live in Light of the Lord's Return?* (2:28a, 29; 3:3) By abiding in Him, practicing righteousness, and purifying ourselves. Second, *Why Should We Live this Way in Light of The Lord's Return?* (2:28; 3:2) So that we'll have confidence when He comes; we'll not be ashamed at His coming; we'll be like Him; and we'll see Him. In this lesson we'll learn:

The Reasons Christ Came (vv 5, 8b)
The Results for Those Who are His (vv 6a, 7)
The Results for Those Who are Not His (vv 4, 6b, 8a)

In verse three John reminds his readers of the importance of striving for purity in light of the Lord's return, and just in case they don't get it, he reminds them of the danger they are in if they continually commit sin, if they do not purify themselves as He is pure. And so we begin with our first result for those who do not belong to the Lord.

The Results for Those Who are Not His
1 John 3:4

> Whoever commits sin also commits lawlessness, and sin is lawlessness (1 John 3:4).

Notice that John begins with the word *whoever*. Ladies, this is universal; there is no exception here. No one is exempt—not the pastor, not the pastor's wife, no one. *Whoever commits sin commits lawlessness*. What does it mean to *commit* sin? Commit here is in the tense which means to continually practice. It actually reads this way: "whoever is continually doing sin is doing lawlessness." What is *sin*? Sin is anything that offends the righteous standard of God—it is an offense. It also means to miss a goal, like a warrior who tries to strike an opponent and misses; or an archer who tries to hit a target but misses; or a traveler who misses his way. All of these point to missing a goal or standard that is attempted but missed. Sin is missing the mark. And may I say that every sin we commit is sin. Sins of commission (those who know they're doing wrong and still do it), and sins of omission (those who don't know what they're doing is sin) it is still sin. Anything that is against God's holy law is a sin.[51]

You might say, "Well, that isn't fair. What if I don't know that what I am doing is sin?" Paul tells us in Romans that we do know. Romans 2:15 states, "who show the work of the law written in their hearts, their conscience also bearing witness, and between themselves their thoughts accusing or else excusing them." Paul says the law is written in our hearts. That is part of the promise of the new covenant according to Ezekiel 36:26-27: "I will give you a new heart and put a new spirit within you; I will take the heart of stone out of your flesh and give you a heart of flesh. I will put My Spirit within you and cause you to walk in My statutes, and you will keep My judgments and do them." God says, I will put my Spirit in

[51] cf. 1 John 3:4-7. There is an obvious connection of thought between the pursuit of purity (1 John 2:28-3:3) and an understanding of the nature of sin. The contrast is more obvious in Greek, with a construction of pas (English, *everyone*) + article + participle in 2:29 (i.e., "everyone that doeth righteousness," KJV) and 3:4 (i.e., "whosoever committeth sin," KJV), reflecting this dualism of the concepts of righteousness and sin. J. C. Ryle mentions this connection as he writes on this passage: "He that wishes to attain right views about Christian holiness must begin by examining the vast and solemn subject of sin. He must dig down very low if he would build high. A mistake here is most mischievous. Wrong views about holiness are generally traceable to wrong views about human corruption." Then Ryle gives his own definition of sin: "The slightest outward or inward departure from absolute mathematical parallelism with God's revealed will and character constitutes a sin, and at once makes us guilty in God's sight" (cf. *Holiness: It's Nature, Hindrances, Difficulties and Roots* (Durham, England: Evangelical Press, 1991), p 1). *The Westminster Larger Catechism* defines: "Sin is any want of conformity unto, or transgression of any law of God, given as a rule to the reasonable creature."

you; you will have a new heart; you will know right from wrong. The problem is not in knowing what is sin, but in determining not to sin.

John says if you continually practice sin, then you *commit lawlessness*. This means you transgress or violate the law. "Why?" you might ask. John says because *sin is lawlessness*. What does that mean? Well, sin is breaking the law.[52] But John is not talking here about someone who knows there is a law and chooses to break it. Rather, he's talking about someone who lives as if there is no law at all. This reminds me of the end of the book of Judges where it says "everyone did what was right in his own eyes." (Judges 21:25) Actually, it reminds me of a lot of what I see today. People live as if there are no moral laws or even any laws of the land. Everyone seems to be doing what is right in their own eyes, not considering anyone besides themselves, especially God! Now, John is once again attacking the heresy of the day, Gnostism. The Gnostics taught and lived that you could be involved in sin, as well as be indifferent to any acts of sin, and still know God. John says that is ludicrous. Sin is transgression of the law. The first result for those who do not belong to God—they are sinners, they are lawbreakers. John then reminds his readers that Christ came to take away our sins, not to have us become engrossed in sin. Read verse 5.

---

[52] What does it mean that "sin is the transgression of the law"? The NASB and NIV translate the phrase "sin is lawlessness" (Greek, he hamartia estin he anomia), for the idea is that the nature of sin is breaking the law (cf. Psalm 32:1; 51:3, 5; 2 Cor. 6:14-15). The direct opposite of lawlessness is *righteousness* or behaving in conformity to the standards of the law. John R. W. Stott observes: "The heretics seem to have taught that the enlightened Christian questions of morality were a matter of indifference; today our sins are excused either by euphemisms like *personality problems* or by the plea of *cultural relativity*. In contrast to such under-estimates of sin, John declares that it is not just a negative failure (hamartia, sin, meaning literally *missing the mark,* and adikia, unrighteousness, a deviation from what is right or just), but essentially an active rebellion against God's known will. It is important to acknowledge this, because the first step towards holy living is to recognize the true nature and wickedness of sin." cf. John R. W. Stott, *Tyndale New Testament Commentary: The Letters of John* (Grand Rapids, MI: Eerdmans, 1988), pp 126-127.

The Reasons Christ Came
1 John 3:5

> And you know that He was manifested to take away our sins, and in Him there is no sin (1 John 3:5).

John says *and you know that He was manifested to take away our sins*. What does *manifested* mean? It means he appeared; Christ came to earth. He was in heaven, but He left His glory and came to earth. And He came, He appeared, for a reason. Because the term *manifested* is used for Christ's incarnation (cf. 1 John 1:2; 3:8; John 1:31; 3:11; 7:4; 1 Peter 1:20), Christ's words and works (cf. John 2:11; 17:6), Christ's appearance after the resurrection (cf. John 21:1, 14; 1 John 3:2, 8), and even Christ's second coming (cf. 1 John 3:2; Colossians 3:4; 1 Timothy 3:16), the term could refer to all of the above manifestations of Christ, viewed as one culminating act (Greek, aorist tense). Westcott helpfully explains, "His Birth, and Growth, and Ministry, and Passion, and Resurrection, and Ascension. Each part of the revelation contributed in some way to the removal of sins." [53]

And the reason was to take away our sins. This is the first reason Christ came—to take away our sins. What does it mean for Him to *take away* our sins? It means that we have our sins lifted up and carried away. What did the Psalmist say in Psalm 103:12? "As far as the east is from the west, so far has He removed our transgressions from us." Ladies, He came to take away our sins! Remember the account of Joseph when the angel appeared to him in a dream in Matthew 1:20? The angel told him not to be afraid to take Mary as his wife because "that which is conceived in her is of the Holy Spirit." And then the angel says in the next verse, verse 21, "And she will bring forth a Son, and you shall call His name JESUS, for He will save His people from their sins." And later, after Christ's birth and before His public ministry, John the Baptist sees

---

[53] B. F. Westcott, *The Epistles of St. John: the Greek Text with Notes* (Grand Rapids, MI: Eerdmans, 1966), p 103.

Jesus coming to Him and says "Behold! The Lamb of God who takes away the sin of the world!" (John 1:29). That's why Christ came! I firmly believe that when we celebrate Christmas we should focus not so much on the baby in the manger, but on the Savior on the Cross. That is why He came—to take away our sins! You and I have been forgiven a debt we can never repay. All of our wretched, filthy sins have been taken away and forgiven. There is only one person who can take away our sins: the spotless Lamb, Jesus Christ. Why is that? Why is it that only Jesus Christ can take away our sins? Because, John says, *in Him there is no sin*. Literally this reads, "In Him sin is not." He is essentially and forever without sin. The verb tense suggests that Christ was sinless in the past, in the present, and in the future. Christ never has and never will sin. Paul states this fact in 2 Corinthians 5:21, "For He made Him who knew no sin to be sin for us, that we might become the righteousness of God in Him." John has just made mention in verse 3 that Jesus is pure, and so it only makes sense that He has no sin. The Gnostics taught that Jesus did, in fact, sin. Remember, they taught that Jesus was material and so He sinned. They denied that Jesus was the Christ. Because Christ is sinless, because He came into the world to take away our sins, then it only makes sense that those who know Him will not sin habitually. And with that idea, John gives us the first result for those who belong to the Lord.

The Results for Those Who are His
1 John 3:6a

Whoever abides in Him does not sin (1 John 3:6a).

Again John points us to the fact that *whoever* is universal, just like the whoever in verse 4. John says *whoever abides in Him does not sin*. The word *abide* is a word John has used several times thus far in 1 John, and it simply means to remain, and to permanently remain. This is a person who has a continual relationship with God, and is one who is in the habit of doing the will of God. Those who abide in Him *do not sin*, as John says. You might be thinking, "John must be crazy, there is no way I cannot sin. Why, I have sinned today already! How can this be? How can a Christian not sin?"[54] Well, some well meaning people have taken this to mean that Christians never sin; they call it the doctrine of perfection. I have met a lot of Christians, but I must say I have never met one who does not sin. If you find one, let me know! I would like to meet them and, of course, I would like to ask their spouse or their children or their best friend if they sin. Christians sin! Even Paul admits to that fact in Romans 7, where he talks about the ongoing war he has against sin in his life, and where he mentions that he wants to do the right thing but ends up doing the wrong thing. He then comes to the end of his dilemma and says in verse 24, "O wretched man that I am! Who will deliver me from this body of death?" Even Moses, who was the meekest man in the earth, sinned. He got angry, and the result was that he didn't get to go into the Promised Land. David, who was a man after God's own heart, also sinned. He sinned grossly by committing adultery with Bathsheba and then having her husband murdered to try to cover it up! If you look at the saints of the Old and the New Testaments, you will not find one without sin. Even John, who wrote this epistle, admits that we sin in 1 John 1:9. He was the one of the disciples that wanted to call fire down from heaven to blast a Samaritan village out of existence when they rejected Christ, to which Christ rebuked him (Luke 9:51-56). So what is John saying when he states that whoever abides in Him *does not sin*? John is talking about a habit of sin, just as he has mentioned in verse 4. John is saying that those who abide in Christ—those who are true Christians—do not carry their past ongoing sin into their new life. Sinful patterns do not characterize their new relationship with Christ. An unbroken state of sinful behavior from the past into the present, which continues in the present, characterizes the children of the devil, but is not the character of one who has been begotten of God. This is the first result of those who know God—they do not practice sin.

[54] This passage has a long history of interpretation and is central to the Epistle of First John, as a major test of eternal life is elaborated. We have added a special Appendix, in order to present the various views and argue for the one we believe is biblical. The student should carefully consider this question.

A person who claims to be a Christian, and yet has an ongoing pattern of sin in their life, proves to be a spurious Christian, one who does not have a regenerated heart. If there is no change, if there is no growing toward Christ's likeness, then John would say this person is of the devil, as we will see in verse 8. One man put it well: "The believer may fall into sin but he will not walk in it."[55] Or as Chrysostom said, "To sin is human; but to persevere in sin is not human but altogether satanic." For example, Moses got angry but his life was not characterized by anger. David committed adultery with Bathsheba, but his life was not characterized by adultery. Paul makes it clear in two different places in the New Testament that those who think they can live in a pattern of sin and be believers who are on their way to heaven are dead wrong! In 1 Corinthians 6:9-11 he says,

> Do you not know that the unrighteous will not inherit the kingdom of God? Do not be deceived. Neither fornicators, nor idolaters, nor adulterers, nor homosexuals, nor sodomites, nor thieves, nor covetous, nor drunkards, nor revilers, nor extortioners will inherit the kingdom of God. And such were some of you. But you were washed, but you were sanctified, but you were justified in the name of the Lord Jesus and by the Spirit of our God (1 Corinthians 6:9-11).

And in Galatians 5:19-21 he says something similar,

> Now the works of the flesh are evident, which are: adultery, fornication, uncleanness, lewdness, idolatry, sorcery, hatred, contentions, jealousies, outbursts of wrath, selfish ambitions, dissensions, heresies, envy, murders, drunkenness, revelries, and the like; of which I tell you beforehand, just as I also told you in time past, that those who practice such things will not inherit the kingdom of God (Galatians 5:19-21).

[55] Donald Burdick, *The Letters of John the Apostle* (Chicago, IL: Moody Press, 1985), p 239.

The Results for Those Who are Not His
1 John 3:6b

Whoever sins has neither seen Him nor known Him (1 John 3:6b)

And with this in mind, John says, *whoever sins has neither seen Him nor known Him*. What does this mean, they have not *seen* Him? It means to experience or to discern clearly. John is talking clearly about spiritual vision, not physical vision. Paul speaks of this spiritual vision in 2 Corinthians 4:6 when he states, "For it is the God who commanded light to shine out of darkness, who has shone in our hearts to give the light of the knowledge of the glory of God in the face of Jesus Christ." Those who practice sin not only cannot see Him because they are spiritually blind, but also prove that they have not known Him or come to know Him. If you continue to sin, then John says you have not come to know him. He is talking about a knowledge that is spiritual as well as experiential. Again, John is combating the Gnostics, who claimed knowledge of God and yet lived in sin. They taught that only those with the superior knowledge were in the know. John says, no way! They have not come to know Him! How could they know Him and live in habitual sin? That is contrary to the new nature. The writer to the Hebrews would give us a fearful warning if we held to that view: "For if we sin willfully after we have received the knowledge of the truth, there no longer remains a sacrifice for sins, but a certain fearful expectation of judgment, and fiery indignation which will devour the adversaries" (Hebrews 10:26, 27). And just in case they think they can continue in sin and be in relationship with God, John gives his readers a warning in verse 7.

The Results for Those Who are His
1 John 3:7

Little children, let no one deceive you. He who practices righteousness is righteous, just as He is righteous (1 John 3:7).

Little children, John says, little born ones of God, *let no one deceive you* about this. Literally, "Let no one succeed in deceiving you." John says let no one cause you to roam or be led astray about this. This is an obvious reference to the Gnostics, who justified their sin by saying that it did not matter what one did in the body. As long as you don't harm your spirit then, hey, you're okay, they would say. But John says, don't let them deceive you, little children. The real test for whether one knows God is this: *He who practices righteousness is righteous, just as He is righteous*. Notice, John is not saying that we become righteous as we practice righteousness. Otherwise, our salvation would be by works. But John is saying that doing righteousness is a sign that we are righteous. This is very similar to what Jesus says in the Sermon on the Mount in Matthew 7:17-18, "Even so, every good tree bears good fruit, but a bad tree bears bad fruit. A good tree cannot bear bad fruit, nor can a bad tree bear good fruit." If you have a good tree, then you will have good fruit. Likewise, if you have a bad tree, then you will have corrupt fruit. There is nothing difficult to understand about that. The one that does righteousness is righteous, just as He is righteous. This is the second result of those who know God—they practice righteousness. And just in case it still is not clear to his readers, just in case it is still not clear to some of us, John states that continuing in sin not only proves that we are not born of God, but it also proves that we are children of the devil.

The Results for Those Who are Not His
1 John 3:8a

> He who sins is of the devil, for the devil has sinned from the beginning (1 John 3:8a).

John says if you continually practice sin you are *of the devil*. Who is the *devil*? The Greek is diabolos, which means across, and to throw or cast. His Hebrew name, Satan, comes from the word satanas, which means accuser, adversary, slanderer. He is also called the evil one, the wicked one, the enemy, a murderer, a deceiver,

Beelzebub, the prince of demons, and the ruler of this world. He is the fallen angel we read about in Isaiah 14. John has already mentioned the devil in 2:13, where he referred to him as the wicked one. He is certainly someone I would not want to be identified with, and yet those who continually practice sin are identified with him. That's why John says in verse 6 that those who abide in Him do not sin; the pattern of sin has been broken or interrupted in the life of the believer.

John goes on to say that the devil *sinned from the beginning*. The devil has sinned from the beginning and is still sinning. So you might ask, from the beginning of what? Some think this means from the beginning of the world, or from the first account we have of him, which would be in the Garden of Eden. The meaning is that the devil introduced sin into the universe, and that he has continued to practice it ever since. It could also mean from the beginning of his devilish career, as it is revealed in Isaiah 14 when he tried to set himself up as God:

> How you are fallen from heaven, O Lucifer, son of the morning! How you are cut down to the ground, you who weakened the nations! For you have said in your heart: "I will ascend into heaven, I will exalt my throne above the stars of God; I will also sit on the mount of the congregation on the farthest sides of the north; I will ascend above the heights of the clouds, I will be like the Most High." Yet you shall be brought down to Sheol, to the lowest depths of the Pit (Isaiah 14:12-15).

Another possible meaning of from the beginning, is from the beginning when Cain killed his brother, as seen in verses 9-12 which we will cover in our next lesson. This view goes along with what Jesus said to the unbelieving Jews in John 8:44, "You are of your father the devil, and the desires of your father you want to do. He was a murderer from the beginning, and does not stand in the truth, because there is no truth in him. When he speaks a lie, he speaks from his own resources, for he is a liar and the father of it." We know for sure it does not mean that he sinned from the beginning of his existence, because God created him holy like the other angels, according to Ezekiel 28:15, "You were perfect in your ways from the day you were created, till iniquity was found in you." This is the second result of those who do not know God: they are of the devil.

The Reasons Christ Came
1 John 3:8b

> For this purpose the Son of God was manifested, that He might destroy the works of the devil (1 John 3:8b).

John goes on to state another purpose for which Christ came. We have already seen the first reason in verse 5 and that was to take away our sins. Now John says, *for this purpose the Son of God was manifested, that He might destroy the works of the devil*. The second reason Christ came was to destroy the works of the devil. To *destroy* the works of the devil means to dissolve or loose them; to render them inoperative, to nullify them, or deprive them of their power. Christ came to undo Satan's evil works and free people from the awful consequences of their sin. *The works of the devil* are the deeds or acts that he is behind. Jesus came to destroy them! Jesus Himself stated this in the beginning of His earthly ministry in Luke 4:18, "The Spirit of the Lord is upon Me, because He has anointed Me to preach the gospel to the poor; He has sent Me to heal the brokenhearted, to proclaim liberty to the captives and recovery of sight to the blind, to set at liberty those who are oppressed." Those held by Satan were in bondage, they were blind, and they were bruised and brokenhearted. And when Jesus commissioned His disciples to go out and do ministry He commanded them to "preach, saying, 'The kingdom of heaven is at hand.' Heal the sick, cleanse the lepers, raise the dead, cast out demons. Freely you have received, freely give" (Matthew 10:7, 8). Even the Apostle Paul was given marching orders from Christ to do the same in Acts 26:18: "to open their eyes, in order to turn them from darkness to light, and from the power of Satan to God, that they may receive forgiveness of sins and an inheritance among those who are sanctified by faith in Me." Christ came to destroy the works of the devil and one day we know Satan's works will finally come to end, as he and all those who followed him will be cast into the lake of fire. The battle will be over and Satan will be defeated! Christ came to destroy the works of the devil.

Summary

We have seen: *The Reasons Christ Came* (vv 5, 8b): to take away our sins and to destroy the works of the devil. *The Results for Those Who are His* (vv 6a, 7): they do not practice sin and they do practice righteousness. *The Results for Those Who are Not His* (vv 4, 6b, 8a): they practice sin and they are of the devil.

As we close this chapter, the question that is foremost on my mind is this: Are you a child of God or a child of the devil? The question really is not a hard one to answer. Is your life characterized by doing what is right, by fighting hard against sin? Have you seen change and growth in your walk since you first believed in Christ? If you hate sin, and are convicted when you sin, if you confess your sin, and determine to turn away from it, then more than likely, you are a child of the King; you have been born of God. However, if you continually practice sin, if you have no conviction when you break God's holy law, if you can easily behave as if there is no law, if you have not seen change in your life since you became a Christian, then I would say, as John would say, you have not come to know him.

But ladies, it does not end here. You can come to know Him. There is no time like today to come to know Him. Today could be the day of your salvation. Paul gives us a very simple plan of how to come to know Him in Romans 10:9-10, "that if you confess with your mouth the Lord Jesus and believe in your heart that God has raised Him from the dead, you will be saved. For with the heart one believes unto righteousness, and with the mouth confession is made unto salvation." You must believe that Jesus is the Christ, that

God raised Him from the dead. You must confess with your mouth the Lord Jesus. To confess Him as Lord means that He is now the owner, the master, of your life; He is in charge of your life. This means that you turn away from your sin, you repent, and you now determine to follow what His Word says. If you have not done this, will you today? It is my deepest desire and prayer that all of you will know the blessing of why Christ came—to take away your sins and to destroy the works of the devil. It is a wonderful thing to know Him, to no longer be of the devil and enslaved to sin. Instead, you can become one who knows God, who does not practice sin, but practices righteouness. Will you, if you have not already, come to know Him?

Questions to Consider

The Children of God Contrasted With the Children of Satan: Part 1

1 John 3:4-8

1. Read 1 John 3:4-8. (a) For what two reasons does John say that Christ was manifested? (b) What contrasts do you see between those who are born of God and those who are not born of God? (c) What does this passage teach you regarding sin?

2. Memorize 1 John 3:5.

3. (a) What are some other biblical terms for sin? See Psalm 51:1-4; Psalm 119:3; 1 Timothy 1:9 (KJV); 1 John 5:17. (b) How would you personally define sin? (c) How does the unbelieving world define sin? (Or should I say "redefine"?)

4. (a) Why was the law given, according to Romans 7:1-8:4? (b) What characteristics does Paul use to describe the law? (You should find at least four.) (c) How could you use this passage to confront those who say we are not under the law today or that we need not abide by it?

5. (a) What do you think John means when he says that the devil sinned from the beginning? (b) How did Lucifer (Satan) fall, according to Isaiah 14:12-17? (c) What will be the final fate of Satan, according to Isaiah? (d) What warning(s) are there for us in this passage?

6. John states that Christ will destroy the works of the devil (1 John 3:8). (a) Give some biblical examples in which Christ did this. (Hint: Look in the Gospels.) (b) When and how will Satan finally be destroyed, according to Revelation 20:7-10? (c) Where is Satan's final destiny? (d) How will he spend eternity?

7. In what ways does your life manifest that you are indeed a child of God?

8. Will you determine to share with at least one person this week that Jesus Christ came into the world to take away his/her sins? You might want to share this with others so that they can be praying.

9. Meditate on 1 John 3:5 and write out with a prayer of thanksgiving to God based on your meditation on this verse.

Chapter 12

The Children of God Contrasted with the Children of Satan: Part II

1 John 3:9-12

Years ago, when my mother was still living, I remember telling my husband that Mom reminded me more and more of my Grandma, who was with the Lord. Doug quickly agreed; she was looking more like her mother as she aged, and she also had many of her mannerisms. Why was that? It was because my mother was my Grandmother's offspring. Most of us would agree that it doesn't take too long after children start growing up to realize that they not only look like their parents but they also start acting like their parents. Why is that? It's because they are the offspring of their parents. My son not only looks like his Dad, but he acts like him as well. And now he has a son who is his spitting image! Scientists who study genetics tell us that our genes, passed on from generation to generation, greatly determine the nature and characteristics of our offspring.

We can relate this to the spiritual world as well. Those who are born of God, as they grow in their relationship to Christ, begin to behave like He does. They are righteous, just as He is righteous; they take on a resemblance to Christ. Why? Because they are born of God; because they are His offspring! But sadly, the same thing is true of the children of Satan. They too begin to resemble him; they are wicked and evil, just as Satan is. Why? Because they are children of the devil. As we continue on in our study of 1 John, we look at the contrast between the children of God and the children of the Satan. Read verses 9-12.

1 John 3:9-12

> Whoever has been born of God does not sin, for His seed remains in him; and he cannot sin, because he has been born of God. [10]In this the children of God and the children of the devil are manifest: Whoever does not practice righteousness is not of God, nor is he who does not love his brother. [11]For this is the message that you heard from the beginning, that we should love one another, [12]not as Cain who was of the wicked one and murdered his brother. And why did he murder him? Because his works were evil and his brother's righteous (1 John 3:9-12).

In our last lesson we saw: *The Reasons Christ Came* (vv 5, 8b): to take away our sins and to destroy the works of the devil. *The Results for Those Who are His* (vv 6a, 7): they do not practice sin and they do practice righteousness. *The Results for Those Who are Not His* (vv 4, 6b, 8a): they practice sin and they are of the devil. John will continue to contrast the children of God with the children of the devil in this lesson. We will see:

Three Characteristics of God's Children (vv 9, 11)
Three Characteristics of Satan's Children (vv 10, 12)

Three Characteristics of God's Children
1 John 3:9

> Whoever has been born of God does not sin, for His seed remains in him; and he cannot sin, because he has been born of God (1 John 3:9).

John begins by repeating something he has already said in verse 6, that the person who *has been born of God does not sin*. What does it mean to be *born of God*? The word born means procreate. Being born of God is an act that happened once, but it has continuous and lasting results. So John says whosoever is born of God *does not sin*. We saw in our last lesson that this means that those who are born of God do not practice sin. Yes, they sin, but the pattern of sin has been broken and habitual sinful behavior is not a part of their new life in Christ. This is the first characteristic of those who are God's children—they do not practice sin! There is a reason why genuine believers do not remain the same, why they do not practice sin. John says it's because *His seed remains in him*. What does this mean? What is the *seed*? The Greek word for seed is sperma. It is the seed or germ of the divine life. So what is the seed that has been sown in us? Peter gives us a hint in 1 Peter 1:23: "having been born again, not of corruptible seed but incorruptible, through the word of God which lives and abides forever." The seed that has been implanted in us is the Word of God.[56] Ladies, those who are born of God have God's seed in us and it is one that remains. Paul mentions this is Hebrews 8:10: "For this is the covenant that I will make with the house of Israel after those days, says the LORD: I will put My laws in their mind and write them on their hearts; and I will be their God, and they shall be My people." This is the second characteristic of those who are God's children—God's seed remains in them. The idea that John is trying to convey is that because we have been born of God, and because His seed has been implanted in us and remains in us forever, we, therefore, remain His children. We can never again be children of the devil and therefore retain a sinful habit of life. It's the same idea as I brought out in the introduction to this lesson: My children are my children; they are the offspring of my husband and me; and they will never be anyone else's children. That's impossible. They are our children and they bear our likeness.

---

[56] In John's writings, the Word of God is an active force, which makes the disciples clean (cf. John 15:3) and abides in the Christian (cf. John 15:7; 1 John 2:14, 24). Elsewhere, the Word of God, or Gospel, relates to the begetting of Christians, in Luke 8:12; James 1:18; 1 Peter 1:23; and 1 Corinthians 4:15. To lost men, Jesus mentioned that they "have not His word abiding in you" in John 5:38. Also, the Word of God is called spora or sporos in Luke 8:11. (cf. Augustine, Luther, Alford, IV, pp 468-469; Lenski, pp 462-463; Barclay, p 94). This is John's intended meaning, for within the genuine believer is the infused understanding and love for the law or Word of God (cf. Hebrews 8:10 with Jeremiah 31:31-34). As we have seen, the believer delights in the law of God as his/her greatest delight and longs to live in obedient conformity to it (cf. Psalm 1:1-3; Rom. 7:12, 22; compare with Psalm 119:34, 77, 97, etc.). Obviously, this is contrary to the nature of man in his/her lost condition as they despise the law.

John then repeats what he began with: *and he cannot sin, because he has been born of God.* Notice John says he *cannot sin.* What does this mean? Because, the fact is that we do sin! John is not saying that a Christian never commits acts of sin, but that he is continually unable to engage in continual sinning without letup. He may and does commit acts of sin, but that is not the unbroken pattern of his life. John MacArthur says: "A Christian habitually practices righteousness but occasionally sins; he doesn't habitually sin but occasionally practice righteousness."[57] A genuine Christian should not be comfortable with sinning. I think Joseph is a great example of this, when he was being pursued by Potiphar's wife to commit adultery with her. Joseph says in Genesis 39:9, "There is no one greater in this house than I, nor has he kept back anything from me but you, because you are his wife. How then can I do this great wickedness, and sin against God?" Joseph knew that to do such an evil deed was a wicked sin, and so he fled and got out. By the way, it cost him something, as he was thrown into prison. But it is better to suffer for doing what is right than to suffer for doing what is wrong. That's the heart of a believer, one who will go to all costs to avoid sin, even if it costs him or her dearly. But some believers struggle with sin unnecessarily, because they put themselves in tempting situations, which are dangerous. Many refuse to be held accountable by someone older and wiser than they are. Others lack knowledge of what is sinful due to the fact that they are not in the Word enough to know what *God* says is sinful. Without these things in place, our fight against the flesh is terribly difficult and we become anemic in our walk and certainly cannot live in victory as God intends that we should. John has made it crystal clear to his readers and to us that children of God do not practice sin.

The Characteristics of Satan's Children
1 John 3:10

> In this the children of God and the children of the devil are manifest: Whoever does not practice righteousness is not of God, nor is he who does not love his brother (1 John 3:10).

[57] http://www.biblebb.com/files/mac/2111.htm

John says it is pretty obvious—it is apparent, which is what *manifest* means—who are *the children of God and the children of the devil*. Watch a person's life: Are they in the habit of ongoing sin? Then they are a child of the devil. Are they in the habit of righteousness? Then they are a child of God! Jesus made this very clear when He was in the midst of a showdown with the Pharisees over their thinking that they could somehow make some claim to God and yet live otherwise. (Sometime, read over John 8.) Listen to some of the things Jesus says to them from John 8: "Then Jesus said to those Jews who believed Him, 'If you abide in My word, you are My disciples indeed'" (John 8:31); "Jesus answered them, 'Most assuredly, I say to you, whoever commits sin is a slave of sin'" (John 8:34); "Therefore if the Son makes you free, you shall be free indeed" (John 8:36); "They answered and said to Him, 'Abraham is our father.' Jesus said to them, 'If you were Abraham's children, you would do the works of Abraham'" (John 8:39): "Why do you not understand My speech? Because you are not able to listen to My word. You are of your father the devil, and the desires of your father you want to do. He was a murderer from the beginning, and does not stand in the truth, because there is no truth in him. When he speaks a lie, he speaks from his own resources, for he is a liar and the father of it" (John 8:43, 44). Jesus is claiming the validity of who He is to the Pharisees, and as He does so He gets to the real issue, the issue of their sinful heart. They become so angry that, in verse 59, they want to stone him!

If you were to divide the whole entire world into two categories, and there would only be two, you would have category one, children of God, and you would have category two, children of the devil. There is no third category. Everyone belongs in one category or the other. You might be saying, Susan, you are so black and white! Aren't there any categories in between? No, according to God's Word, there isn't! John says that *whoever does not practice righteousness is not of God*. (We've had this before in 2:29 and 3:7.) *Righteousness* refers to doing what is right, and it denotes that this is the character of one's life. This is the first characteristic of those who belong to Satan—they do not practice righteousness.[58]

John then mentions the second characteristic of those who belong to Satan—they do not love their brother.[59] In addition to not practicing righteousness, John says the one who is Satan's *does not love his brother*. You might wonder why John now transitions his thoughts from not practicing righteousness to not loving one's brother. He does so because the core of our Christianity is love. It is one of the greatest litmus tests that we are the sons of God. What did Jesus say in John 13:35? "By this all will know that you are My disciples, if you have love for one another." The word that John uses here for *love* is agape. There is a church tradition which says that when John was an old man in Ephesus, he had to be carried to the church in the arms of his disciples. At these meetings, he was accustomed to say no more than, "Little children, love one another!" After a time, the disciples wearied at always hearing the same words and asked, "Master, why do you always say this?" "It is the Lord's command," was his reply, "and if this alone be done, it is enough!" This is not something new to John's readers, as he says it again in verse 11.

---

[58] That is, they observe their actions and deduce their spiritual parentage (i.e., God or the devil) by two ways: first by either the practice of righteousness or the practice of sinning; second, by either the practice of loving the brethren or not loving the brethren. This second way their spiritual parentage is manifested transitions into the social test of genuine faith, i.e., loving (Greek, present participle) and other believers (cf. 1 John 3:11-18). Verse 10 is a hinge passage, and perhaps John's thinking is that central to a person's righteousness is the showing of love to others.

[59] Who are the *brothers*? In the Apostle John's three epistles he uses adelphos or the plural form 20 times: 1 John 2:7, 9, 10, 11; 3:10, 12 (two times), 13, 14 (two times), 15, 16, 17; 4:20 (two times), 21; 5:16; 3 John 3, 5, 10. Only in John's illustration of Cain and Abel (3:12), where the obvious meaning is a physical blood relationship (cf. Genesis 4:1ff.) is the term used in a broader way. In Revelation he uses the term 5 times and always in a limiting way, signifying fellow believers (cf. Revelation 1:9; 6:11; 12:10; 19:10; 22:9). It is interesting that out of the 14 times adelphos is used in the Gospel of John, only in 20:17 and 21:23 does the word refer to spiritual brothers. All other references are to physical blood relatives (cf. 1:10, 41; 2:12; 6:8; 7:3, 5, 10; 11:2, 19, 21, 23, 32). What is significant is that the Apostle John never uses adelphos to refer to fellow humans!

The Characteristics of God's Children 1 John 3:11

> For this is the message that you heard from the beginning, that we should love one another, (1 John 3:11).

John says *this is the message*; this is the announcement which you heard from the beginning. What does *from the beginning* mean? From the beginning of what? John is referring to the time they first heard the gospel message. The gospel message itself is a message of love. John himself recorded Jesus' words in John 3:16: "For God so loved the world that He gave His only begotten Son, that whoever believes in Him should not perish but have everlasting life." God so loved the world that He gave His only Son. Later on in 1 John, John will say, "Beloved, if God so loved us, we also ought to love one another" (1 John 4:11). The word for *love* here again is agape. It makes logical sense; if God loved us so much that He gave His son to die for us, then we too should not only love Him but also *love one another.*

They not only heard this message from the beginning, i.e., when they heard the gospel, but they also would have heard it and known of it because it was spoken from the lips of our Lord to His twelve disciples. John 13:34-35, "A new commandment I give to you, that you love one another; as I have loved you, that you also love one another. By this all will know that you are My disciples, if you have love for one another." And then later on in John 15:12 Jesus states, "This is My commandment, that you love one another as I have loved you." And again in John 15:17, "These things I command you, that you love one another." Jesus keeps repeating this command to love one another because it is so important. Throughout His entire earthly ministry Christ had been exhibiting how to love one another, but now as He is getting ready to face the cross, He reminds them of this great commandment to love one another. Of course He didn't just tell them to do this, but by washing their feet He gave them a tangible example of what He meant. Jesus and John are not the only writers who speak of this. In Romans 13:8-10, Paul also tells us that loving the brethren is fulfilling the royal law: "Owe no one anything except to love one another, for he who loves another has fulfilled the law. For the commandments, 'You shall not commit adultery,' 'You shall not murder,' 'You shall not steal,' 'You shall not bear false witness,' 'You shall not covet,' and if there is any other commandment, are all summed up in this saying, namely, 'You shall love your neighbor as yourself.' Love does no harm to a neighbor; therefore love is the fulfillment of the law." James also reminds us of this important commandment in James 2:8: "If you really fulfill the royal law according to the Scripture, 'You shall love your neighbor as yourself,' you do well."

This loving of one another applies to all of mankind, not just to our Christian brothers, even though Paul tells us in Galatians 6:10, "Therefore, as we have opportunity, let us do good to all, especially to those who are of the household of faith." In fact, Jesus even raises the standard higher in the Sermon on the Mount. Listen to His words in Matthew 5:43-48,

> You have heard that it was said, "You shall love your neighbor and hate your enemy." But I say to you, love your enemies, bless those who curse you, do good to those who hate you, and pray for those who spitefully use you and persecute you, that you may be sons of your Father in heaven; for He makes His sun rise on the evil and on the good, and sends rain on the just and on the unjust. For if you love those who love you, what reward have you? Do not even the tax collectors do the same? And if you greet your brethren only, what do you do more than others? Do not even the tax collectors do so? Therefore you shall be perfect, just as your Father in heaven is perfect (Matthew 5:43-48).

Ladies—this really goes without saying—a true Christian loves others! This is the third characteristic of those who are God's children—they love others. And with that in mind, John gives his readers an example of the first individual mentioned in the Word of God who failed to love his brother—Cain.

The Characteristics of Satan's Children
1 John 3:12

> not as Cain who was of the wicked one and murdered his brother. And why did he murder him? Because his works were evil and his brother's righteous (1 John 3:12).

John is referring to an account that his readers would be very familiar with, in Genesis 4. *Cain* and Abel were Adam and Eve's first sons. Abel brought a sacrificed that pleased God because it was an animal sacrifice. Cain, however, did not please God with his sacrifice, as he brought fruits and grains. After rejecting Cain's sacrifice, God gave Him another chance to do what was right, and to do it with a right attitude. (Our worship is important, but our attitude regarding worship is important as well!) But Cain rejected God's encouragement to do what was right, and because he was jealous and hated his brother, he *murdered* him. Cain represents a child of the devil, mentioned in verse 10, and Abel represents a child of God, also mentioned in verse 10. It is interesting that Jude uses Cain as an example of the wickedness of false teachers. "Woe to them! For they have gone in the way of Cain" (Jude 11). (Remember, John is also combating false teachers.) In other words, Jude says false teachers are haters of their brethren, and they that are such are murderers just like Cain; and by their false doctrine they corrupt and destroy the souls of the people.

John goes on to say that Cain *was of the wicked one*. He has already stated in 2:9 that if anyone hates his brother he is in darkness. Cain was in darkness and he was of the wicked one. What does it mean he was of the wicked one? *Wicked* is a word which, in the Greek, pertains to organized evil. This refers to a person who has a desire to corrupt others and is willing to drag everyone else down with him. This certainly describes Satan, doesn't it? Eve, Cain and Abel's mother, is a good example of someone that Satan tried to bring down and corrupt. Remember, Satan tried to convince her that it was okay to eat the forbidden fruit. He wanted to corrupt her and bring her down with him. Satan is still trying to do the same to all of mankind today. Ladies, we must be on the alert against the evil schemes of the wicked one. It can affect those around us, including our children, just as it did in the case of Eve! That's why Paul tells us in Ephesians 6:11, "Put on the whole armor of God, that you may be able to stand against the wiles of the devil." Satan is the wicked one, and Cain was like his father, the devil. Like father, like son. Speaking about Satan Jesus said in John 8:44, "he was a murderer from the beginning." And that is what John said of Cain—he murdered his brother. *Murder* is a word which means to butcher or slaughter, to slay by cutting the throat, and it indicates it was a violent death. Up until now, there had been no murder. The only method of killing that Cain would have been familiar with was the sacrificial slaughtering of an animal. So he actually, according to the word used here, cut his brother's throat and let his blood run out from the slit of his neck. You might say, that is really gross; why would he do such a wicked deed? John asks the same question: *And why did he murder him?* John answers by saying that it was *because his works were evil and his brother's righteous*. What does this mean? It means that Cain hated his brother because Cain's evil deeds were exposed by his brother's righteous deeds. Cain perverted what should have been an animal sacrifice of worship into a murderous act of hatred and jealousy.

Alcibiades used to say to Socrates, "Socrates, I hate you, because every time I meet you, you show me what I am."[60] That is exactly what happened with Cain and Abel. Abel's sacrifice and proper attitude in worship showed Cain exactly what he was. He was of the wicked one. This is the third characteristic of those who belong to Satan—their works are evil. Now most of us would say, I would never do such a wicked deed—slit someone's throat—never! Well, let's look at Matthew 5:21-26, where our Lord raises the standard from killing someone to those wicked attitudes of our heart and He says they are just as evil:

[60] William Barclay, *The Letters of John and Jude* (Louisville, KY: Westminster John Knox Press 2002), p 95.

> You have heard that it was said to those of old, "You shall not murder, and whoever murders will be in danger of the judgment." But I say to you that whoever is angry with his brother without a cause shall be in danger of the judgment. And whoever says to his brother, "Raca!" shall be in danger of the council. But whoever says, "You fool!" shall be in danger of hell fire. Therefore if you bring your gift to the altar, and there remember that your brother has something against you, leave your gift there before the altar, and go your way. First be reconciled to your brother, and then come and offer your gift. Agree with your adversary quickly, while you are on the way with him, lest your adversary deliver you to the judge, the judge hand you over to the officer, and you are thrown into prison. Assuredly, I say to you, you will by no means get out of there till you have paid the last penny (Matthew 5:21-26).

Jesus says if you are angry with your brother without a cause, you are in danger of judgment. If you say to him, "Raca!" which means worthless person, empty one, then you are in danger of the council. And if you say, "You fool!"—which means blockhead or stupid—then you are in danger of hell fire. That's why Jesus goes on to say, in verses 23-26, that if you have such an attitude towards someone you need to take care of it and do it quickly. Don't even come to worship the Lord if you have something against someone. Take care of it! Let me pause and say, this is probably one of the biggest griefs that I have in ministry—people who refuse to be reconciled with one another. They go on in their bitterness and anger, refusing to do what is right. This is a great evil in the sight of our Lord, and I know it must grieve His heart. We must be careful, ladies, when those first thoughts of jealousy or hatred or anger are aroused it our hearts. We must refuse to go there, and we must put on righteous thoughts. For example, if someone gets picked to do a ministry that you really wanted to do, instead of being jealous of them, rejoice with them, pray for them, and look for ways to help them succeed. If your husband forgets your anniversary or birthday, instead of getting angry in your heart, look for ways to do good to him, and pray for his memory. We must kill sin the moment it comes to our mind. We must grasp hold of these dreadful sins of jealously, anger and hatred in our hearts. They are a sign that we are being prompted by Satan himself and there is no limit to what these sins will lead us to do if we leave them unchecked. Instead we must be transformed by the renewing of our mind, as Paul says in Romans 12:2.

Summary

In this lesson the Apostle John has shown us: *Three Characteristics of God's Children* (vv 9, 11): they do not practice sin; God's seed remains in them; and they love others. And *Three Characteristics of Satan's Children* (vv 10, 12): they do not practice righteousness; they do not love their brother; and their works are evil.

Once again John has made it crystal clear to us. If we are born of God, we cannot live a sinful life; if we are of Satan, we will live a sinful life. If we are born of God, we will love others; if we are of Satan, we will hate others. If we are born of God, His seed remains in us forever; if we are of Satan, his evil works reside in our hearts. Are you a child of God or a child of the devil? It is my deepest desire that every one of you is indeed a child of the King.

Questions to Consider

The Children of God Contrasted with the Children of Satan: Part 2

1 John 3:9-12

1. Read 1 John 3:9-12. (a) What phrases do you see that are similar to phrases John has already used in this epistle? (b) What three ways are listed in this passage to determine whether one is a child of God? (c) What three ways determine whether one is a child of the devil?

2. Memorize 1 John 3:9.

3. John says in 1 John 3:9 that a genuine believer cannot sin. (a) What do you think this means? (b) Why is this true according to what Paul says in Romans 6? (You should find several reasons.) (c) How does what Paul says in Romans 6 help you to understand in 1 John 3:9?

4. (a) Skim 1 John and make note of how often John speaks of loving our brother. (b) Why do you think this is mentioned so often in this little epistle?

5. John states that one way we can know for certain that we are of God is by our love for the brethren. (a) What are some of the ways, according to the following Scriptures, that we love one another? Romans 12:10; 14:13; 15:14; 2 Corinthians 13:12; Galatians 5:13; Ephesians 4:1-3; 4:32; 1 Thessalonians 5:11; Hebrews 3:13; 10:24. (b) Practically speaking, what are some other ways in which we can show love to the brethren?

6. Read the account of Cain and Abel in Genesis 4:1-15. (a) Why did Cain kill his brother, Abel? (b) What sin(s) did Cain first commit before he committed murder? (c) After he murdered his brother, what further sin(s) did he commit? (d) What does this teach you about unconfessed, unrepentant sin? (e) In your opinion, what should Cain have done in the beginning to avoid sinning in the first place?

7. (a) How does a believer's life manifest a hatred of sin? (b) Does your life manifest that you take sin seriously? (c) How do you fight sin in your own life? (d) In what areas of sin in your life have you seen victory?

8. (a) What are some ways you think we should show love to the brethren? (b) What are some ways we show a dislike of the brethren? (c) Is there anyone you are refusing to love? (d) What will you do about this?

9. (a) Make it your prayer to show love to the brethren. (If you need some help in how to do this, refer back to question 5.) (b) Be prepared to share how God has blessed you by your obedience.

10. Reflect on either question 7 *or* 8, and write out a prayer request based on your need.

Chapter 13

Is Your Life Characterized by Love or Hate?

1 John 3:13-18

In recent years I had the privilege of traveling to Pune, India to teach the Bible to women at the National Expositors Conference which is sponsored by "Grace to You" of India. One thing that has stood out to me as I've visited is their love for one another and for me. Even though our cultural differences are vast, the love of Christ joins us together. I have been struck repeatedly by the reminder that in Christ there is neither Jew nor Greek, male or female, but we are all one in Christ Jesus. Jesus said that love would be the mark that would show the world that we belong to Him (John 13:35). Love of the brethren is a precious, precious benefit for those of us who know Christ. But for those who are in darkness, they are not able to experience such love. Their lives are characterized by something different; their lives are characterized by hate. This is a character quality of those who do not know God, and just as it is in America, so it is in India. One young man in India recalled his life before Christ, stating that he used to beat Christians, strip them half naked and beat them until they were profusely bleeding. He burned their Bibles. He hated Christians. Another true story is told of a young couple in India who both put their faith in Jesus Christ. One day the husband dropped his wife off at her parents' house. The young woman sat down to eat with her family, and within moments she was dead because her parents had poisoned her food. The world hates Christians, whether they are in India or in America. John puts it this way:

1 John 3:13-18

> Do not marvel, my brethren, if the world hates you. [14]We know that we have passed from death to life, because we love the brethren. He who does not love his brother abides in death. [15]Whoever hates his brother is a murderer, and you know that no murderer has eternal life abiding in him. [16]By this we know love, because He laid down His life for us. And we also ought to lay down our lives for the brethren. [17]But whoever has this world's goods, and sees his brother in need, and shuts up his heart from him, how does the love of God abide in him? [18]My little children, let us not love in word or in tongue, but in deed and in truth (1 John 3:13-18).

In our last lesson we saw *Three Characteristics of God's Children* (vv 9, 11): they do not practice sin; God's seed remains in them; and they love others. In contrast, we saw *Three Characteristics of Satan's Children* (vv 10, 12): they do not practice righteousness; they do not love their brother; and their works are evil. We left off with the awful example of Cain, who slit his brother's throat because of his jealousy and hatred toward him. In this lesson, we'll examine:

The Nature of Those Who Love Others (vv 13, 16-18)
The Nature of Those Who Hate Others (vv 14, 15)

The Nature of Those Who Love Others
1 John 3:13

> Do not marvel, my brethren, if the world hates you (1 John 3:13).

John begins this section by saying *do not marvel*—cease wondering or stop wondering about this. Don't think it is so unusual that the world hates you. In fact, it would be unusual if the world did love us, wouldn't it? It would probably be an indicator that something is out of kilter with us. After all, the world and its system are opposed to God and all He stands for. The *world* here would obviously represent Cain, who we dealt with in our last lesson. Why should we expect any different treatment than what Abel received from his brother Cain? Evidently, the readers were surprised at this hatred. Maybe they had forgotten the words of our Lord, who said this would happen to us, in John 15:18, 19, "If the world hates you, you know that it hated Me before it hated you. If you were of the world, the world would love its own. Yet because you are not of the world, but I chose you out of the world, therefore the world hates you." It is very similar to what Peter says to his readers in 1 Peter 4:12, where he states, "Beloved, do not think it strange concerning the fiery trial which is to try you, as though some strange thing happened to you."

What does John mean here that the world *hates* us? It means they detest us. John says don't be surprised if the world hates you, as it does. John reminds them of what Jesus had already told them in John 15. Remember, John was there in the upper room when Jesus stated this and he wrote those words down in the Gospel of John. The world hates us just as Cain hated Abel! Why? As we saw in verse 12 in our last lesson, it's because Cain's works were evil, but his brother's were righteous. Jesus put it this way in John 3:19, 20: "And this is the condemnation, that the light has come into the world, and men loved darkness rather than light, because their deeds were evil. For everyone practicing evil hates the light and does not come to the light, lest his deeds should be exposed."

When the world comes in contact with those in the light, its evil deeds are brought to the light. Because of that, the world hates the light and anyone who represents the light. Unbelievers are not comfortable around us because we cause them to feel guilt and shame as their evil deeds are exposed. So they lash out at us in hatred. This is the first mark of those who love—they are hated by the world! As believers in Jesus Christ, our attitude toward others is to be different. John puts it this way in verse 14.

The Nature of Those Who Hate Others
1 John 3:14, 15

> We know that we have passed from death to life, because we love the brethren. He who does not love his brother abides in death (1 John 3:14).

What does it mean to have *passed from death to life*? It means to change place, literally to pass over or migrate. It is a word that means to geographically move from one location to another. It is also in the present tense in the Greek, which indicates that the transfer has already taken place, but its effects are still continuing.[61] John is saying that we have been transferred out of death, and we have entered into life. Paul puts it this way in Colossians 1:13: "He has delivered us from the power of darkness and conveyed us into the kingdom of the Son of His love." We have gone from darkness to light. So how can we know this transfer has indeed taken place? How can I know I have geographically moved from darkness to light? John says we can know this is true if *we love the brethren*. This makes sense because when we embrace Christ, we embrace His family, His kingdom. We have a whole new family that is very different from our physical family. And I might add that our spiritual family is far closer many times than our physical family! John says we know we have passed from death to life when we *love* the brethren. The Greek word that John uses here for love is agape. Now John is not saying that eternal life is earned by loving the brethren, but rather that we show evidence that we have eternal life by our

[61] Notice there are only two spheres which are possible: *the death* (Greek, tou thanatou) or *the life* (Greek, ten zoen). Some translate the spheres with the definite article as, "the death which is truly death" and "the life which is truly life." cf. B. F. Westcott, *The Epistles of St. John: the Greek Text, with Notes and Addenda* (Grand Rapids, MI: Eerdmans, 1966), p 112; cf. R. C. H. Lenski, *The Interpretation of 1 and 2 Epistles of Peter, the Three Epistles of John and the Epistle of Jude* (Minneapolis, MN: Augsburg Publishing House, 1966), p 469; cf. Henry Alford, *The Greek Testament* (Chicago, IL: Moody Press, 1958), vol. IV, p 473. This is similar to the imagery of changing from death to life in Paul's writings. cf. Ephesians 2:1, 5; Colossians 2:13; 2 Timothy 1:10. The term metabebekamen usually is used to describe geographical movement from one location to another. Here it is figuratively used to suggest movement from one spiritual sphere to another spiritual sphere.

loving of the brethren. By the way, this loving the brethren is not just once in a while when I am having a good day or have some free time to show love; it is a continual habit of our lives. A Christian just loves others. If one does not love the brethren, then John says that one *abides in death*. What does it mean to abide in death? It means we remain there and that we have never made that geographical move from death to life. The transfer has never been made. This is the first characteristic of those who hate—they abide in death! John now moves from loving one's brother to hating one's brother. We should not be surprised at the world hating us, as John already mentioned in verse 13. However, hatred from a professing brother or sister is another matter. It should not be. God forbid!

> Whoever hates his brother is a murderer, and you know that no murderer has eternal life abiding in him (1 John 3:15).

John says, in verse 15, if you hate your brother, then you are a murderer! The word *hates* means to detest and it is a continual hatred, a continual detesting. John is not speaking of someone who has a temporary moment of anger toward someone, but someone who is in the habit of hating his brother. One man says that "The person whom one hates, or desires to see disappear. Hatred is the desire to get rid of someone, whether or not one has the nerve or the occasion to perform the act."[62] This is a person that you wish to be dead. It might even be your husband: "I wish he would get killed in the plane or have a car accident or have a heart attack and die." Or maybe it's a neighbor you can't stand, or someone who has hurt you deeply and you wish them out of your life. John says if you hate your brother you are a murderer. Hatred is the same as murder and murder is cause for damnation. This is the second mark of those who hate—they are murderers! John equates hatred with murder, just like Jesus does in the Sermon on the Mount, in Matthew 5:21-22: "You have heard that it was said to those of old, 'You shall not murder, and whoever murders will be in danger of the judgment.'

---

62 Donald Burdick, *The Letters of John the Apostle* (Chicago, IL: Moody Press, 1985), p 266.

But I say to you that whoever is angry with his brother without a cause shall be in danger of the judgment. And whoever says to his brother, 'Raca!' shall be in danger of the council. But whoever says, 'You fool!' shall be in danger of hell fire."

What does *murderer* mean here? It means manslayer, or man killer. This person has the spirit of Cain, whom John already wrote about, and is of the devil. John goes on to say that no murderer *has eternal life abiding in him. Eternal life* means perpetual life. John is crystal clear: you cannot hate someone and think you are on your way to heaven. John and Jesus (in the Sermon on the Mount) equate hate with murder and murder with eternal damnation.

John writes in another place, the last book of the Bible, to remind us again that murder equates with eternal separation from God. Consider the following: Revelation 21:7-8, "He who overcomes shall inherit all things, and I will be his God and he shall be My son. But the cowardly, unbelieving, abominable, murderers, sexually immoral, sorcerers, idolaters, and all liars shall have their part in the lake which burns with fire and brimstone, which is the second death." Revelation 22:14-15, "Blessed are those who do His commandments, that they may have the right to the tree of life, and may enter through the gates into the city. But outside are dogs and sorcerers and sexually immoral and murderers and idolaters, and whoever loves and practices a lie." This is the third mark of those who hate—they will spend eternity in hell.[63]

Hating others is a very, very serious sin. Ladies, we must be so careful, because even thoughts of not liking someone, their personality, the way they do things, their religious beliefs, can turn

63 Early in human history a temporal judgment of physical death was pronounced upon anyone who committed murder. cf. Genesis 9:5-6; Exodus 20:13 with 21:12; Proverbs 1:10-19. God "requires it" (cf. Gen. 9:6) and providentially will bring the murderer to a premature death, unless repentance takes place or other outstanding circumstances exist. e.g., David's adultery with Bathsheba and murder of Uriah should have resulted in God's temporal judgment of death, but evidently, because God has graciously promised grace in the Davidic Covenant, the usual penalty was acquitted and fell upon the Davidic house. cf. 2 Samuel 7:8-17 with 12:7-15.

to hatred if we are not careful. We need to change our attitude and seek forgiveness and repentance. I remember once confronting someone who was exhibiting harshness and hatred toward me. This was happening way too often, in fact, almost every time I was with them. The person kept saying they were sorry, and they didn't know why they kept on behaving that way, or why it was consistently happening. As I studied this lesson, I thought, "If they don't get a grip on this, it could be a very serious indicator of something far more concerning than hating me—an indictor of eternal damnation!" Of course, the opposite of hating others is loving others. And John gives us the greatest example of love ever known to mankind, the love of God.

The Nature of Those Who Love Others
1 John 3:16-18

> By this we know love, because He laid down His life for us. And we also ought to lay down our lives for the brethren (1 John 3:16).

John says we have come to know and we still know the love of God. How did they *know* the love of God? How is it that you and I know the love of God? John says we know *because He laid down his life for us*! What greater love could there be? Romans 5:7, 8, says, "For scarcely for a righteous man will one die; yet perhaps for a good man someone would even dare to die. But God demonstrates His own love toward us, in that while we were still sinners, Christ died for us." What does it mean that He *laid down* His life? Laid down means to lay aside something, like a garment that one takes off. It is the imagery of Christ putting off his life as though it were a garment. It is the verb that is used in John 13:4, where it states that Christ "rose from supper and laid aside His garments, took a towel and girded Himself." And, of course, we know He did this so that he could wash the disciple's dirty feet. John obviously is thinking of Calvary and the cross and the fact that Christ did all that voluntarily. Christ made this statement in John 10:11: "I am the good shepherd.

The good shepherd gives His life for the sheep." And then again in John 10:17-18: "Therefore My Father loves Me, because I lay down My life that I may take it again. No one takes it from Me, but I lay it down of Myself. I have power to lay it down, and I have power to take it again. This command I have received from My Father." The laying down of Jesus' life was for the benefit of others, so that they might live; and He laid down his life for those who certainly did not deserve it. So John says because Christ willingly and voluntarily laid down His life for us, then *we also ought to lay down our lives for the brethren.* What does this mean, since obviously we can't lay down our lives in the same way Christ did? We know that we cannot atone for someone else's sins, but we can lay our lives down in the same sense when we go to great lengths to sacrifice on behalf of others. We should be willing to risk our own lives for others, even if we think they don't deserve it. I remember a time when someone called in need of something and I turned them down because I had a prior commitment. Doug asked me later, "If that was one of your closer friends, would you have cancelled the prior commitment?" That really got me thinking and it brought great conviction. This is the second mark of those who love—they are willing to lay down their lives for others.

Now let me point out here that John's readers would have understood martyrdom. We don't see much of that in our country, but in other nations it is not uncommon for believers to die for their faith. In John's day believers dying for each other would not have been unusual, and in other parts of our world it is not uncommon today. And so John is saying that some of them may literally have to lay down their physical lives for someone else, and they should do so willingly. Evidently, some were willing to do this and it was commonplace. For example, Paul says in Romans 16:3-4, "Greet Priscilla and Aquila, my fellow workers in Christ Jesus, who risked their own necks for my life, to whom not only I give thanks, but also all the churches of the Gentiles." Priscilla and Aquila evidently risked their lives for the life of Paul. This is not something we see a lot of in our day, but it does not mean that the day won't come when we might have to lay down our physical lives. Love will not only give up one's life if needed, but it will also give up one's possessions, time and energy for one who is in need. In fact, John goes on to elaborate on this a little more.

> But whoever has this world's goods, and sees his brother in need, and shuts up his heart from him, how does the love of God abide in him (1 John 3:17)?

John says if you have this world's goods, if you have means of livelihood, if you have enough to sustain your life, and see your brother has a need, and you don't meet it, how does God's love dwell in you? *We* would say, for those who have leftovers, and two houses, four boats and eight cars … then give to someone else. But that is not what John is saying here. It is the very same Greek word that is used of the widow in Mark 12:44, who was being contrasted with the others as they gave their money. Jesus said of her: "for they all put in out of their abundance, but she out of her poverty put in all that she had, her whole livelihood." She gave all that she had. That's what John is saying when he says you have the *world's goods*. He's saying you have enough to live. So, if you have this world's goods, if you have enough to live, and see your *brother in need*, and you don't meet that need, how does God's love dwell in you?[64] By the way, the word for *brother* here is not physical or spiritual brother, but anyone who is a human being. And when John says they have a *need*, it means that you discern that need. This does not mean that you're casually discerning, but that you deliberately contemplate that this person has a need. You have investigated the situation long enough to know and understand the case. So you understand this person has a need. A need here is something thay is a requirement for living, such as food, clothing or shelter.

[64] Both the Old Testament and the New Testament appeal to our care for the poor and needy. cf. Exodus 22:22-25; Leviticus 19:9-10; 23:22; 25:35-37; Deuteronomy 15:11; 24:14-15, 19-22; Isaiah 10:1-2; Ezekiel 22:29; Amos 2:6-7; 5:11-12; 8:4-6; Matthew 11:5; 15:32; 19:21; 20:34; Luke 14:13, 21; Acts 2:45; 4:34-35, etc.

Now let me stop and say that we do need to investigate, as many times what one person calls a need is nothing more than a want. We must discern a real need from a want. My husband will often get calls from people who want the church to give them money for bills or food. We would be unwise not to investigate each of these needs. Paul says in 1 Timothy 6:8 that we should be content with food and raiment. ("And having food and clothing, with these we shall be content.") The problem with some people is that they are not content with what they have, and we would be wise not to give to their fleshly desires. Unfortunately, we are dealing with a culture that thinks their needs include a plasma TV, new car, I-pad, I-phone, I-pod, I-this and I-that. (Funny, it's all *I*!) Those are all wants; they are not needs. Also, when discerning a need we need to investigate the person's work ethic, as Paul also commands in 2 Thessalonians 3:10 that if people don't work, then they should not eat. ("For even when we were with you, we commanded you this: If anyone will not work, neither shall he eat.") But let's assume that you have done all the investigating and you realize it is indeed a need and you *shut up your heart from him*, then how does God's love dwell in you? Literally, this phrase reads, "And shuts his inner parts from him." The inner parts or bowels of compassion were the heart, lungs and liver, and so they came to indicate the affections, the place where our emotions are.

So literally, if you see a brother has a legitimate need, and then you close the door of your compassions, or the seat of your emotions, then *how does the love of God abide in you*? This means what is the use? How can one love God if he doesn't love his brother? He can't. The love of God does not dwell in him or her. John will mention later in 1 John 4:20, "If someone says, 'I love God,' and hates his brother, he is a liar; for he who does not love his brother whom he has seen, how can he love God whom he has not seen?" James says in his epistle something very similar: "What does it profit, my brethren, if someone says he has faith but does not have works? Can faith save him? If a brother or sister is naked and destitute of daily food, and one of you says to them, 'Depart in peace, be warmed and filled,' but you do not give them the things which are needed for the body, what does it profit? Thus also faith by itself, if it does not have works, is dead" (James 2:14-17). In his commentary on 1 John, Jay Adams gives an example of this. He's talking to the counselee:

> "Have you felt pity or concern for Bradley and his family?"
> "Certainly, He was in real need."
> "Well, what did you do about it?"
> "Oh, I don't know. I guess at the time I prayed for him."
> "But you could have done something concrete to meet his need, couldn't you?"
> "Hmmm. I suppose so."
> "But you didn't?"
> "No."
> "Any reason you can think of that kept you from doing so?"
> "Well, I was very busy with my business at that time. Things were going so well that I was snowed under."
> "In other words, you stifled your emotions, turned your back on their need and pursued your own concerns?"
> "It sounds pretty cold when you put it that way."
> "Well, how would you put it?"
> "I guess you are right. I was cold about the whole matter."
> "Then what do you suppose you ought to do about it now?"[65]

On Judgment Day, one of the great indicators of those who are truly of God will be those who have met legitimate needs. Jesus will then separate the sheep from the goats, and the marks of genuine faith will be what Christ says to the sheep in Matthew 25:35, 36: "for I was hungry and you gave Me food; I was thirsty and you gave Me drink; I was a stranger and you took Me in; I was naked and you clothed Me; I was sick and you visited Me; I was in prison and you came to Me." The marks of those who are not His, the goats, will be marked by what He says to them in verses 42-43: "for I was

---

[65] Jay Adams, *The Christian's Counselor's Commentary: The Gospel of John and The Letters of John and Jesus* (Woodruff, SC: Timeless Texts, 1998), p 238, 239.

hungry and you gave Me no food; I was thirsty and you gave Me no drink; I was a stranger and you did not take Me in, naked and you did not clothe Me, sick and in prison and you did not visit Me." The third quality of those who love—they meet the needs of others. John continues on with his appeal in verse 18.

> My little children, let us not love in word or in tongue, but in deed and in truth (1 John 3:18).

My little children, John says, let us not just love with our mouths but with action. Did you notice that John includes himself with this appeal by the pronoun *us*? John knew that this is a mark of one who truly loves God and he was not above warning himself in this. What does it mean to *love in word and tongue*? *Word and tongue* would indicate what you say. John says don't just say love, but do love. John says, "Practice what you profess." Let your words be followed up with deeds, with activity. Biblical *love* is not a lazy love; it gets up off the couch and does something. Words are fine, but they're cheap when they're not followed up with *deeds*, with works, which is what that word means. Actions many times do speak louder than words, and here is one of those situations. John says, instead, let us love in deed and truth. *Truth* would be a love that is shown in agreement with the truth that person professes, the truth of the gospel and the love of Jesus Christ who gave Himself for our sins. He laid down His life for us—so we should lay down our lives for others! Love in this way, in deed and in truth.

Summary

So what is *The Nature of Those Who Love Others* (vv 13, 16-18)? They are hated by the world; they are willing to lay down their lives for others; and they meet the needs of others in deed and truth! What is *The Nature of Those Who Hate Others* (vv 14, 15)? They abide in death; they are murderers; and they will spend eternity in hell.

I don't know if you ever struggle with the assurance of your salvation, but if you do, you can either take great comfort from these verses or you can take great concern from these verses. Does the world we live in warmly embrace you? If it does, then perhaps you need to reexamine your salvation. Does the world we live in persecute you; do they think you are strange? If so, then you can take comfort in this—that you indeed know Christ. Do you have a continuous and habitual love for others? If you do, then you can take comfort that you know God. Do you have a continuous and habitual hate for others? If so, then you should be concerned that you don't know God. Do you habitually give out of a generous heart of compassion to others from your time, your energy, and your resources? If you do, then you can take comfort that you know God. Do you habitually begrudge the time, money, and energy you give to others; would you rather be watching TV, surfing the net, catching up on your Facebook, chilling out, and doing your own thing? Are you indifferent to the needs of others? If these things describe you, then you should be concerned that perhaps you don't know God. These are issues I would encourage you to ponder before the Lord in the quietness of your heart—they are matters of life and death.

Questions to Consider

Is Your Life Characterized by Love or Hate?

1 John 3:13-18

1. (a) According to 1 John 3:13-18, what specific words or phrases does John use to describe how we are to manifest love toward others? (b) What are the words or phrases he uses to describe our hatred or indifference toward others?

2. Memorize 1 John 3:16.

3. Why should believers not be surprised at the world's hatred for them? See Matthew 10:24, 25, 34-36; John 15:18-25; John 16:1-3.

4. (a) Do you think that the laying down of Christ's life was easy for Him? Support your answer with Scripture. (b) How does this help you as you think about laying down your own life? (c) What do you think John means when he says we are to "lay down our lives for the brethren"?

5. In each of the following examples, share *who* was in need, *what* was needed, *who* met the need, and *how* the need was met in deed and in truth? Exodus 1:22-2:10; 1 Samuel 22:1-4; Luke 10:30-37; John 19:25-27; Philippians 2:25-30. (b) What principles can you glean for your own life when endeavoring to love others?

6. (a) What are some ways in which the world manifests its hatred toward believers today? (b) In the workplace? (c) In your neighborhood? (d) In your family? (e) In your church?

7. (a) Is there anyone you hate? (b) What does John say in this passage about those who hate? (c) What are you going to do about your sin?

8. (a) What could you do this week to exhibit love to someone, according to the standard of love John sets forth in 1 John 3:16-18? (b) Do it!

9. After contemplating this week's lesson, come with a prayer request to share.

Chapter 14

Five Valid Tests that We are Born of God

1 John 3:19-24

Over the years as I have counseled women, I've encountered many who have struggled with assurance of their salvation. With some, after working with them over a period of time, it is easy to see that no actual regeneration has taken place in their hearts and there is no fruit in their lives. When I have presented my concerns to them regarding the validity of their faith, some have bowed their knee to Christ, but others have become angry. There are also those who struggle with assurance who are indeed believers, but because of past sins in their life they struggle with self-condemnation. Even so, there is fruit in their Christian walk and a regenerated heart. With these ladies, I try to encourage them to forget the past and help them with their oversensitive conscience. Perhaps you do not struggle with assurance, or even if you do, we have come to a portion of 1 John that can either be of great comfort to you or of great concern. The passage we are studying, as we finish chapter three, gives us five valid tests that we are indeed born of God.

Test #1: Loving the Brethren (vv 19, 23)
Test #2: Answered Prayer (v 22)
Test #3: Obedience to His Word (v 22)
Test #4: Belief in Jesus Christ (v 23)
Test #5: The Indwelling of the Holy Spirit (v 24)

1 John 3:19-24

And by this we know that we are of the truth, and shall assure
our hearts before Him. 20For if our heart condemns us, God is
greater than our heart, and knows all things. 21Beloved, if our
heart does not condemn us, we have confidence toward God.

> [22]And whatever we ask we receive from Him, because we keep His commandments and do those things that are pleasing in His sight. [23]And this is His commandment: that we should believe on the name of His Son Jesus Christ and love one another, as He gave us commandment. [24]Now he who keeps His commandments abides in Him, and He in him. And by this we know that He abides in us, by the Spirit whom He has given us (1 John 3:19-24).

In our last lesson we saw *The Nature of Those Who Love Others* (vv 13, 16-18): they are hated by the world; they are willing to lay down their lives for others; and they meet the needs of others in deed and truth! We also saw *The Nature of Those Who Hate Others* (vv 14, 15): they abide in death; they are murderers; and they will spend eternity in hell. John reminded us that hatred from the world toward believers is to be expected. However, hatred from believers toward others is not expected and should never be! John equated hatred with murder and murder with eternal condemnation. He then gave us the example of Christ in how to love our brother, and that is by laying down our lives. We also saw how important it is when meeting needs to make sure they are needs and not wants. Finally, we ended with the admonition from John to not just love with our mouths, but with our actions, in deed and truth. John has been speaking about loving in deed and in truth and now he continues on with the theme of truth in verse 19. John has told us to love one another in truth and now he tells us how we can know that we are indeed of the truth. Here is our first valid test that we are indeed born of God.

Test #1: Loving the Brethren
1 John 3:19

> And by this we know that we are of the truth, and shall assure our hearts before Him (1 John 3:19).

The first question we need to ask of this verse is, "By *what* do we know that we are of the truth?" This statement forces us back to the previous verse, verse 18. By loving the brethren in deed and in truth, this is how *we know that we are of the truth.* So this is test number one that assures us that we are of God—loving the brethren. The word *know* means to be sure. John says we no longer have to doubt our salvation, we no longer have to wonder if we are of the truth, we can be assured of this if we love the brethren. John then adds *and shall assure our hearts before Him*. What does this mean? *Assure* means to persuade or to tranquilize our hearts or our consciences before God. Do you ever wonder if you indeed are a believer? You can be assured you are a believer if you love the brethren. As we have seen in previous lessons, children of the devil do not love others.

Now ladies, I know I'm going to step on some toes. (It won't be the first time at least!) I'm puzzled when people come to church and sit in the pews or chairs week after week but don't really get involved in the body life of the church or in serving others. That is a concerning sign of an unregenerate heart.[66] We should love others and we should be growing deeper and more fervent in our love with each passing year that we know God. We should have a growing desire to love one another and serve one another. We should desire to be ministering to others more than we desire to be ministered to. An idle Christian is a concept that is foreign to the New Testament. We will have confident assurance before God that we are His, and that we are of the truth, if we love others. My friend, this is a comforting thought, because at times our conscience condemns us. But as our love for others grows, and as we have a desire to sacrifice on their behalf, we can be assured that we are His and He is ours. Now some of us struggle with self-condemnation, even if we are truly of God. That's why John goes on to say in verse 20,

[66] Contemporary evangelical practice has done a disservice in stressing assurance of salvation, immediately following a public confession of faith. The wrong impression received is that a person's salvation is assured because of walking an aisle, sincerely saying a prayer or making a decision for Christ. According to the New Testament, however, assurance comes from objectively evaluating the fruits of a new nature, i.e., the life of obedience, love and doctrinal integrity.

> For if our heart condemns us, God is greater than our heart, and knows all things (1 John 3:20).

Now this is not an easy verse to interpret, but, after much study, I will give you the conclusion I have come to. The word *condemn* means to blame or to find fault. John is speaking here of a believer who has a troubled heart and conscience. This condemning heart could be because of past sins or because of failure to love the brethren as you should. But John says, *if our heart condemns us, God is greater than our heart, and knows all things*. This means that God is greater or larger than our heart and He knows all things. Ladies, many times we can't know our heart, but God does. As Jeremiah says in Jeremiah 17:9, 10, "The heart is deceitful above all things, And desperately wicked; Who can know it? I, the LORD, search the heart, I test the mind, Even to give every man according to his ways, According to the fruit of his doings." Or as Proverbs 20:27 states, "The spirit of a man is the lamp of the LORD, Searching all the inner depths of his heart." God knows all things. He is omniscient. Even when the Apostle Peter was being questioned by the Lord about his love for Christ, the apostle said, "Lord, You know all things; You know that I love you" (John 21:17). So, what is John saying here? He's saying our hearts may condemn us at times, or an oversensitive conscience can cause us to have unnecessary feelings of guilt. This may be reflected in our thinking that we are not doing enough or that we are not loving our brother the way we should. But God is greater than our conscience and He knows all things. God discerns everything and He will be the ultimate judge. Many times I am not able to meet a need because I cannot be all things to all people, and so I feel guilty and self-condemned. I cannot possibly meet every need of every person, but God knows and He is greater than my heart. However, if I should be meeting the need, and am able to do so, and don't do it, that guilty conscience is probably from God. Again, He is greater than my heart and He will judge me on that day according to the deeds I have done in my flesh, whether they be good or evil.

Some of you may have an oversensitive conscience or some of you may have a truly guilty conscience. That's why it is essential to educate your conscience with the Word of God. I must admit that I have an oversensitive conscience at times, even though I know that the Lord has grown me in this area. Sometimes my conscience condemns me and sometimes it is the Lord. If my conscience condemns me, I need to remember that God is greater than my conscience and He knows all things. Sometimes we would be wise to remind ourselves of Romans 8:1, where Paul says, "There is therefore now no condemnation to those who are in Christ Jesus, who do not walk according to the flesh, but according to the Spirit." Paul makes it clear: if you are walking in the Spirit, there is no condemnation; if you're walking in the flesh, there is condemnation. But we should not allow our conscience to condemn us when God does not. God is greater and much more superior than our hearts, and ultimately He is the one who knows all things and will bring all things to light. Paul helps us tremendously with this in 1 Corinthians 4:4, where he says, "For I know of nothing against myself, yet I am not justified by this; but He who judges me is the Lord." Paul says, "My conscience is clear, but that does not make me innocent. It is the Lord who judges me." Even though Paul had a pure conscience before God and man, he knew, as we all should, that he could be deceived. But we can rest in the fact that the Lord is the judge and He will make all things right on that day. We should never fool ourselves into thinking we know our own heart; we don't. John goes on to say,

> Beloved, if our heart does not condemn us, we have confidence toward God (1 John 3:21).

We have applied verse 20 to a believer with an oversensitive conscience, who is feeling guilty over not helping a believer when he thinks he should have. In verse 21 we have the opposite happening. This believer is not feeling guilty about what they have or have not done. Their conscience is clear, and therefore they can have boldness before God. For the one who is feeling guilty before God, he needs to confess his sins and or educate his conscience, so that he too can have confidence before God as well. So, *if our heart does not condemn us, we have confidence toward God.* What does this mean? It means that if we are sincere, if there is no hypocrisy in us, if we are what we proclaim ourselves to be, then we can *have confidence toward God.* What does it mean to have *confidence* toward God? It means to have frankness, assurance or boldness. Notice that this confidence is *toward God*, not toward ourselves and not toward others. Our confidence is based on sins forgiven, not on some favor we think we deserve. This word *toward* is very significant. In the Greek it is pros ton theon, which implies a face-to-face intimacy, as one would enjoy in prayer to God. It is so beautifully put in Hebrews 10:22: "Let us draw near with a true heart in full assurance of faith, having our hearts sprinkled from an evil conscience and our bodies washed with pure water." When we rid ourselves of our evil conscience, then we can come boldly to the throne of grace. This confidence toward God allows us to approach His throne in prayer and receive the things we ask for. And that is John's point as he goes on in verse 22. And here we find the second and third valid tests of our faith.

Test #2: Answered Prayer
Test #3: Obedience to His Word
1 John 3:22

> And whatever we ask we receive from Him, because we keep His commandments and do those things that are pleasing in His sight (1 John 3:22).

These words are very similar to what Jesus said in John 15:7: "If you abide in Me, and My words abide in you, you will ask what you desire, and it shall be done for you." The Greek tense here in verse 22 indicates that *ask* means to keep on asking and *receive* means to keep on receiving. The believer's life should be one of constant prayer—praying without ceasing. And the Lord's response to that asking is to be constantly giving and giving and giving. It is

God's desire to give good gifts to His children and to keep on giving them according to Matthew 7:11 and James 1:17. This is the second valid test that we are children of God—He answers our prayers!

Now, a lot of people stop right there in the middle of this verse and claim that they can ask whatever they want from God and they will have it. They fail to read the rest of the verse. There are conditions in this asking. John says, *because we keep His commandments and do those things that are pleasing in His sight.* By the way, the Greek tenses of these phrases give the idea that we keep on keeping His commandments and we keep on doing those things that please Him. This is to be a habit of our lives. (You might take time to look at these other conditions for answered prayer, found in the following verses: Psalm 66:18; Mark 11:25; John 16:23, 24; James 1:6; 4:2, 3; 1 Peter 3:7; 1 John 3:22; 5:14.) Now let's stop and think through this for a minute. For example, what if you are praying for a million dollars? If you are asking for a million dollars to expand the kingdom and glorify God, then go for it. If you are asking for selfish reasons, then you do not understand the verse here. Why? Because "you shall not covet" is a commandment. You are not keeping His commandments when you're asking for a million dollars for your own selfish purposes. Prayer has to be in accordance with God's will. Also, John says another condition of answered prayer is not only obedience to His commandments, but also doing *those things that are pleasing in His sight*. Coveting a million dollars is not pleasing in God's sight. God's Word says that with food and raiment we are to be content. It says nothing about being content with a million dollars. In fact, if you had it, I could almost guarantee you would not be content with it! It is interesting that the word for *receive* here means to accept. Whatever we ask of Him, we accept from Him. Could it mean that sometimes He answers in ways we do not expect? One man has said,

> I asked God for strength, that I might achieve, I was made weak, that I might learn humbly to obey; I asked for health, that I might do greater things, I was given infirmity, that I

> might do better things; I asked for riches, that I might be happy, I was given poverty, that I might be wise; I asked for power, that I might have the praise of man, I was given weakness, that I might feel the need of God; I asked for all things, that I might enjoy life, I was given life, that I might enjoy things; I got nothing that I asked for—but everything I had hoped for, Almost despite myself, my unspoken prayers were answered, I am among all men, most richly blessed.[67]

Many times, the things we ask God for are answered with the unexpected. But we can rest assured as children of God that if we are obeying Him and pleasing Him He will answer our prayers. In fact, each day as we commit our ways to Him we should see God moving in our lives and answering prayer on our behalf. So we can take courage, as we obey Him and please Him He will answer our prayers. And of course it only makes sense that as we obey Him and please Him then we will be asking for those things that would please Him and are in accordance with His Word. The more that we are growing in our knowledge of God and have His mind, the more we will ask for things that we know are in His will.

Now you might ask, "Is there any difference between keeping His commandments and doing those things which are pleasing in His sight?" Yes, to *keep His commandments* means to keep those things that God has specifically demanded of us, while doing *those things that are pleasing in His sight* is to doing those things that He has not necessarily told us to do but which we know would please him. For example, my husband may say, "Susan, I don't want you to clean house today. I want you to spend time with me." That is a command, which, by the way, he has never said. However, let's say it is my housecleaning day and yet I know that I haven't spent much time with my husband and he is freer than usual, and so I forgo my housework to be with him because I know it would please him. See the difference? In fact, *in His sight* means in God's presence or

[67] Author Unknown.

in His face. In other words, we do things as if His presence were there, and indeed it is. We do everything as unto the Lord, as Paul says in Colossians 3:17. You and I should be so close to our Lord that we know what would please Him. We don't need to ask Him, as we know His heart and His mind. A believer will indeed watch and carefully observe what her Lord has asked, and she will do that not only occasionally, but as a habit of her life. Our will should be completely surrendered to the Father. Just as a parent, you are more apt to give good things to a child who is obedient, so it is with our Heavenly Father. And just as you withhold privileges from a disobedient child, so it is with our Heavenly Father. This is the third test of a genuine believer—obedience to His commandments. So if my answered prayer is conditioned upon my obedience to his commandments, then what are those commandments? I'm glad you asked! John sums up all the commandments in one commandment in verse 23. And here we find our fourth valid test that we are born of God.

Test #4: Belief in Jesus Christ
1 John 3:23

> And this is His commandment: that we should believe on the name of His Son Jesus Christ and love one another, as He gave us commandment (1 John 3:23).

Now you might have scratched your head on this and said, "John just said commandments (plural) in verse 22, and now he just says commandment (singular). Why?" It's because faith and obedience cannot be separated. Faith and love are not separate issues. What we believe has an effect on how we behave. If we believe in Christ, then it is only makes sense that flowing from that belief will be obedience. We also can't love the brethren in the sense that John is saying here without the faith in Christ that enables us to love our brothers. It is the idea that Christ mentions in Matthew 22:34-40 and Mark 12:28-31, where he says we are to love the Lord our God with all our heart, soul and mind, and we are to love our neighbor as ourselves. Jesus says all the commandments can be summed up in one! So what does John mean when he says that we are to *believe on the name of His Son Jesus Christ*? It means we are to have faith, to trust on the name of Jesus. His name would be representative of His authority, nature and character. To *believe* here is once and for all and it means to continually believe. I don't just believe in Jesus today and decide tomorrow I think He's a fake. This is the fourth valid proof that you belong to God—you believe in Christ, and it is lasting. This belief in Christ affects the very nature of who I am and it fleshes out in my *love* for others. When John says love *one another*, it is the Greek word allos, which means one of the same kind. This would be referring to those who are in Christ, those who are like us. Paul even tells us in Galatians 6:10, "Therefore, as we have opportunity, let us do good to all, especially to those who are of the household of faith." We are to be ministering especially to those like us, those who are in Christ. Christ has commanded us to love one another in John 15:12: "This is my commandment, that you love one another as I have loved you." John repeats here in this verse the important aspect and valid test of our relationship with Christ—we love others. John goes on in verse 24 with his theme of keeping God's commandments, as well as giving us the fifth valid test that we know God.

Test #5: The Indwelling of the Holy Spirit 1 John 3:24

> Now he who keeps His commandments abides in Him, and He in him. And by this we know that He abides in us, by the Spirit whom He has given us (1 John 3:24).

John says whoever *keeps His commandments abides in Him* and He is *in him*. What does it mean to *abide in Him*, and He in us? The word *abide* means to dwell, to stay in a given place. What is John saying? He's saying that if we are keeping His commandments, then we have the assurance that He stays with us and we stay with Him. He sticks with us and we persevere to the end. It is like Hebrews

13:5: "I will never leave you, nor forsake you." The Greek is more literally rendered, "I will never, no never, no never leave you!" It is a triple negative in the Greek. Jesus Himself mentions this idea of abiding in Him and keeping His commandments in John 15, which is the discourse of the vine and the branches: "If you keep my commandments, you will abide in my love, just as I have kept my Father's commandments and abide in His love" (John 15:10).

Just in case you still are in doubt as to your eternal destination, John says, *and by this we know that He abides in us, by the Spirit whom He has given us*. This is the fifth test that John gives which determines if we are born of God—the indwelling of the Holy Spirit. John says we can know, we can be sure, that God abides in us, that He stays in us, by the Spirit whom He has given us. By the way, this is the first mention of the Spirit in this epistle. And it is interesting that John mentions the Holy Spirit now, at this point in the epistle, as it is He who enables us to love our brother as we should (verses 18, 19 and 23); it is He who assists us as we pray (verse 22); it is He who sets the sinner apart (sanctifies) from his act of unbelief to the act of faith in the Lord Jesus (verse 27); it is He who gives us unrest when we are not obeying as we should (verse 22); it is He who has been given to us as a gift from God (verse 24); it is He who lives and dwells within us; it is He who convicts us when we're doing wrong and assures us and prompts us to love the brethren. As we obey the commandments of God we are assured of God the Holy Spirit residing in us. These are the things that John has been speaking of and now he ends with the blessed promise of the indwelling Spirit.

Summary

What a powerful portion of the Word of God that should aide in helping you examine yourself to see if you are in the faith. There are five valid tests to see if we are in the faith. *Test #1: Loving the Brethren* (vv 19, 23). Do you love the brethren more today than you did last year? How does it manifest itself? Are you more sacrificial in your love for others? *Test #2: Answered Prayer* (v 22). Do you pray? Constantly? Consistently? Do you see God answering prayer in your life daily? *Test #3: Obedience to His Word* (v 22). Do you obey and please God? Do you know the Word so that you don't have to wonder what it is that God has asked of you? Do you delight to do the will of God? Are you disobeying God in any area of your life this day? *Test #4: Belief in Jesus Christ* (v 23). Do you really believe the facts concerning Christ and who He is? Does it affect how you live? *Test #5: The Indwelling of the Holy Spirit* (v 24). Does God the Holy Spirit dwell within you? How do you know? Do you sense His presence, His conviction, His comfort, and His enabling in your life? If you have any unrest after this lesson, my friend, I would encourage you to talk with the Lord, talk with your husband or your closest friend. Find an accountability partner to pray with you and to help you discern where you are in your walk with Christ. Today, if you will hear His voice, please do not harden your heart!

Questions to Consider

Five Valid Tests that We are Born of God

1 John 3:19-24

1. (a) In 1 John 3:19-24, John gives several criteria whereby we can be assured that we truly are born of God. What are they? (b) Do these tests give you confidence that you know God, or do they concern you that you might not know God? (c) What will you do about it?

2. Memorize 1 John 3:22. (How have these verses helped you in your walk?)

3. What do you think John means in 1 John 3:20, 21?

4. (a) How would you answer someone biblically who claimed that 1 John 3:22 was a blank check for asking and receiving anything they wanted? (b) What are the conditions for answered prayer, according to this verse, and what do you think they mean? (c) Are you meeting those conditions? (d) Extra Credit: What are some other conditions for answered prayer, according to the Scriptures?

5. How does Mark 12:28-33 relate to what John says in 1 John 3:23?

6. John says in 1 John 3:24 that we can know we are of God because of the Spirit He has given us. (a) What facts do you already know about the Holy Spirit? (b) What does the Bible teach us about the Holy Spirit according to John 3:6-8; John 14:16-17, 26; John 15:26; John 16:7-15; Romans 8:1, 2, 14-16, 26-27; and Ephesians 1:13, 14? (c) How do these verses assure you that you have the Holy Spirit?

7. (a) What "things" do you think please the Lord? (b) Would you say your life is pleasing to the Lord? (c) How could you change your life to be more pleasing to the Lord?

8. (a) Does the Lord answer your prayers? (b) What prayer(s) has He answered this week? Be prepared to share some of those with your group! Come prepared to tell of His wondrous works!

9. What would you like to ask the Lord for this week? Please put it in the form of a prayer request to share. (Remember to keep His commandments and do those things that are pleasing in His sight!)

Chapter 15

Discerning Truth from Error

1 John 4:1-6

Several summers ago, around the time I was studying for this particular lesson in 1 John, I went outside to get the mail. As I brought it in, my eyes fell on a newsletter my husband receives. But for some reason (I am sure the Lord had something to do with it), I began to read the first page. It started like this: "It is getting a little depressing to attend the various messianic conferences around the nation. There seems to be the acceptance of virtually every new wind of doctrine and almost every year there is a new wind blowing. Sadly, some people do not have the discernment to evaluate doctrine on the basis of Scripture. In fact, too often truth is determined by how good it makes one feel and/or accepted on the basis of the personality and forcefulness of the one presenting the doctrine. Due to a lack of proper discipleship, so many Christians never move from milk to meat and even the milk seems to be diluted with a lot of water."[68] Around the same time, I had been emailing my friend, Martha Peace, about a matter, and happened to mention my concern for a friend who had gotten caught up in the teaching of a popular writer and speaker. Her response was funny, but sad; she said, "Your friend must have a theological disconnect."

With those things in mind, my question to you as we begin chapter four of 1 John is this: Can a genuine believer be led into error? Can a genuine believer be led astray by false prophets? I'm grateful that I don't personally have to answer that question for you, as God the Holy Spirit through the aged old Apostle John gives us the answer. Let's read together the first six verses of 1 John, chapter 4.

---

68 Ariel Ministries Newsletter, Summer 2002.

1 John 4:1-6

> Beloved, do not believe every spirit, but test the spirits, whether they are of God; because many false prophets have gone out into the world. [2]By this you know the Spirit of God: Every spirit that confesses that Jesus Christ has come in the flesh is of God, [3]and every spirit that does not confess that Jesus Christ has come in the flesh is not of God. And this is the spirit of the Antichrist, which you have heard was coming, and is now already in the world. [4]You are of God, little children, and have overcome them, because He who is in you is greater than he who is in the world. [5]They are of the world. Therefore they speak as of the world, and the world hears them. [6]We are of God. He who knows God hears us; he who is not of God does not hear us. By this we know the spirit of truth and the spirit of error (1 John 4:1-6).

In our last lesson we saw that John gave five valid tests that we are born of God: *Test #1: Loving the Brethren*; *Test #2: Answered Prayer*; *Test #3: Obedience to His Word*; *Test #4: Belief in Jesus Christ*; *Test #5: The Indwelling of the Holy Spirit*. Our outline for this lesson will include:

Our Responsibility to Discern False Teachers (v 1)
Our Method for Discerning False Teachers (vv 2, 3)
Our Promise to Overcome False Teachers (v 4)
Our Vast Differences with False Teachers (vv 5, 6)

The transition here seems to be from the thought of the Spirit whom God has given us, in 3:24, to testing the spirits, in 4:1. Those who truly possess the indwelling of the Holy Spirit will be able to discern truth from error. God has given us His Holy Spirit, this is true, but we must also be very discerning, because there are other spirits out there, which have nothing to do with The Holy Spirit. John begins to warn his children and reminds them of their responsibility to discern false teachers.

Our Responsibility to Discern False Teachers
1 John 4:1

> Beloved, do not believe every spirit, but test the spirits, whether they are of God; because many false prophets have gone out into the world (1 John 4:1).

Beloved here means dearly beloved. John is using this term of endearment because he is prompted by his love for them to warn them about the false teachers of their day, the Gnostics. His readers would have sensed his affection and concern for them. Remember, John is very old as he writes this epistle, and most of the first generation Christians were gone, and those reading this epistle would have been second and third generation believers. Most of them had not actually seen Christ, and so perhaps some were having doubts about what was truth and what was error. Many generations have come and gone since then, and how much more careful must we be! So John says, beloved, *do not believe every spirit*. Stop believing every spirit; do not have faith in every spirit; don't accept every spirit as true. Apparently many were being led away by these false teachers. So instead of believing everything that comes down the pike, instead of believing every spirit, John says we are to *test the spirits*. What does it mean to test the spirits?[69] It means to approve, examine, try,

[69] The plural "spirits" (Greek, pneumatti) could be either: 1) Beings that inspire men but are distinct from men, using human personalities to express themselves. Those holding this view (Alford, IV, p 483, and Brown, pp 486-487) suggest the context following refers to the wicked spirit of deceit and the Holy Spirit. The weakness of this view is that it is inconsistent to take the reference to be spiritual beings here and human beings in the rest of the paragraph; 2) By metonymy, men in whom spirits exist. This second view is John's intended meaning as the testing of the spirits is similar to Deut. 13:1-6 and 18:15-22, where men are tested. Also, verses 2b and 3 are clearly talking about people (cf. Robertson, VI, p 229; Plummer, p 142; Stott, pp 153-154; Bruce, p 103). John uses pneuma in two ways in this paragraph to refer to either the Holy Spirit or the spirit of men (vv 2, 6) and to refer to the spirits of men who are influenced by these spirits (vv 1, 2 3). "The author's shifting of references from one to the other so quickly, sometimes within the same sentence, shows the close association between the human spirits and the two supernatural spirits which inspire them. Since the emphasis of the paragraph is upon the external phenomena by which spirits are recognized primarily attention is focused on human beings, and the reference of the two occurrences of pneuma in vs. 1 is to men." cf. Robert L. Thomas, *Exegetical Digest of First John* (Copyright by Robert L. Thomas, 1984), p 333.

and prove them. Put them to the acid test; or, like coins, prove them in the fire. It is interesting that the word *test* also has the idea that the test is performed with an optimistic attitude that hopes for the best. For example, when gold coins were tested, they were tested with the hope that they were indeed genuine. This makes sense, as we should always hope that those who are professing Christ do indeed possess Christ. And John says we test them to see if *they are of God*. We must test to see if their origin is from God or not. And according to the present tense in which this word is written in the Greek, this testing is to be done continually. We can never let our guard down because false teachers are abundant and every day new ones come onto the scene. And by the way, once we've tested them, we should be like the Berean believers and keep on testing them. Some teachers start out with good intentions and sound doctrine but will later go astray. So, always be testing the spirits. You might be saying, "Well, why should I spend my time doing that, Susan? I have enough things to do! I have laundry to do and diapers to change and a house to clean! Can't I leave that job to my pastor; isn't that what I pay him for?" Certainly pastors have a greater responsibility to guard their sheep from the wolves, but John doesn't give a qualifier here. He just says beloved, which means that his words are applicable to all of God's children.[70]

John then gives the reason why we must test the spirits. He says, *because many false prophets have gone out into the world.* Notice John says *many*, which means abundant. And, of course, we

[70] Careful principles of interpretation are essential today. I would recommend the following reading: *Reckless Faith: When the Church Loses Its Will to Discern*, by John MacArthur, Jr. (Wheaton, IL: Crossway Books, 1994). Included in the book is an excellent commentary on another central New Testament passage on the three commands of discernment from First Thessalonians 5:21-22, i.e., to judge everything, to cling to what is good and to shun what is evil (pp 69-81). Also, Appendix 2 of the same work, "Jonathan Edward's Theology of Discernment," based on 1 John 4:1, pp 219-231. *Heresies: the Image of Christ in the Mirror of Heresies and Orthodoxy from the Apostles to the Present*, by Harold O. J. Brown (Garden City, NY: Doubleday & Company, 1984). General reading on the science of interpretation: *Protestant Biblical Interpretation*, by Bernard Ramm (Grand Rapids, MI: Baker, 1970); *Hermeneutics: Principles and Processes of Biblical Interpretation*, by Henry A. Virkler (Grand Rapids, MI: Baker, 1981); *Biblical Hermeneutics*, by Milton S. Terry (Grand Rapids, MI: Zondervan, 1974).

know from what Jesus said in the Olivet Discourse that false prophets will increase more abundantly as the end of the age comes (Matthew 24:24). Now what is a *false prophet*? The word means a religious imposter. More than likely, these false prophets in John's day were the Gnostic teachers who were invading the church. Evidently, by this time there were many false prophets and false teachers and false doctrines in the world. In our day, we would say they're more than abundant; we would say there is a super abundance of false teachers, prophets and doctrines. So what is our responsibility in discerning false teachers? It is to not believe but test every teacher. You might say, "Well, how will I know a false prophet or not?" John tells us how in verses 2 and 3 and here we have our method in discerning false teachers.

Our Method for Discerning False Teachers 1 John 4:2, 3

> By this you know the Spirit of God: Every spirit that confesses that Jesus Christ has come in the flesh is of God (1 John 4:2).

John says *by this you know* false teachers from the true teachers. The word *know* means knowledge that is obtained by observing the evidence and then drawing the conclusion. How can we know if someone is of *the Spirit of God* or not? John says those who are the genuine thing will *confess that Jesus Christ has come in the flesh*. What does it mean that *Jesus Christ has come in the flesh*? It means He was once a spirit, but that He took on a body. He had a human form just like you and me. He had flesh.[71] It was what John

[71] This is why the first four and a half centuries of the Christian Church were given to precise theological debate, centering on the Person of the Lord Jesus Christ, culminating in the *Chalcedonian Creed* of 451. It was there that Jesus Christ was declared to be "of one substance with us, according to His humility, in all things like us, saving sin." Although the historical context of our First John passage applied to identifying the Gnostic heresy, it helps discern between the true and the false among contemporary, 1) Liberal Theology, which denies the full deity of Jesus Christ; 2) Neo-orthodoxy, which denies the nature and historical fact of the incarnation; and 3) Modern Cults, such as Jehovah's Witnesses, who deny the incarnation, i.e., Christian Science, New Thought and Unity School, etc.

spoke about in the very first verse of his letter, when he said, "That which was from the beginning, which we have heard, which we have seen with our eyes, which we have looked upon, and our hands have handled, concerning the Word of life" (1 John 1:1). Those that are of God will confess this truth. Now, what does it mean to *confess*? It means to covenant or to assent. To confess is also a reference to a public proclamation, which expresses a commitment and an obligation. It is an open confession. This confession is continual and it demonstrates itself not just by what is said but also in what is shown by the life. When I make a covenant with God, He becomes my Master and it shows itself in how I obey Him. You should be able to watch a person's life as well as listen to her lips, and say, yes, she is of God. It's just like in a marriage; you make a covenant when you get married and it means you are to be faithful to the one you marry. I can confess that I am married all I want with my mouth, but if my behavior doesn't show that I am a married woman, (i.e., running around with other men, going to single bars and clubs, etc.), then you probably won't believe me. And so one's confession of Christ coming in the flesh should manifest itself in their commitment to Christ. You should be able to see it. If the life and the lips match up, then you know they are of God. If not, then you know they are not of God, as John states in verse 3.

> And every spirit that does not confess that Jesus Christ has come in the flesh is not of God. And this is the spirit of the Antichrist, which you have heard was coming, and is now already in the world (1 John 4:3).

Anyone who *does not confess that Christ has come in the flesh*, and whose life does not back it up, John says, has *the spirit of the Antichrist*. *Confess* speaks of a habitual practice, a personal conviction which is openly expressed. The Gnostics would fall under this category, as they taught that Christ was separate from the man Jesus, and denied that He had *come in the flesh*. They also lived unrighteous lives and took no responsibility for it. So if any one, not just the Gnostics, denies the incarnate Christ, then John says, first of all, that person *is not of God*, and second, they have *the spirit of the Antichrist*. What does it mean to have the spirit of the Antichrist? *Antichrist* is an opponent of the Messiah. This is any one or any system that would be opposed to Christ. Any false religion that is opposed to Christ is antichrist. And John says, *which you have heard was coming, and is now already in the world*. John says, you are not ignorant of this, just as you and I should not be ignorant that there are antichrists in the world today. Now you might be asking, when did they hear about this? Think back to when we dealt with this in a previous lesson, when we were studying 1 John 2:18: "Little children, it is the last hour; and as you have heard that the Antichrist is coming, even now many antichrists have come, by which we know that it is the last hour." We saw then that they heard it before through apostolic teaching. (We won't take the time to review these here, but the following verses are listed in case you have forgotten: Acts 20:29, 30; 2 Thessalonians 2:3-10 and 1 Timothy 4:1. You might also refer back to our lesson in chapter 8 of this book.)

Now ladies, before we go on, let me say that this does not mean that this is the only test of a false prophet, as you saw in the "Questions to Consider" for this lesson. But John is giving this particular test to these readers because of the heresy of Gnostism. Now in the "Questions to Consider," I gave you the main passages in the Word of God which should help you to discern false teachers. But before we go on, I would also like to give you 7 more helps, from the Application Bible Commentary, which I thought would be helpful, especially when it comes to discerning a cult. It seems like there are new ones springing up almost daily.

> 1. *They allow a human authority to make the decisions.* David Koresh, Rev. Moon, Jim Jones. It is not the Bible which is the authority in their teaching, but a man or woman.
>
> 2. *They claim to have new truth or special revelation.* Many times this teaching contradicts what the Scripture

already teaches. Tulsa, Oklahoma, where I live, has many of these false teachers.

3. *They attack the Christian church.* They call Christians hypocrites, racists, or immoral. They do this in order to attack Christians and say they are not the true church.

4. *They twist Christian doctrine.* They twist doctrines like the doctrine of the trinity or the deity of Christ or the virgin birth.

5. *They undermine Scripture.* They twist the Scripture in order to prove some way-off viewpoint.

6. *They promote salvation by works.* Salvation, to them, is not by faith but by meetings, training, and the promotion of their cult.

7. *They undermine the assurance of eternal life in God's grace.* They teach that salvation happens when you adhere to their teaching, not in the saving grace of Christ.[72]

If a man or woman draws people to themselves and not to God—watch out! If a man or woman does not teach consistently from the Word of God and contradicts what Scripture says—watch out! If a man's or woman's moral character does not back up what they teach—watch out! If a man or woman only says what pleases the ear, and not the Lord—watch out! So what is our method for discerning false teachers? Anyone who confesses Jesus Christ came in the flesh is of God, and those who do not confess that Jesus came in the flesh are not of God! You might be saying, "Susan, you are scaring me! I mean, what if I am not able to discern all the false teachers out there?" Well, John has some encouragement for us, that we who are of God can discern false teachers. Notice what he says:

---

[72] Principles derived from *Life Application Bible Commentary: 1, 2, & 3 John* (Carol Stream, IL: Tyndale House Publishers, 2010), p 84.

Our Promise to Overcome False Teachers
1 John 4:4

> You are of God, little children, and have overcome them, because He who is in you is greater than he who is in the world (1 John 4:4).

Notice the tenderness in John's words: *you are of God, little children*, and because you are of God, little children, *you have overcome them*. Overcome who? The false prophets. What does it mean that they have *overcome* them?[73] It means they have subdued them with a calm confidence of final victory. The tense here of the word overcome means that the Christians John is writing to had stood against the false heresy sometime in the past and they were still standing against it. But John is also encouraging them to continue to stand against it. This affirms to us that those who know Christ cannot be led astray by false teachers. You and I, as genuine believers, will not be swept away by false teaching. It is also comforting that Jesus says the same thing in Matthew 24:24: "For false christs and false prophets will rise and show great signs and wonders to deceive, if possible, even the elect." Jesus says it's not possible—praise be to God!

Now you might ask, "Why will I will be able to discern false teachers? Why will I overcome them?" John says, *because He who is in you is greater than he who is in the world*! Just in case you start thinking, "Well, I sure have discernment against error, but I wonder why so and so doesn't," or, "I must be someone special or have a special gift," remember that it is the Spirit that is in you that gives

[73] The Greek perfect verb neikekate (cf. 1 John 2:13) means to carry off victorious or come off victorious, suggesting a past victory that endures until the present. As we discovered in 2:13, the victory took place at conversion, when the believer's past relationship to Satan and his kingdom was severed by the death and resurrection of Christ. All believers have *overcome* in this sense (cf. 1 John 5:4-5; compare with Rev. 2:7, 11, 17, 26; 3:5, 12, 21). But here John says we have overcome *them* (Greek, autous), which refers to those in verse 3, who *do not confess that Jesus Christ is come in the flesh* and so are *antichrist*. These are the false prophets (v 1) who are devastating the area with their Gnostic doctrines.

you that discernment! It is not of us; it is of God. And God is greater than Satan, who is behind all antichrists, all false teachers, and all false teaching![74] False teachers, antichrists and the like all have their origin in Satan. They are indeed his mouthpieces. Paul warns us about Satan and all his demons in 2 Corinthians 11:13-15: "For such are false apostles, deceitful workers, transforming themselves into apostles of Christ. And no wonder! For Satan himself transforms himself into an angel of light. Therefore it is no great thing if his ministers also transform themselves into ministers of righteousness, whose end will be according to their works." So John gives us promise here in this verse that we will overcome false teachers because greater is the One in us than the one in the world. John goes on to describe the vast differences that believers have with false teachers, in verses 5 and 6.

Our Vast Differences with False Teachers
1 John 4:5, 6

> They are of the world. Therefore they speak as of the world, and the world hears them (1 John 4:5).

Who is *of the world*? The false teachers, the antichrists, those who deny that Jesus came in the flesh—the Gnostics—they

[74] Some evangelical writers suggest that genuine Christians can be indwelt spatially by demons: Merrill Unger (cf. *What Demons Can Do to Saints,* 1990); Neil Anderson (cf. *The Bondage Breaker,* 1990; *Victory Over the Darkness,* 1990); Mark Bubeck (cf. *The Adversary,* 1975; *Overcoming the Adversary,* 1984); C. Fred Dickason (cf. *Demon Possession and the Christian,* 1987); Ed Murphy (cf. *The Handbook for Spiritual Warfare,* 1992); Frank Peretti (cf. *This Present Darkness*, 1988; *Piercing the Darkness,* 1989). According to the New Testament, there are four terms used for indwelling demons [notice the *ownership* is not the point]: *one with an unclean spirit* (Greek, echon), used 16 times, cf. Mark 11:18; Mark 3:30; 5:15; 7:25; 9:17; Luke 4:33; 7:33; 8:27; John 7:20; 8:48-49; 8:52; 10:20; Acts 8:7; 16:16; 19:13; *one who is demonized* (Greek, daimonizomai), used 13 times, cf. Matthew 4:24; 8:16, 28, 33; 9:32; 12:22; 15:22; Mark 1:32; 5:15-16; 5:18; Luke 8:36; John 10:21; *one with an unclean spirit* (Greek, en), used two times: Mark 1:23; 5:2; *one vexed with unclean spirits* (Greek, ochloumenous), used once, in Acts 5:16. cf. Alex Konya, *Demons: A Biblically Based Perspective* (Schaumberg, IL: Regular Baptist Press, 1990), pp 20-23. Comparing the New Testament data, there is not one case where a genuine believer is said to be indwelt by a demon or demons.

are of the world. Because they are of the world, *they speak as of the world, and the world hears them*. What does it mean that they *speak of as the world*? It means they talk about trivial pursuits and worldly matters. Their conversation is not at all centered on Christ or His kingdom. Why would it be? This should make us all consider our conversations and the things we spend our time discussing. Do we spend the bulk of our conversations with others centered on the trivial pursuits of life? Or do we focus in on the things of Christ and pursue how we can provoke one another to love and good deeds? Do we socialize or do we fellowship? I think we can often tell a lot about a believer by their conversation and the direction it goes. In fact, I have always loved that verse in Malachi 3:16 which mentions those who fear the Lord and speak often to one another about the Lord. Malachi says that there is a book of remembrance written for them who fear the Lord and think on His name. But those who are of the world, they talk about the world, *and the world hears them.* What does it mean that the world hears them? It means that those who listen to false teachers are of the world. Believers don't listen to such nonsense and have the spiritual discernment to realize it is not of God. As Jesus put it in John 15:19, those who are of the world love their own. In contrast to those who have the spirit of antichrist and who are of the world, we now have, in verse 6, those who are of Christ and who are not of the world.

> We are of God. He who knows God hears us; he who is not of God does not hear us. By this we know the spirit of truth and the spirit of error (1 John 4:6).

In contrast to those who hear the false teachers, we have those who hear the true teachers. And these individuals *are of God.* John says the one *who knows God hears us*. *Know* here speaks of a progressive but not complete knowledge. If you know God then you listen to the truth. One who knows God is habitually growing in that knowledge and understanding of who He is. When you think back to when you first became a Christian and what you knew then about God, and then reflect on what you now know about Him, there should be a tremendous increase in your knowledge and understanding of who God is. That is the meaning behind this word. But, John says, the one *who is not of God does not hear us*. Those who are not of God will not pay any attention to truth or to those who are proclaiming it. God's people will listen to God's message and to God's messengers. A true Christian will hear and receive the doctrines of Christ. What are our vast differences with false teachers? They are of the world; they speak like the world; and the world hears them. Those who are of God, however, know God and listen to the true teachers.

John now ends his thoughts on discerning the true from the false, the antichrists from those who are of Christ, by saying: *by this we know the spirit of truth and the spirit of error*. How do we know truth from error? John has spelled it out for us. Truth equals confessing that Jesus came in the flesh, which manifests itself in a growing knowledge of God and discernment of truth and love of truth. Error equals denying that Jesus came in the flesh and manifests itself in being of the world and speaking like the world.

Summary

In this lesson we have considered: *Our Responsibility to Discern False Teachers* (v 1). So what is our responsibility in discerning false teachers? It is to not believe but to test every teacher. *Our Method for Discerning False Teachers* (vv 2, 3). So what is our method for discerning false teachers? Those who confess that Jesus is the Christ and came in the flesh is of God, and those who do not confess that Jesus came in the flesh are not of God! *Our Promise to Overcome False Teachers* (v 4). John promises that we will overcome false teachers because greater is the One in us than the one in the world. *Our Vast Differences with False Teachers* (vv 5, 6). What are our vast differences with false teachers? They are of the world; they speak like the world; and the world hears them. Those who are of God, however, know God and listen to the true teachers.

I have had a growing concern over the past few years seeing the number of professing believers who are being swallowed up by false teachers has multiplied. People are following a name, but do not consider the message that is being preached. I have heard several speakers over the past few years take liberties with Scripture, pervert the gospel, and use the Bible for their own means, giving no thought or study to its original meaning or context. What is so sad about this is that men and especially women, sorry to say, sit in the audiences with mouths wide open, receiving what is heard as if it is truth. Be careful about following the masses and those who teach the crowds. Those who faithfully teach God's Word are not going to win a popularity contest, because people do not want to hear about sin or the demands that Christ makes on them, or how to change their lives. Be careful about people who are cunning and try to convince you by their experiences or by the miraculous things they claim have happened to them. Some people are swallowed up and duped when they hear others share their experiences. Experience alone is worth nothing! All kinds of cults and false teachers can give you their "experience" stories, but the crucial questions to ask are not, "What is your experience?" but, "What do you teach? Can it be backed up with the Word of God? Do you live out what you teach?"

These are the questions to ask. Be careful, ladies, about believing everything you hear. There's a lot of stuff out there, even in the Christian bookstores, that has nothing to do with Christianity. Don't be gullible, and don't believe everything you read and hear. You must protect yourself, and you must do that by being prepared, by knowing God and by knowing His Word. You and I should be like the Berean believers, of whom Paul says in Acts 17:11, "These were more fair-minded than those in Thessalonica, in that they received the word with all readiness, and searched the Scriptures daily to find out whether these things were so."

Questions to Consider

Discerning Truth from Error

1 John 4:1-6

1. (a) What are the differences between those who are false and those who are true, according to 1 John 4:1-6? (b) Who is behind false prophets, antichrists, and those who teach error? (c) What test does John give us in this passage that helps us to discern false teachers?

2. Memorize 1 John 4:1.

3. John gives us some ways to test false prophets in 1 John 4:1-6. However, there are other ways to discern false prophets. What are they, according to the following passages? Deuteronomy 13:1-5; Deuteronomy 18:20-22; Isaiah 8:19, 20; Matthew 7:15-23; Galatians 1:8; 1 Timothy 4:1-3; 2 Peter 2; Jude 4, 8, 10, 16.

4. (a) Do you think all believers can discern false teachers? See Matthew 24:24; John 16:13; 1 John 4:6. (b) How should Christians respond to false teachers? See Deuteronomy 13:1-5; Titus 3:10, 11; 2 John 7-11. (c) Why should we respond that way? (Answer this question according to the preceding passages.)

5. (a) What is going to happen to false teachers? See 2 Peter 2:1, 12, 13, 17; Jude 11-15. (b) How can you encourage or exhort those who are engrossed in error?

6. How does 1 John 4:4 give you comfort?

7. (a) Do you think you can discern false prophets? (b) How can you be more discerning after this lesson? (c) Who are some of the false teachers and/or some of the false religions in our day, and how did you discern that? Do you know anyone who has been swept away by false teaching and/or false teachers? How might we pray for them? Please write your burden down in the form of a prayer request.

Chapter 16

How Deep the Father's Love for Us!

1 John 4:7-12

There is a hymn that was written in the 1800's that we don't sing much anymore, but it is quite appropriate for the text we'll be studying in this lesson. The hymn is entitled *The Love Of God*, and it perhaps expresses God's love for us more vividly than any other hymn I know of. An interesting fact about this hymn is that the first two verses were written by the composer, Frederick Lehman; the third verse, however, was found on the wall of a patient's room in an insane asylum after the patient's death. Since I will close this chapter with the words to this hymn, I won't share the entire song now but will just introduce it to you by including the third stanza and the refrain that was found in the patient's room.

> Could we with ink the ocean fill,
> And were the skies of parchment made,
> Were every stalk on earth a quill,
> And every man a scribe by trade;
> To write the love of God above
> Would drain the ocean dry;
> Nor could the scroll contain the whole,
> Though stretched from sky to sky.
> Oh, love of God, how rich and pure!
> How measureless and strong!
> It shall forevermore endure—
> The saints' and angels' song.

The love of God—a wonderful truth for the believer in Jesus! John mentions in his letter just how deep God's love is for us, so deep, in fact, that He sent His son to die for us! And as we think about the depth of the Father's love, we should bow our hearts in an attitude of humble thanksgiving and express our thanks in a tangible way. How do we say thanks for such love? I'm glad you asked! John says our gratitude is shown by our attitude toward others—an attitude of love! Let's read what John has to say about this love.

1 John 4:7-12

> Beloved, let us love one another, for love is of God; and
> everyone who loves is born of God and knows God. [8]He who
> does not love does not know God, for God is love. [9]In this the
> love of God was manifested toward us, that God has sent His
> only begotten Son into the world, that we might live through
> Him. [10]In this is love, not that we loved God, but that He loved
> us and sent His Son to be the propitiation for our sins. [11]Beloved,
> if God so loved us, we also ought to love one another. [12]No one
> has seen God at any time. If we love one another, God abides in
> us, and His love has been perfected in us (1 John 4:7-12).

In our last lesson we saw: *Our Responsibility to Discern False Teachers* (v 1); *Our Method for Discerning False Teachers* (vv 2, 3); *Our Promise to Overcome False Teachers* (v 4); and *Our Vast Differences with False Teachers* (vv 5, 6). In contrast to the false teachers we now have those who are true, the beloved. Those who are beloved and belong to God behave differently because they are born of God. And in this lesson, we'll consider the two-fold reason why we should love others.

We Love Others Because Love is the Nature of God (vv 7-10)
We Love Others Because God Loves Us (vv 11, 12)

Let's look first at our obligation to love others based on the fact that love is the nature of God.

We Love Others Because Love is the Nature of God
1 John 4:7-10

> Beloved, let us love one another, for love is of God; and everyone who loves is born of God and knows God (1 John 4:7).

This is the third time that John has mentioned the importance of loving the brethren. The first time was in 1 John 2:7-11, where John wrote about loving our brother because of our connection with the True Light. The second time was in 1 John 3:10-24, where John wrote of loving the brethren as an evidence of our salvation. But here, John connects loving our brother with the very nature of God. He says that love is of God. But first he begins with that term we have become very familiar with, *beloved*, which means dearly beloved. It is a term of endearment. John uses this term 10 times in this epistle. An interesting fact, however, is that he never uses it in the Gospel of John. The term beloved is very appropriate at this point, because only those who are beloved of God can love one another as they ought.

After calling them beloved, John then gives them a command, and the command is to *love one another*. And the tense in the Greek indicates that the command is to love one another continually. Let us go on loving each other. *Love* is the Greek word agape, which indicates a consuming passion for the well being of others. *One another* is the Greek word allos, which means another of the same kind. John is again referring to our love for the brethren, those who are of the same kind. This does not mean they have to look and act just like we do, but they are of God, they are children of God. There is a two-fold reason behind this command. The first reason is because *love is of God*. I love others because love is of God. Love flows from God and it flows in such a way that the source remains unbroken. What does it mean that love is of God? John made mention of this in 1 John 3:1: "Behold what manner of love the Father has bestowed on us, that we should be called children of God!" What kind of love is this? It is an amazing love! Manner here is an interesting word in the Greek. It is used to describe something foreign like a country or a race. John is saying, "What kind of foreign love is this that the Father has bestowed on us that we should be called the children of God!" God's love is a kind of love that is certainly foreign to the world in which we live. It is a love which comes from another country indeed, a heavenly country! John is saying, this is amazing love, that we should be named the children of God! It's amazing! It's foreign. What does God's love look like? Well, you saw some of that in the "Questions to Consider" when you looked at the gospel accounts. God's love looks like this: being spit on, beaten, mocked, ridiculed, having a crown of thorns on His head without retaliating or running. It looks like nails in His hands and feet. It looks like bearing the sins of the whole world. It looks like separation from His Father, which He had never known. It looks like the wrath of a sin-hating God being poured out on Him. That's what God's love looks like. May I say to you that if you are having a difficult time loving someone then perhaps you need to return to the source of love? Take a good look at God and His Son Jesus Christ and the love that was shown at Calvary! Amy Carmichael once wrote, "If I have not compassion on my fellow servant even as my Lord had pity on me … then I know nothing of Calvary's love."[75]

The second reason we love others is because we are *born of God* and we reflect His nature. It is only natural that we reflect the God we are related to because we are born of God, and so we resemble Him. John puts it this way: *everyone who loves is born of God and knows God.* That does not mean that if I love my husband or dog or aunt then I am of God. Lost people love each other. I have lost family members whom I see genuinely loving others. But lost people cannot love others with the kind of love that God intends. A lost husband, for example, cannot love his wife the way Christ loved the church. Why? Because God's love is very different from the world's love. God's love is undeserved and unrestricted. In fact, the Greek tense of this phrase is that of past action with continuing results. In other words, if we have been born of God in the past,

75 Amy Carmichael, *If* (Grand Rapids, MI: Zondervan, 1980), page number unknown.

the results of it will still be evident, and one result is love of the brethren. So to those who love the brethren, John says, you are born of God. To be born of God means to be regenerated. And not only are you born of God, but you *know God.* This is a rebuke to the Gnostics, who claimed a knowledge of God and yet did not possess love for one another. They were known to look down on others as being spiritually inferior. That, my friend, is not love. So, you might ask, what if I don't love my brother? Well, John says you are in big trouble!

> He who does not love does not know God, for God is love (1 John 4:8).

John says the one who *does not love does not know God.* The Greek translates literally as did not know from the beginning, and absolutely did not know God. In other words, this person never knew God, has no acquaintance with God, and never did get acquainted with him. If you did know Him, then you would love. Why? *For God is love*! John has already stated in 1 John 1:5 that God is light. We saw that light is who God is. He is not a light or even the light; light is the essence of who God is. John also mentions in John 4:24 that God is Spirit. Love represents God's nature, just as light and spirit do. Love also is an attribute or a characteristic of God; He is love. It is worthy to mention here that the Gnostics believed that God was a spirit and that God was light, but they never taught that God was love. How convenient for their warped theology! God is love, and so it only makes sense that as His children love would be preeminent in our lives. How do I know God is love? How was His love shown? John tells us in verse 9.

> In this the love of God was manifested toward us, that God has sent His only begotten Son into the world, that we might live through Him (1 John 4:9).

God's love *was manifested*, or rendered apparent, which is what this word means, when God *sent* His Son. Sent means to send out on a mission. And John lets the readers know that the one sent on this mission was God's *only begotten Son*! What does only begotten mean? It means only born-soul. There is a reason God sent His Son, and the reason John mentions is so that *we might live through Him*. This means in Him and Him alone we have life. Without Him there is no life. Without Him we are dead spiritually, but in Him we are alive. I know my life since my conversion is so different than my life before conversion. I have purpose and meaning to life, whereas before there was no meaning to life, no joy, no peace. I live through Him and because of Him. Speaking of living through Him, John now mentions how we got from being spiritually dead to spiritually alive. And, just in case you think you got there on your own good merit, just in case you think loving God was all your idea, John says something different in verse 10.

> In this is love, not that we loved God, but that He loved us and sent His Son to be the propitiation for our sins (1 John 4:10).

Did you know that God *loved us* first?[76] Jesus put it clearly in John 15:16, "You did not choose Me, but I chose you and appointed you that you should go and bear fruit, and that your fruit should remain, that whatever you ask the Father in My name He may give you." Some people think it is their intellect or their decision to choose God or love Him first. But the Bible clearly teaches God chose us first, and He loved us first. John will mention in 1 John 4:19, "We

---

[76] D. A. Carson gave an insightful four part series on *The Difficult Doctrine of the Love of God* at the W. H. Griffith Thomas Lectures at Dallas Theological Seminary, February 3-6, 1998. These were published in the theological journal *Bibliotheca Sacra,* volume 156, Number 621 and 622. In these lectures, Carson mentions that the Bible speaks of the love of God in five distinguishable ways: 1) The love of the Father for the Son and of the Son for the Father; 2) God's providential love over all He has made; 3) God's love for the fallen world and concern for their salvation; 4) God's particular, selecting love toward His elect; and 5) God's love for His own people in a provisional or conditional way. *Ibid.,* January-March, Number 161, pp 7-10. There is a case to be made for an additional distinction, i.e., God's love for the lost in a provisional or conditional way, but this is a helpful outline of the vast Scriptural doctrine of the love of God. 1 John 4:7-12 is on the fourth distinction of God's love, with a special emphasis on its initiating of our response. God's children love because they are first loved!

love Him because He first loved us." God loved us first and we did not deserve that love. As Paul puts it in Titus 3:4, 5, "But when the kindness and the love of God our Savior toward man appeared, not by works of righteousness which we have done, but according to His mercy He saved us, through the washing of regeneration and renewing of the Holy Spirit." How did He show that love? John says, He *sent His Son to be the propitiation for our sins*. *Sent* means the same thing it meant in verse 9, to send out on a mission. What was that mission? It was to be the *propitiation* for our sins. We had this word when we were in 1 John 2:2. We saw then that Christ Himself is the atonement for our sins. He is the atoning sacrifice for our sins. The word propitiation was used in secular writing for a sacrifice that would appease the wrath of an angry god. This would seem to suggest that God is justifiably angry at sin. God is angry with the wicked every day, as Psalm 7:11 demonstrates.[77] His Son, Jesus Christ, being the atoning sacrifice, the propitiation, made it possible to appease the wrath of God upon man's sin. Because God's nature is love, and because He does love us, then an outcome of that love

[77] Morris summarizes the Old Testament teaching on the wrath of God: "There are more than twenty words used to express 'wrath' as it applies to Yahweh (in addition to a number of other words which occur only with to human anger). These are used so frequently that there are over 580 occurrences to be taken into consideration. This constitutes such a formidable body of evidence that we cannot hope to deal with it fully, and can only indicate in general terms the results of detailed examination." cf. Leon Morris, *The Apostolic Preaching of the Cross* (Grand Rapids, MI: Eerdmans, 1965), p 150. The New Testament also records abundant passages on the wrath of God: Romans 1:18-3:20; 2:5-9; John 3:36; Ephesians 5:6; Colossians 3:6 1 Thessalonians 2:16; 5:9; 2 Thessalonians 2:16; 5:9; 2 Thessalonians 1:7-9; Hebrews 12:29; Revelation 11:18; 14:10; 16:19; 19:15, etc.

would be to send His son to die for our sins.[78] And so, John turns to the second reason why we should love others. We should love others because God loves us.

We Love Others Because God Loves Us
1 John 4:11, 12

> Beloved, if God so loved us, we also ought to love one another (1 John 4:11).

By the way, this is the last time in this epistle that John uses the word *beloved.* The word *if* here means since. Since *God so loved us*, dear ones, *we also ought to love one another. Ought* is a word we had before in 1 John 2:6, and it means we are under moral obligation. If I borrow money from you, I ought to pay it back; it is my moral obligation. So it is our moral obligation to love others, because God loves us, and believe me we aren't that easy to love at times. This command to love one another is a continuous obligation, as we have brought out before. Now, sandwiched in between God loving us and us loving God and the brethren, John puts this strange statement in verse 12.

---

[78] John R. W. Stott explains: "In the ancient world outside Christianity, it was thought appropriate to love only those who were regarded as worthy of being loved. But God loves sinners who are unworthy of His love, and indeed subject to His wrath. He loved us, and sent His Son to rescue us, not because we are loveable, but because he is love. So the greatness of His love is seen in the costliness of His self-sacrifice for the wholly undeserving (cf. Romans 5:7-8). A clearer manifestation of God's love could not be imagined." cf. John R. W. Stott, *Tyndale New Testament Commentary: The Letters of John* (Grand Rapids, MI: Eerdmans, 1988), pp 165-166. In the Old Testament, the particular gracious aspect of God's initiating love is centered in the nation of Israel. For example: "For thou art an holy people unto the LORD thy God: the LORD thy God hath chosen thee to be a special people unto himself, above all people that are upon the face of the earth. The LORD did not set his love upon you, nor choose you, because ye were more in number than any people; for ye were the fewest of all people: But because the LORD loved you, and because he would keep the oath which he had sworn unto your fathers, hath the LORD brought you out with a mighty hand, and redeemed you out of the house of bondmen, from the hand of Pharaoh king of Egypt." cf. Deuteronomy 7:6-8. "Behold, the heaven and the heaven of heavens is the LORD's thy God, the earth also, with all that therein is. Only the LORD had a delight in thy fathers to love them, and he chose their seed after them, even you above all people, as it is this day." cf. Deuteronomy 10:14-15.

> No one has seen God at any time. If we love one another, God abides in us, and His love has been perfected in us (1 John 4:12).

Now I must admit I looked at the phrase *no one has seen God at any time*, and wondered why John put this statement here. I thought, well it must be because John has now mentioned God 11 times, but that was a dumb conclusion. Then I thought, perhaps it is because of the Gnostics who claimed some special relationship with God, and they were saying to these church members, "I have seen God, I have seen God," and John says, "No, you haven't; no one has." But that still did not make sense in the context. The context of this verse is loving others because love is the nature of God, and loving others because God loves us. John is trying to get the point across that since He is invisible others can only see God as they see Him manifested in our love for each other. What did Jesus say in John 13:35? "By this all will know that you are My disciples, if you have love for one another." How will others know God? Or how will they know His followers? Not by physically seeing Him, and saying, "Oh, that must be God," but by seeing Him through us as we love each other. As the saying goes, you are the only Jesus some will ever see! Now to make it clear to his readers, John says no man, absolutely none, not a single one, has seen God. The word *see* comes from the Greek word tetheatai, which means to look at closely, to be entranced, to perceive and, as a result, admire. Its root word, thea, means theater, a place where one admires what he sees. It is not some vision someone claims to have that proves his or her relationship with the living God, it is loving the brethren. This also is perhaps why this portion of John's letter on loving the brethren follows the portion on false teachers and how to discern who they are.

Now I know some questions have probably come to your mind as a result of the "Questions to Consider" that accompany this chapter. So let's look at some of those passages. From John 1:18 it is clear that no man has seen God at anytime. From John 4:24 we read that God is a spirit. So how can anyone see Him? John

6:46 says, "Not that anyone has seen the Father, except He who is from God; He has seen the Father." The Apostle Peter also mentions twice in 1 Peter 1:8 that no one has seen God. And Paul tells us, in 1 Timothy 1:17, that God is invisible. Now some of you might be thinking about the example of Moses and Jacob. Didn't they see God? Let's consider those examples. In Genesis 32:24-30, it says a Man wrestled with Jacob in verse 24. Verse 28 clarifies who this man is—God (NKJV). In other words, God met Jacob in the form of a Man, an angel. According to Hosea 12:2-5, this Man is identified as the Angel of the Lord: "The LORD also brings a charge against Judah, and will punish Jacob according to his ways; according to his deeds He will recompense him. He took his brother by the heel in the womb, and in his strength he struggled with God. Yes, he struggled with the Angel and prevailed; he wept, and sought favor from Him. He found Him in Bethel, and there He spoke to us—That is, the LORD God of hosts. The LORD is His memorable name." In Moses' case, in Exodus 33:18-23 God said to Moses that no man will see Him and live. Moses only saw the back, and not the face, of God. Moses saw God's glory but he did not see God Himself. We need to be very careful and very leery of people who claim to see God—no man has seen God at any time. God can be seen in the manifestation of His Son, Jesus Christ, but no man has actually seen God.

With that in mind, John goes back to his theme of love, and ends with *if we love one another, God abides in us, and His love has been perfected in us*. What does it mean that God *abides in us* or dwells in us? To abide or dwell means to stay in a given place. It also means that God is at home or comfortably dwelling in us. Is Christ comfortable in you? Robert Munger once wrote a book called *My Heart, Christ's Home*[79], wherein he pictures the Christian life as a house, in which Jesus goes from room to room. In the library, which is the mind, Jesus finds trash and all sorts of worthless things, which He proceeds to throw out and replace with His Word. In the dining

[79] Robert Boyd Munger, *My Heart, Christ's Home* (Downer's Grove, IL: InterVarsity Press, 2001).

room of appetite, he finds many sinful desires listed on a worldly menu. In the place of such things as prestige, materialism and lust, He puts humility, meekness, love and all the other virtues for which believers are to hunger and thirst. He goes through the living room of fellowship, where He finds many worldly companions and activities; through the workshop, where only toys are being made; into the closet, where hidden sins are kept; and so on, through the entire house. Only when He has cleansed every room, closet and corner of sin and foolishness, can He sit down and be at home. Is Christ at home with you? He should be at home with you. He should be comfortable there. And so, if we love one another God dwells in us and *His love is perfected in us*. This means his love is complete. One man helps us to understand the essence of this phrase; he says "His love comes to its intended goal in us when it reaches out through us and treats another brother lovingly."[80]

Summary

So to wrap it up, *We Love Others Because Love is the Nature of God* (vv 7-10); and *We Love Others Because God Loves Us* (vv 11, 12). Ladies, the idea of loving others comes from the One who is love Himself—God. Without Him, love would not even be a concept that we could understand. Once again, John is stressing the importance of loving others, and the motive to love others is God, who is Himself love, and who loves us. I want to end by focusing on the love of God. To do so, I would like for us to meditate on the words of the song, *The Love Of God.*

> The love of God is greater far
> Than tongue or pen can ever tell;
> It goes beyond the highest star,
> And reaches to the lowest hell;
> The guilty pair, bowed down with care,
> God gave His Son to win;

80 Donald W. Burdick, *The Letters of John the Apostle* (Chicago, IL: Moody Press, 1985), p 326.

His erring child He reconciled,
And pardoned from his sin.

Refrain:
Oh, love of God, how rich and pure!
How measureless and strong!
It shall forevermore endure—
The saints' and angels' song.

When hoary time shall pass away,
And earthly thrones and kingdoms fall,
When men who here refuse to pray,
On rocks and hills and mountains call,
God's love so sure, shall still endure,
All measureless and strong;
Redeeming grace to Adam's race—
The saints' and angels' song.

Could we with ink the ocean fill,
And were the skies of parchment made,
Were every stalk on earth a quill,
And every man a scribe by trade;
To write the love of God above
Would drain the ocean dry;
Nor could the scroll contain the whole,
Though stretched from sky to sky.[81]

[81] Words by Frederick M. Lehman; Verse 3 was penciled on the wall of a narrow room in an insane asylum by a man said to have been demented. The profound lines were discovered when they laid him in his coffin.

Questions to Consider

How Deep the Father's Love for Us!

1 John 4:7-12

1. Read 1 John 4:7-12. (a) How many times does John mention the word *love* or some form of the word? (b) What are the different ways that John uses the word *love*? (c) What other word(s) do you notice that John repeats several times?

2. Memorize 1 John 4:10.

3. John says that God showed His love by sending His son to die for us. Choose one of the gospel accounts of the death of Christ and summarize in your own words what Christ endured on your behalf (Matthew 26 and 27; Mark 14 and 15; Luke 22 and 23; or John 18 and 19). (b) Do you love others to that extent? (c) How can you sacrificially love others? (d) What do you think John means in 1 John 4:11?

4. (a) According to 1 John 4:10 and 1 John 4:19, who loved first, God or us? (b) According to Romans 5:7-9, was there anything in us that solicited that love from God? (c) How does Paul describe our sinful condition in Romans 3:9-18? (d) How does this passage in Romans help you to understand the depth of God's love for you? (e) What is the promise (regarding the love of God) to those whom Christ has saved, according to Romans 8:31-39? (f) What is your response to God as you consider your salvation?

5. (a) Why has no man seen God at any time? See John 1:18, John 4:24, John 6:46 and 1 Timothy 1:17. (b) With those passages in mind, how do you explain Genesis 32:24-30 (especially verse 30)? (c) How does one see God, according to what Jesus said to Philip in John 14:7-12?

6. (a) How have you grown in your love toward others? (b) In what ways does the love of God motivate you to love others? (c) In what ways do you think the church could improve in loving others? (d) How can you be a part of that improvement? (e) What will you do about it?

7. Write out your testimony of how God saved you. Especially bring out the aspects of God's love that you saw as He drew you to Himself.

8. What does God's love mean to you personally? Write a praise of thanksgiving to God, writing down your thoughts to Him.

Three Spectacular Gifts for God's Children!

1 John 4:13-18

By way of introduction to this lesson, I want to begin by giving you a slice of my life, which I believe sets the ground for this lesson in 1 John. After I graduated from high school in Tulsa, Oklahoma, I went off to Moody Bible Institute. The day I arrived I was at the registration table where all the new students were to register, and I met this guy named Doug Heck. Two weeks later we began to date and the rest is history. Several things stand out to me as vivid memories about our dating relationship during our college days. One specific memory is from the school cafeteria.

One day Doug and I were eating a meal together when he brought up the topic of the rapture. I don't remember all of what he said, but I do remember my response. I began to cry and I asked him not to bring it up again. I told him I didn't like to talk about it, and my excuse was that I was brought up on a steady spiritual diet of prophecy from my Dad who loved and still loves Bible prophecy. I told him that I did not enjoy talking about it. The truth of the matter was this: I was absolutely terrified at the thought of the coming of Christ. In fact, I would get weak in the knees and knots in my stomach when it was brought up. Why, you might ask? Well, I should have been asking myself the same question, but I never did. The fact that I was terrified when thinking about the rapture should have been a clue to me that I was not a child of God. John makes it very clear in the text we are going to cover that those who are born of God have no fear of the coming judgment or the rapture. Read together with me 1 John 4:13-18.

1 John 4:13-18

By this we know that we abide in Him, and He in us, because He has given us of His Spirit. [14]And we have seen and testify that the Father has sent the Son as Savior of the world. [15]Whoever confesses that Jesus is the Son of God, God abides in him, and he in God. [16]And we have known and believed the love that God has for us. God is love, and he who abides in love abides in God and God in him. [17]Love has been perfected among us in this: that we may have boldness in the Day of Judgment; because as He is, so are we in this world. [18]There is no fear in love; but perfect love casts out fear, because fear involves torment. But he who fears has not been made perfect in love (1 John 4:13-18).

We saw last time that *We Love Others Because Love is the Nature of God* (vv 7-10), and *We Love Others Because God Loves Us* (vv 11, 12). Our outline for this lesson will include three spectacular gifts for God's children. (By the way, they all begin with the letter S, and they are all wonderful tests of assurance as well.)

The Gift of the Spirit (v 13)
The Gift of His Son (vv 14-16)
The Gift of Self-Confidence in the Day of Judgment (vv 17, 18)

John has just mentioned in verse 12 that the only reason we can love one another the way God intends is because of the fact that God dwells in us. John continues on with the theme of the indwelling of the Holy Spirit in verse 13.

The Gift of the Spirit
1 John 4:13

By this we know that we abide in Him, and He in us, because He has given us of His Spirit (1 John 4:13).

Here we have the first gift given by God: the gift of the Spirit. John begins by saying *by this we know that we abide in Him, and He in us, because He has given us of His Spirit*. The words *we know* are in the present tense. In other words, John is saying that this is a continual experience that we have as believers. We experientially know that we dwell in Him, and He in us, and it is ongoing. How do we know we are *in Him*? We know because *He has given us of His Spirit*. The word *given* is a word that means to freely give of one's own accord and goodwill. Ladies, the Holy Spirit is a wonderful gift of God that was given to you at the time of your conversion. The present tense indicates that this gift is still in our possession and that the results of it are evident in our lives.[82] Paul relates this truth to us in Ephesians 1:12-14 when he says, "that we who first trusted in Christ should be to the praise of His glory. In Him you also trusted, after you heard the word of truth, the gospel of your salvation; in whom also, having believed, you were sealed with the Holy Spirit of promise, who is the guarantee of our inheritance until the redemption of the purchased possession, to the praise of His glory." We are sealed with the Holy Spirit at the time of our conversion and this is a mark of His ownership of us. He is still in us and the results should be evident in our life. The Scriptures are replete with examples of what the work of the Spirit is in our life. (The Upper Room Discourse, John 13-17, is a great place to start your study of the Holy Spirit.) And thinking of the indwelling Spirit, John turns His thoughts toward salvation and the cost to the Father, in verse 14.

---

[82] The subjective work of the Spirit of God producing assurance in the heart of the child of God is based on the objective evidence produced by His ministry within us. I would disagree with Dodd, who says, "Probably, then, we are intended here to think of the interior witness of the Holy Spirit, the immediate, spontaneous, unanalysable awareness of a divine presence in our life." cf. C. H. Dodd, *The Moffatt New Testament Commentary: The Jonannine Epistles* (London: Hodder & Stoughton, 1946), p 115. As Romans 8:12-17 suggests, the internal subjective witness of the Holy Spirit is manifested by an objective accomplishment, i.e., He mortifies (i.e., the process of dying; not death itself) the flesh. Implication: if our flesh isn't being mortified then we have no basis for assurance of eternal life. Or, in John's case, if we are not loving other believers and our sense of the love of God for us isn't being matured in us, then we have no basis for assurance of eternal life.

The Gift of His Son
1 John 4:14-16

> And we have seen and testify that the Father has sent the Son as Savior of the world (1 John 4:14).

This is the second gift that John mentions in these verses, the gift of His Son. (It's interesting to note that all three persons of the trinity are mentioned in these verses.) So John says, *we have seen and testify that the Father has sent the Son as Savior of the world.* The word *seen* means to look closely, as well as to gaze at something remarkable. John says they not only saw, but they also *testify*. What does that mean? It means to bear record, or to witness. To bear witness means to testify to the reality of what they saw. For a witness to be accepted in a court of law, he must first be of sound mind and know personally what he is talking about. He also has to have seen and experienced what he is testifying about. It must be a first hand experience and it must be believable. That is what John is saying: we saw and testified that the Father sent the Son to be the Savior of the world. Does this sound familiar to you? We had this in our introductory lesson when we studied 1 John 1:1-3: "That which was from the beginning, which we have heard, which we have seen with our eyes, which we have looked upon, and our hands have handled, concerning the Word of life—the life was manifested, and we have seen, and bear witness, and declare to you that eternal life which was with the Father and was manifested to us—that which we have seen and heard we declare to you, that you also may have fellowship with us; and truly our fellowship is with the Father and with His Son Jesus Christ." The apostles saw Christ, they touched Him, and they gave testimony or witness to what they had seen and heard. John says we have seen and testified *that the Father has sent the Son as Savior*, or the deliverer, of the world. By the way, this is the only time John has used this word *Savior*. In New Testament times, the word savior could be used for men and for gods. Even Caesar was called the savior of the Roman world. But Jesus is the Savior in that He saves His people from their sins. Even though John says the Son was the Savior *of the world*, not all the world will be saved. John is not a Universalist, and he makes this very clear in verse 15.[83]

> Whoever confesses that Jesus is the Son of God, God abides in him, and he in God (1 John 4:15).

Whoever is an interesting word in the original language, meaning anyone at anytime. As an individual and as prompted by the Holy Spirit, there must be a confession *that Jesus is the Son of God* in order for one to be saved. This, of course, as brought out many times in our study of 1 John, was a rebuke to the Gnostics, who denied that Jesus was the Son of God. What does it mean to *confess*? It has the idea of a covenant or a promise. To confess is also to give a public proclamation, which expresses a commitment and an obligation. It is an open confession which is once and for all and shows itself in a life of obedience. It does not mean I go around with some theological confession that Jesus is the Son of God, but it is in essence a personal trust in Him. This word means a personal acceptance, not a verbal assent. It is not just a prayer that you pray, but it is an awareness of the acceptance of the work of Christ in your heart. It is interesting that the Apostle Paul brings out in 1 Corinthians 12:3 that no man can say or confess that Jesus is Lord but by the Holy Spirit. The two go hand in hand. If you have the Holy Spirit, then you have confessed Jesus as Lord, and if you have confessed Jesus as Lord, then you have the Holy Spirit. So John says, if one confesses that Jesus is the Son of God, than there is great news: *God abides in him, and he in God.* In case you didn't get

83 The doctrine of Particular Atonement can be supported by Scripture. cf. Matthew 20:28; John 10:14-15; 15:13; 17:6, 9, 10; Acts 20:28; Ephesians 5:25, etc. However, passages such as 1 John 4:14; 2:2; and 1 Timothy 2:3-4, cannot be pressed into the tight Limited Atonement understanding but broaden to include the work of Christ's death as having benefit for lost humanity. Compare with 2 Peter 2:1-4. This does not mean that the work of Christ satisfied the demands of God's justice for the non-elect, for that would be a contradiction of logic. As Charles H. Spurgeon said, "if Christ has died for you, you can never be lost. God will not punish twice for one thing. If God punished Christ for your sins He will not punish you. 'Payment God's justice cannot twice demand; first at the bleeding Savior's hand, and then again at mine.' How can God be just if He punished Christ, the substitute, and then man himself afterwards?"

John's point, he repeats himself in verse 16, only this time he adds the element of God's love.

> And we have known and believed the love that God has for us. God is love, and he who abides in love abides in God, and God in him (1 John 4:16).

John says *we have known*, which means we have come to know and we still know. This is a permanent knowledge that does not leave us. John says, we know, we have a permanent knowledge of *the love that God has for us*. One who believes in God knows the love God has for him. May I add that it also means we are aware that the love is undeserved? When I think of the depth of my sin and my life before Christ, I am overcome with the love of God! Why should God love me so? John says, because *God is love*. Love is an attribute of God. He is love. God's love is not some warm fuzzy feeling for us, but it is a love which gives not what man wants but what he needs. It is agape love, which is the love that man needs for the forgiveness of his sins, which can only be provided by our Savior. As John says in another place, "For God so loved the world that He gave His only begotten Son, that whoever believes in Him should not perish but have everlasting life" (John 3:16). That's how much God loves us. And because of that, for the one who has confessed Him as their Lord and *abides in love*, or has received that love, John says he *abides in God, and God in him*. The abiding in love could refer to the love of God in us, or to the love we have for one another, as mentioned by John numerous times in this letter. Both are true. And as he is speaking of love, John next speaks of our love being made perfect in verse 17 and moves on to our third wonderful gift from the Father!

The Gift of Self-Confidence in the Day of Judgment 1 John 4:17, 18

> Love has been perfected among us in this: that we may have boldness in the Day of Judgment; because as He is, so are we in this world (1 John 4:17).

The idea of what John is saying here is that those who are born of God have a love that is complete and therefore they have no fear of judgment to come, because they live as He lived. This is the third gift given to us by God, the gift of self-confidence, or boldness, in the Day of Judgment. Did you know that boldness is a wonderful gift from God? Listen to what Paul says in Romans 8:15: "For you did not receive the spirit of bondage again to fear, but you received the Spirit of adoption by whom we cry out, 'Abba, Father.'" And again in 2 Timothy 1:7: "For God has not given us a spirit of fear, but of power and of love and of a sound mind." Both of these refer to the fact that God has not given us fear, but boldness! Boldness, or self confidence, is a gift from God!

John says, you want to know for sure that your *love has been perfected*? Here's how you can know: Your love is made perfect if you have *boldness in the Day of Judgment*. What does it mean to have *boldness* in the Day of Judgment? It means to have frankness or to be outspoken. John made mention of this already in 1 John 2:28: "And now, little children, abide in Him, that when He appears, we may have confidence and not be ashamed before Him at His coming." We brought out then that this word entails boldness in speaking. It was a word that had a range of meanings: speaking openly rather than secretly; speaking truth rather than lies; speaking courageously rather than keeping quiet out of fear or respect; and speaking plainly rather than obscurely. In fact, it was a word that described the martyrs in the early church as they faced their killers—they had confidence. It was also used to describe the free citizens of Athens who were allowed to freely speak their mind with boldness in the assembly. Why do we have boldness in *the Day of Judgment*? How can this be? John says it's because we are living like He lived. John says, *because as He is, so are we in this world*. What does this mean? It means that likeness to Christ will give us that boldness we need in the Day of Judgment. John has written about this numerous times already in 1 John. In 1 John 1:7, he made mention that we are to walk in the light as He is in the light; in 1 John 2:6, John said we are to walk as He walked; in 1 John 3:3, he mentioned that we are to purify ourselves as He is pure; in 1 John 3:16, we were admonished to lay down our lives as He laid down His. Ladies, as we endeavor to live our lives as He lived, then we have no fear of judgment. This does not mean that we live a life of perfection as He did, but it does mean that we are continually striving to be holy as He is holy. When you think about it, believers shouldn't be asking the question: "How much can I sin and still get into heaven?" but they should be asking, "How little can I sin?" Believers should hate sin, and strive to be like Jesus. If you have confidence or boldness when you think about facing judgment, then John says your love is perfect, or mature or complete. This means that you have grown or matured in love. John goes on in verse 18 to say that it is impossible for fear and love to coexist together.

> There is no fear in love; but perfect love casts out fear, because fear involves torment. But he who fears has not been made perfect in love (1 John 4:18).

John says *there is no fear in love*, there is not alarm or fright in love. The word *fear* comes from the Greek word <u>phobos</u>, from which we get our English word phobia. In fact, the Greeks had a god who was called Phobos, who was said to be dreaded because of the terror he inspired. A believer does not have that dread or fear. Fear is the dreaded experience of a slave or a criminal. True love has no fear, because it is not concerned about self-preservation but surrenders to the one who is loved. The man or woman who loves God and whom God loves has no fear. They don't dread the judgment to come. They know they will be able to stand boldly in the Day of Judgment because of the shed blood of Christ. They have been justified, and they have assurance of that. That was why I was terrified and got sick to my stomach every time the subject of the rapture was brought up. I was literally terrified. Why? Because I had not been justified and I had no assurance of that, even though I thought I was a believer. That's why it is not only a gift, but also a test of assurance.

A child of God will have boldness in the Day of Judgment. There will be no fear. Now let me say that John is not talking about the fear we should all have for God, which is a reverence or a holy awe. This is something every child of God should have. John is talking about a fear in judgment. This should be foreign to a believer, and John states why that is so at the end of the verse when he says he who fears has not been made perfect in love. In contrast to those who are fearful, John says, *perfect love casts out fear*. What does it mean that perfect love casts out fear? To cast means to throw or to turn out of doors. John is saying that love flings fear out the door! Why? Because *fear involves torment*. What does that mean? It means that fear is associated with punishment. It is a word that refers to punishment of various kinds. *But he who fears has not been made perfect in love*. Literally, this reads, the fearer is not perfected in love. It means that you are not born of God. That's what was wrong with me, only I was so spiritually blind I could not see that. Perfect love casts out fear, not only in the Day of Judgment, but in this life as well. I know that before Christ I had all types of fears: fears of storms, fear of flying, fear of the dark, fear of being alone, fear, fear, fear! But that is not of God! When you think about it, fear and love cannot be partners. If you are fearful you cannot love. What John is saying here is that those who fear that coming day of judgment have not been made perfect in their love for God. As one man said, "If a person is afraid of God, this is because the love of God has not yet filled his heart and driven out all fear."[84]

As we love God and He loves us, fear is driven out. A person who has a continual fear of the coming judgment is one in whom the Spirit does not reside, otherwise he or she would by the Spirit of God have a love that has been made complete or perfect. It is the unbeliever that has a terror of the judgment to come, and they should. But one who is walking with the Lord should not have that continual fear of judgment to come. Now, I do want to stop here and say that there may be times that you do have some fears about

[84] I. Howard Marshall, *The Epistles of John* (Grand Rapids, MI: Eerdmans, 1978), p 224.

the judgment to come, and this might be due to unconfessed sin or unrepentant sin or relationships you need to make right. I would encourage you to take care of those issues so that your fear will flee. You might have some fears regarding loved ones that won't be in heaven. But, if your life is one of overall fear of the coming judgment, then perhaps you might want to examine yourself very carefully to make sure you are in the faith.

Summary

What great gifts from a great God—*The Gift of the Holy Spirit* (v 13); *The Gift of His Son* (vv 14-16); and *The Gift of Self-Confidence in the Day of Judgment* (vv 17, 18). Have you received these gifts? Given by God Himself, these gifts are a wonderful assurance for the believer that she is born of God. Does the Spirit dwell within you? Do you know the Son? Do you have confidence when you consider the Day of Judgment?

As I mentioned before, these three wonderful gifts are also three tests to examine our hearts. I wish someone had challenged me in my college days with questions like these: "Susan, do you have the Holy Spirit living in you? If you do, what are the evidences that He resides within your heart?" "Susan, have you received the gift of God's Son? If so, does your commitment to Christ manifest itself by a life of submission to His Lordship?" "Susan, do you have self-confidence when you think about the judgment that is to come or do you fear the day of the Lord?" The great news is that now I can answer those questions with complete confidence. And you know what? You can talk to me all you want about the rapture, and I won't get weak in the knees or sick to my stomach. Why? Because I have no fear of the rapture of Jesus Christ! God's love in my heart has flung those fears completely out of my life and I look forward to glory and eternity with the Father, and with each of you who have confessed Him as Lord!

Questions to Consider

Three Spectacular Gifts for God's Children!

1 John 4:13-18

1. (a) Read 1 John 4:13-18 and make note of all the names that are used for the Godhead. (b) Write down any facts you see regarding each person of the trinity (the Father, the Son, and the Holy Spirit), according to this passage.

2. Memorize 1 John 4:15.

3. Read John 14:16, 17, 26; 15:26; 16:7, and answer the following questions. (a) When did Jesus promise the gift of the Holy Spirit? (b) Where did Jesus say the Spirit would come from? (c) When did the Holy Spirit come, according to Acts 1:1-9 and 2:1-21? (d) What things happened when He came?

4. (a) What do the following passages teach you about our Savior? Luke 2:11; Acts 5:31; Ephesians 5:23; Philippians 3:20, 21; 2 Timothy 1:8-10; Titus 2:13, 14; 3:4-6. (b) What does "Savior" mean to you? (c) Do you think it is possible or impossible to receive Christ as Savior but not as Lord? Support your answer with Scripture.

5. (a) What do the following verses teach you about the day of judgment? Matthew 12:35-37; 2 Peter 2:9; 3:7; Jude 6; Revelation 20:11-15. (b) What do you think John means when he says that those whose love is perfected "will have boldness in the Day of Judgment" (1 John 4:17)?

6. (a) Do you have a fear of the judgment to come? (b) If so, what do you think is producing that fear? (c) What will you do about it?

7. (a) What are some ways we can know that the Spirit is in us? (b) What are some ways we can know we have confessed Christ as Lord? (Scriptural support please!)

8. What would you say is your greatest spiritual need as a result of studying this lesson? Please put it in the form of a prayer request.

Chapter 18

Loving Others by Loving God

1 John 4:19-21

In the 38 years my husband and I have been in the ministry, we have encountered some very unpleasant experiences. Some of those unpleasant experiences stand out as extremely painful. They're painful in the sense that we see "believers in Jesus Christ" who refuse to forgive, refuse to reconcile, and refuse to love others with the type of love which Christ says will "turn the other cheek," "give his brother his coat," "go with his brother an extra mile," "live peaceably with all men," and "forgive as they have been forgiven." Is it possible to have those types of attitudes toward other Christians and love God at the same time? Can people with those attitudes truly be born of God? What does God say through the Apostle John about these things? Let's see what He says as we finish chapter 4.

1 John 4:19-21

> We love Him because He first loved us. [20]If someone says, "I love God," and hates his brother, he is a liar; for he who does not love his brother whom he has seen, how can he love God whom he has not seen? [21]And this commandment we have from Him: that he who loves God must love his brother also (1 John 4:19-21).

In our last lesson together we learned that that there are three gifts given by God to His children: *The Gift of the Holy Spirit* (v 13); *The Gift of His Son* (vv 14-16); and *The Gift of Self-Confidence in the Day of Judgment* (vv 17, 18). We ended that lesson by bringing out the important truth that those who are fearful concerning the Day of Judgment have not been made perfect in their love; they have not been born of God. In contrast to those who are fearful and therefore do not have a perfect love, we now turn to those who have been made perfect in their love in verse 19. Our outline for this lesson will include:

Why We Love God (v 19)
How We Love God (vv 20, 21)

Why We Love God
1 John 4:19

We love Him because He first loved us (1 John 4:19).

Instead of being afraid of God, as we saw in our last lesson, we love God. Those who love God have a perfect love. John says *we love Him*. Yes, this is true, but we did not love Him first, even though some people think they did. John says we love Him—why?—*because He first loved us*! When John says we love Him, the words *we love* are better rendered we are able to love. In other words, we are able to love Him because He first loved us. Ladies, if He did not love us first, we would in no way be able to love Him. Paul put it well in Romans 3:10-12: "As it is written: 'There is none righteous, no, not one; There is none who understands; there is none who seeks after God. They have all turned aside; they have together become unprofitable; there is none who does good, no, not one.'" Not one of us sought God first; He sought us and He loved us first. We were all depraved souls seeking our own agenda and rebelling against God. He reached down and drew us to Himself.

The word *love* is in the present tense, which means we continually love Him. It's not like some young girls, who love one boy one day but don't care for him the next day. They are on again, off again, on again, off again. This love that John is speaking of is not like that; instead, it is a consistent love. Love here is also the Greek word agape. Many people say they love God and to them that means they have some warm fuzzy feeling when they sing a worship song or see a picture of Jesus or think of Him dying on the cross. But agape love has nothing to do with that fuzzy love but is a love that shows itself in action. How do we show love to God? We show our love to God not by working ourselves up in some emotional frenzy, or having a warm fuzzy feeling up and down our spine, but by our obedience to God. I've met many people who base their love for God by some worship experience, and yet when you watch their lives, there is no obedience to the Word of God and no desire to be obedient to the Word of God. Something is very wrong with that picture.

John says we love God *because He first loved us*. John has already indicated this in 1 John 4:10, where he stated, "In this is love, not that we loved God, but that He loved us and sent His Son to be the propitiation for our sins." When John says He first loved us it means His love was foremost, in front of, prior. The tense points back to verse 14 to God's incredible demonstration of love, the sacrifice of His Son. John has already mentioned that love is the very nature of God. Look again at 1 John 4:8: "He who does not love does not know God, for God is love." And 1 John 4:16: "And we have known and believed the love that God has for us. God is love, and he who abides in love abides in God, and God in him." God was first in His love because His nature is love. I think of what God told the nation of Israel in Deuteronomy 7:7-8:

> The LORD did not set His love on you nor choose you because you were more in number than any other people, for you were the least of all peoples; but because the LORD loves you, and because He would keep the oath which He swore to your fathers, the LORD has brought you out with a mighty hand, and redeemed you from the house of bondage, from the hand of Pharaoh king of Egypt (Deuteronomy 7:7-8).

God says, "Look, I did not choose to love you because you were something special or even because you were some great people. In fact, you guys were the fewest of all people. But I chose you because I love you." God chooses to set His love upon those whom He chooses. As Jesus put it well in John 15:16, "You did not choose Me, but I chose you and appointed you that you should go and bear fruit, and that your fruit should remain, that whatever you ask the Father in My name He may give you." So why do we love God? Because He first loved us! Now, because believers possess the love of God, then it only makes sense that our love will be poured out toward others, right? That perfect love, which drives out fear, also drives out hatred of others. You might ask, well, what if it doesn't? What if it I don't love others? Notice what John says in verse 20. We now turn from why we love God to how we love God.

How We Love God
1 John 4:20, 21

> If someone says, "I love God," and hates his brother, he is a liar; for he who does not love his brother whom he has seen, how can he love God whom he has not seen (1 John 4:20)?

Here we have the "if-we-sayers" again—those who are, again, saying things with their lips but not backing those things up with their lives. These people have already said they have fellowship with Him, and yet they walk in darkness (1:6). They have already said they have no sin, and yet they do have sin and they make God a liar (1:8, 10). They have already said that they know Him, but they do not keep His commandments (2:4), they have already said they abide in Him, and yet they do not walk as He walked (2:6). They have already said they are in the light, and yet they hate their brother (2:9). This time they are saying *I love God*, and yet they hate their brother. They're saying, "I love God, but I hate you!" *Hate* means to detest, and it is in the Greek tense which indicates that it means to keep on hating. So John says if you say you love God and yet hate your brother, you are *a liar*. He has already told them if they hate their brother they are in darkness in 1 John 2:9; and in 1 John 3:15 he told them if they hate their brother they are a murderers; and now he tells them if they hate their brother they are a liars. Hatred of one's brother is a proof of being in darkness, being a murderer and being a liar.

These are strong words by the Apostle John, and they should cause each of us to examine our hearts to see if there are any hints of hatred toward others. By the way, the word for *brother* here is for a Christian brother. So if we say we love God, and yet hate our brother, John says we are liars. This is not the only time that John has used this term liar. He also uses the term in 1:6, 1:10; 2:4, 2:22; and 5:10. You might be thinking, "That's a pretty serious accusation," and I would agree that it is! But listen to John's reasoning here: *for he who does not love his brother whom he has seen, how can he love God whom he has not seen?* How ridiculous is that? We say we love God, and yet we have never seen Him. John made it clear in 1 John 4:12 that no man has seen God at any time. In fact, in 1 Peter 1:8, Peter said to the churches scattered abroad, "whom having not seen you love. Though now you do not see Him, yet believing, you rejoice with joy inexpressible and full of glory." We love God, yet we don't see Him. So how can we say we love God, whom we have never seen, and at the same time hate our brother, whom we can see? How can we love God who is invisible, when we cannot even love our brother who is visible? John is saying this logic is absurd. One man helps us here,

> A person may deceive other men by declaring that he loves God; but since God cannot be seen, there is no direct way of telling whether he truly loves God. Even if he goes through the outward motions of devotion to God, prayer, attendance of worship, and so on, it may still be all empty show. But a person cannot so easily deceive others regarding his love for his fellow Christians; since they can be seen, the person's relation with them is also visible."[85]

John is also, once again, confronting the Gnostics, who were claiming to love God but all the while were looking down on their brothers. A genuine faith in Christ will manifest itself in a love for others. So how do we love God? By loving others! John reminds them again of this commandment to love others in verse 21.

---

[85] I. Howard Marshall, *The Epistles of John* (Grand Rapids, MI: Eerdmans, 1978), p 225.

> And this commandment we have from Him: that he who loves God must love his brother also (1 John 4:21).

The word for *commandment* here is an authoritative prescription. And John says we have had this *from Him*. Where did this commandment originate? Way back in Leviticus 19:17 and 18 we read, "You shall not hate your brother in your heart. You shall surely rebuke your neighbor, and not bear sin because of him. You shall not take vengeance, nor bear any grudge against the children of your people, but you shall love your neighbor as yourself: I am the LORD." God made it clear in the beginning that we are not to hate our brother in our heart. But we are to do the more difficult thing and that is to rebuke our brother when there is sin present. Some of us would rather harbor resentment instead of doing the harder thing, which is confrontation. Some think this is the loving thing to do, but many see it as the unloving thing to do. But ladies, that is a wrong, unbiblical concept.

John goes on to say that *he who loves God must love his brother also*. John is saying, don't tell me you love God when you don't love your brother. Don't tell me you love God when you don't love His children. Don't tell me you love God, when you don't love the people that go to your church. Don't tell me you love God, when you don't love your husband. Don't tell me you love God, when you don't love that neighbor next door. Quit saying that! You can't have one without the other. You can't love God and hate your brother. You also can't love your brother and hate God. In fact, Jesus Himself made some very interesting remarks in Matthew 22:35-40 to a lawyer who came and asked Him some questions:

> Then one of them, a lawyer, asked Him a question, testing Him, and saying, "Teacher, which is the great commandment in the law?" Jesus said to him, "'You shall love the Lord your God with all your heart, with all your soul, and with all your mind.' This is the first and great commandment. And the second is like it: 'You shall love your neighbor as yourself.' On these two commandments hang all the Law and the Prophets" (Matthew 22:35-40).

True religion begins and ends in love to God and man. You might be thinking, "Well, I'm off the hook because the people I don't love are not Christians." Well, Jesus has something to say regarding that in Matthew 5:43-48.

> You have heard that it was said, "You shall love your neighbor and hate your enemy." But I say to you, love your enemies, bless those who curse you, do good to those who hate you, and pray for those who spitefully use you and persecute you, that you may be sons of your Father in heaven; for He makes His sun rise on the evil and on the good, and sends rain on the just and on the unjust. For if you love those who love you, what reward have you? Do not even the tax collectors do the same? And if you greet your brethren only, what do you do more than others? Do not even the tax collectors do so? Therefore you shall be perfect, just as your Father in heaven is perfect (Matthew 5:43-48).

Jesus raises the standard here and says, "I want you to love even your enemies." That is a tall order, indeed, but it is not an impossible task with the Lord's help.

Summary

The Apostle John has shown us *Why We Love God* (v 19). We love God because He first loved us. He's also shown us *How We Love God* (vv 20, 21). We love God by showing love to our brethren. Perhaps by now some of you are tired of John's repeated commandment to love one another. Maybe some of you feel like his fellow believers, who in his day said to him, "Give us something new, John." Evidently, they needed to improve on loving one another, just as we do. Or, some of you may be saying, "You know this lesson does not really apply to me because I do love God and I do love my brother. First of all, I am thrilled that you love God and that you love others. But every believer can improve in the area of loving others. I know I can. Remember what Paul says to the church at Thessalonica, a church known for loving the brethren? He states in 1 Thessalonians 4:9, 10, "But concerning brotherly love you have no need that I should write to you, for you yourselves are taught by God to love one another; and indeed you do so toward all the brethren who are in all Macedonia. But we urge you, brethren, that you increase more and more." Paul says, hey, you guys already love, but do it more and more. I would like to close this chapter by challenging you with 8 ways in which you can improve your love. So let's think through this command just a little more.

1. Pursue love. "Pursue love, and desire spiritual gifts, but especially that you may prophesy" (1 Corinthians 14:1). The Apostle Paul has just completed that all too familiar chapter on love, in 1 Corinthians 13. He begins chapter 14 by saying follow after or pursue love. The word means to hunt after, to chase after, and to pursue. This means that we need to take some initiative, as men do when they go out and hunt for game. They plan, they pursue, and they chase the object being hunted. This means we should not just wait for a need to come up, but we should seek out needs. We should ask questions of others, like, "How can I pray for you?" "May I run any errands for you this week?" "Do you need someone to watch your kids this week?" "I would be happy to come over and help you clean your house; I know you haven't felt well lately." These are just some of the ways we can pursue love. Be creative. Pursue love. Chase after opportunities. Don't just wait for one to fall in your lap. I remember once finding out that there were some needs in our church that were not met, and when I commented to my husband that we didn't know there was a need, he said, "That is no excuse; we should have taken the initiative to find out."

2. Be sincere in your love. Paul tells us in 2 Corinthians 8:7-8, "But as you abound in everything—in faith, in speech, in knowledge, in all diligence, and in your love for us—see that you abound in this grace also. I speak not by commandment, but I am testing the sincerity of your love by the diligence of others." Paul says prove the sincerity of your love. Prove your love is genuine. Here, Paul specifically is speaking to those who were poor and in need of financial help. He says prove your love. Again, there are many ways we can do this. Perhaps someone you know is suffering a financial need because of the loss of a job or because of some other reason. Why not buy them some groceries, buy their kids some clothes, take them out for a special treat like lunch or dinner or ice cream, or go through all that stuff you have in your house and give it to someone who is far needier than you are?

3. Abound in love. "… and this I pray, that your love may abound still more and more in knowledge and all discernment" (Philippians 1:9). Paul says I pray that your love may super-abound or be in excess. Would others look at your life and see love that is super-abounding? Do they see you doing as Jesus did, just going about doing good, as mentioned in Acts 10:38? Jesus said in the Sermon on the Mount in Matthew 6:3 that we should not even let our left hand know what our right hand is doing. In other words, just go about doing good and don't even let others know what you are doing. Loving others should be a habit of our life which abounds at all times.

4. Be consistent in love. "… fulfill my joy by being like-minded, having the same love, being of one accord, of one mind" (Philippians 2:2). Paul not only admonishes the church at Philippi to abound in their love, but also to be consistent or the same in their love. This means to be harmonious in our love, like two hearts that beat together, or like clocks that strike at the same time. You know, we can have different opinions about things, but we are to be united in our love. This will flesh itself out in our working together in love for a common goal. When you look at Christ and the apostles, they worked together for the common goal of expanding the kingdom. And yet they were very different in personality. If someone in the church shows an act of love toward someone, and you had the same idea in mind, don't get upset about it or jealous over it. We should work together for the common goal of glorifying God.

5. Increase in love. "… and may the Lord make you increase and abound in love to one another and to all, just as we do to you" (1 Thessalonians 3:12). We should be enlarging our love. Love is not just to be exclusive to a few people we like. We should not be partial in our love. Holy cliques can make for very shallow love. Reach out to many. When you look at the apostles and at Christ, they labored in love to the point of exhaustion for others, even though they also had special times together. They were very close as a group, especially Peter, James, John and Jesus, but they reached out to the multitudes. They were certainly always increasing in their love and seizing all the opportunities to love that were given to them.

6. Provoke each other to love. "… and let us consider one another in order to stir up love and good works" (Hebrews 10:24). This does not mean that we provoke each other in a bad way toward love and good deeds. It doesn't mean that I say to you, "Don't you know that so and so has a need?! Why aren't you doing anything?! What is wrong with you?!" That's not a great motivator! But it does mean that we stimulate or stir up one another to love and good deeds. In other words, we sharpen one another in this area. This might be with words or with actions. For example, I may be unaware of a need that I can meet, and you let me know about it, and you encourage me to meet that need. We also provoke one another to love and good deeds by our example. I think I have learned more about loving others from my husband than from any other human being. His life is a constant rebuke to my own, and he has taught me so much, not by his words only but also as I've watched him. I often think of the time we received a call in the middle of the night, about someone in our church who had taken a fall and was at the hospital. I took the call, since the phone was by my side of the bed. I told Doug about it, and then I turned over to go back to sleep. He turned on the light and got out of bed. I asked him what he was doing and he said, "I'm going to the hospital. Aren't you?" His example spoke volumes to me. He was provoking me to love and good deeds.

7. Continue in love. Another great passage regarding love begins in Hebrews 13:1: "Let brotherly love continue." Let love continue. Let it remain. Don't let it be interrupted. I don't think it is a coincidence that following the admonition to not let our love be interrupted is the admonition to let that love continue. The writer gives us some helps in how this is to continue. First of all, with strangers—yes, we're to love strangers! Look at what is said in verse 2: "Do not forget to entertain strangers, for by so doing some have unwittingly entertained angels." Second, we're to love those in prison, verse 3: "Remember the prisoners as if chained with them—those who are mistreated—since you yourselves are in the body also." Third, we're to love our spouses; look at what is said in verse 4: "Marriage is honorable among all, and the bed undefiled; but fornicators and adulterers God will judge." Fourth, we're to love our Lord; look at verse 5: "Let your conduct be without covetousness; be content with such things as you have. For He Himself has said, 'I will never leave you nor forsake you.'" We must let our love continue with strangers, with those in prison. Don't forget them. That is one way love continues. We must not neglect showing love to our husbands, especially in the sexual area. Let it continue; don't let it be interrupted, unless it is for a time of fasting and prayer, as Paul would say in 1 Corinthians 7:5. And don't let your love to God become cold, to the point that you're not content with what you have. Don't commit idolatry by coveting. Don't let your love to God be interrupted by discontentment.

8. Be fervent in love. 1 Peter 4:8 reminds us, "… and above all things have fervent love for one another, for 'love will cover a multitude of sins.'" Peter says be intentional in your love, be red-hot. This type of love will result in covering one another's sins. Now Peter is not saying love each other so much that you tolerate sin in each other, but do forgive one another. As believers, we are not perfect and we do sin against each other, but we forgive each other for those offenses, or we should. Be so red-hot in your love that you do not keep a record of things done wrong. When others offend you or hurt you, you should be able to forgive them to the point that you never bring it up and you don't even think about it when you see them.

So, do you think you have room for improving your love? We all do, don't we? We all need to follow after love, be sincere in our love, abound in love, be consistent in our love, increase our love, provoke one another to love and good deeds, continue in our love, and be fervent in our love.

The story is told of a young college student named Bill. He was pretty wild, wore jeans with holes and no shoes. While he was in college he became a believer and decided to go to a particular church one Sunday. This church happened to be a very well-dressed, conservative church. By the time he got there, the service had already started and there was no place for Bill to sit, because the sanctuary was packed. Bill walked to the front of the auditorium looking for a seat but found none, so he sat down right on the carpet in the front. Of course, the congregation became uptight and tense. From the back of the church came a deacon in his 80's, slowly walking down the aisle to the front where Bill was sitting. The congregation, of course, was thinking, "Good! He's going to throw that guy out. I mean, how can the preacher preach with that going on?" The elderly deacon made his way to the front and, with much difficulty, sat down on the floor next to Bill. The congregation choked up and many began to cry. When the minister finally gained control, he said, "What I'm about to preach, you will never remember. What you have just seen, you will never forget."[86] As the Apostle John has told us, he who loves God loves his brother also.

[86] Rebecca Manley Pippert, *Out of the Saltshaker and Into the World* (Downer's Grove, IL: InterVarsity Press, 1999), page number unknown.

Questions to Consider

Loving God by Loving Others

1 John 4:19-21

1. Read 1 John 4:19-21. Why do you think loving God leads to loving our brother?

2. Memorize 1 John 4:20.

3. (a) What does it mean to love God, according to the following verses? Deuteronomy 30:20; 1 Kings 3:3; John 14:15 and 21:15-17. (b) What does loving God mean to you? (c) How do *you* see the love for God manifested in a believer's life?

4. John says God loved us first. (a) How do the following verses prove this fact? John 3:16; 15:16; Ephesians 2:1-6; Titus 3:3-5; 1 John 4:10.

5. (a) What are some of the benefits for those who love God, according to John 14:21; Romans 8:28; 1 Corinthians 2:9; 1 Corinthians 8:3; Ephesians 6:24; James 1:12 and 2:5? (b) What happens to those who do not love God, according to 1 Corinthians 16:22?

6. Read Genesis 37 and answer the following questions. (a) Why was Joseph hated by his brothers? (b) What happened as a result of this hatred? (c) Skim the rest of Genesis (chapters 37-50) to see what else resulted from the hatred of Joseph's brothers. (d) What principles can you glean for your own life regarding this serious sin of hating others? (e) Extra credit question: Do you think any of Joseph's brothers claimed to "love God"? Prove your answer biblically.

7. How would you instruct someone who tried to convince you of her great devotion to God while having resentment and bitterness toward others?

8. John writes once again in 1 John 4:20 regarding those who "say" but do not "do." (a) What are some common things we hear believers say but that are not backed up by their actions? (b) Is there anything you say with your mouth but do not back up with your life?

9. (a) Do you love God? (b) Do you love your brother? (c) Where are you falling short in loving God and/or loving your brother? Please commit this to prayer, by writing out a prayer request to share.

Chapter 19

God's Commandments, a Joy or a Burden?

1 John 5:1-3

When my children were growing up, my husband and I set rules for them to follow. These rules were meant to be obeyed if they wished to remain under our roof. We had rules like honoring and obeying us as their parents. We had curfew rules when they became teenagers. We had rules for where they could go, what kind of entertainment was acceptable, and what kinds of friends they were allowed to have. They were also expected to do their part as family members, like helping with the housework, keeping their rooms clean, mowing the yard and carrying out other duties which would need to be done from time to time. We made these rules and we enforced them, because we knew we were responsible before God to bring our children up in the nurture and discipline of His Son. We also enforced these rules so that we would have harmony and peace in our home, and so that they would be taught the benefits and the joy of obedience. On one or more occasions, I can recall comments like, "Mom, you are the only parent who has these rules," or "You are so strict!" My response was usually something like, "I doubt I am the only parent who has these rules, and even if I am, they still remain in effect. You see, Charles, you see, Cindi, some day I as your mom am going to stand before God and give an account for how I parented you, and I do not want to stand before Him ashamed."

Now, you might be wondering, "Is this a lesson on parenting or a lesson on 1 John?" Well, both, in a sense! You see, we who are born of God are in a family, the family of God. God is our parent—our Father, so to speak—and He has set down certain rules for us. They are called commandments and you can find them in His book, the Bible. He gave them to us so that we might live in peace and harmony, so that things would go well with us, and so that we would learn the joy of obeying Him. In fact, Deuteronomy 28 records for us some of the blessings that come from obeying Him as well as some of the curses that come from disobeying Him. Some of us, unfortunately, respond back with comments much like my children did: "God, Christianity is the only religion with such rules," "You are so strict!" "Your rules are a burden to me." My question to you is this: Are these attitudes proper for one who is a child of God? Well, what does God say about this through the Apostle John? Let's read what He has to say as we begin chapter five of 1 John.

1 John 5:1-3

> Whoever believes that Jesus is the Christ is born of God, and everyone who loves Him who begot also loves him who is begotten of Him. [2]By this we know that we love the children of God, when we love God and keep His commandments. [3]For this is the love of God, that we keep His commandments. And His commandments are not burdensome (1 John 5:1-3).

In our last lesson we learned *Why We Love God* (v 19): because He first loved us. And we learned *How We Love God* (vv 20, 21): by showing love to our brethren. As we finished chapter four we saw the absurdity of saying we love God when we hate our brother. We also brought out 8 ways in which we can improve our love for the brethren: follow after love, be sincere in our love, abound in love, be consistent in our love, increase our love, provoke one another to love and good deeds, continue in our love, and be fervent in our love. In this lesson, we'll see that true faith produces:

Love for God (v 1)
Love for God's Children (v 2)
Love for God's Commandments (v 3)

Love for God
1 John 5:1, 2

> Whoever believes that Jesus is the Christ is born of God, and everyone who loves Him who begot also loves him who is begotten of Him (1 John 5:1).

John begins chapter five of his epistle by saying *whoever*. Again, this is universal. Each individual person who *believes* that Jesus is the Christ is born of God. It literally reads, "Whoever is the believing one." So you might be thinking, "Whew! I believe that Jesus is the Christ." Well, not so fast there, pard'ner! (An Okie saying!) Let's define what it means to believe that Jesus is the Christ. The Greek word is pisteuo, which means to believe, to commit, to entrust one's spiritual well being to Christ.[87] It is not just an intellectual belief, but also an individual commitment to a person, the person of Jesus Christ. This belief continues on and on; it is a continuing faith.[88] So John says anyone who believes *that Jesus is*

---

87 Daniel Wallace points out that the present tense of pisteuo (English, *believe*) is used 43 times in the New Testament, most often in the context of salvation. cf. John 1:12; 3:15,16, 18; 3:36; 6:35, 47, 64; 7:38; 11:25; 12:46; Acts 2:44; 10:43; 13:39; Romans 1:16; 3:22; 4:11, 24; 9:33; 10:4, 11; 1 Corinthians 1:21; 14:22; Galatians 3:22; Ephesians 1:19; 1 Thessalonians 1:7; 2:10, 13; 1 Peter 2:6, 7; 1 John 5:1, 5, 10, 13. This is six times as often as the eight aorist tense usages in the New Testament. cf. Mark 16:16; 2 Thessalonians 1:10; Hebrews 4:3; John 7:39; 2 Thessalonians 2:12; Jude 5. "The present tense was the tense of choice most likely because the NT writers by and large saw continual belief as a necessary condition of salvation." cf. *Greek Grammar Beyond the Basics: An Exegetical Syntax of the New Testament* (Grand Rapids, MI: Zondervan Publishing House, 1996), p 621.

88 cf. Matthew 13:3-6, 18-21. Other warnings of temporary faith that is not saving include: "For it is impossible for those who were once enlightened, and have tasted of the heavenly gift, and were made partakers of the Holy Ghost, And have tasted the good word of God, and the powers of the world to come, If they shall fall away, to renew them again unto repentance; seeing they crucify to themselves the Son of God afresh, and put him to an open shame. For the earth which drinketh in the rain that cometh oft upon it, and bringeth forth herbs meet for them by whom it is dressed, receiveth blessing from God: But that which beareth thorns and briers is rejected, and is nigh unto cursing; whose end is to be burned. But, beloved, we are persuaded better things of you, and things that accompany salvation, though we thus speak." cf. Hebrews 6:4-9. "For if after they have escaped the pollution's of the world through the knowledge of the Lord and Savior Jesus Christ, they are again entangled therein, and overcome, the latter end is worse with them than the beginning. For it had been better for them not to have known the way of righteousness, than, after they have known it, to turn from the holy commandment delivered unto them. But it is happened unto them according to the true proverb, The dog is turned to his own vomit again; and the sow that was washed to her wallowing in the mire." cf. 2 Peter 2:20-22. Remember John Bunyan's "Man in the Iron Cage," who felt because of his apostasy that God Himself had imprisoned him in the cage of unbelief because of his lusts and turning to the world! This is a graphic picture of the remorse of the person following a turning from the Lord.

the Christ is born of God. What does it mean to be *born of God*? It means to be regenerated. We now have been given His divine nature. Peter puts it this way in 2 Peter 1:4: "by which have been given to us exceedingly great and precious promises, that through these you may be partakers of the divine nature, having escaped the corruption that is in the world through lust." The tense of this phrase in 1 John indicates that this person has entered into God's family at some point in the past and still is enjoying that family relationship.[89] When you think about it, if you believe in something or someone, it should produce some results, right? Therefore, when you acquire God's nature, then it should produce God-like qualities. John is once again confronting the Gnostics, who denied that Jesus was the Christ. They claimed that Christ descended on Jesus at His baptism but left Him before He was crucified. It's clever of them to believe such ridiculous things about Christ, isn't it? They made their theology convenient, in order to justify their sinful behavior. They claimed they knew God but it did not produce God-like results! Man has a way of doing that.

So if we say that we believe in God then it should produce something, right? This is the point John makes as he lists two results that should be evident when one truly believes in Jesus, when one is born of God. John puts it this way: *everyone who loves Him who begot also loves him who is begotten of Him.* Literally, it reads: "and whoever loves the Father loves the child born of Him." Notice, first, that it is *everyone*, just as it said whoever at the beginning of the

---

89 "The combination of the present tense (ho pisteuon, *believes*) and perfect [i.e., *is born of* God] is important. It shows clearly that believing is the consequence, not the cause, of the new birth. Our present, continuing activity of believing is the result, and therefore the evidence, of our past experience of new birth by which we became and remain God's children." cf. John R. W. Stott, *Tyndale New Testament Commentary: The Letters of John* (Grand Rapids, MI: Eerdmans, 1988), p 175. Others view believing and begetting as simultaneous actions. cf. Brown, p 535; Marshall, pp 226-227; or as Burdick (p 358), that believing results in regeneration. I would agree that the Apostle John's point is not to teach an ordo salutis, or order of salvation, but to affirm that ongoing faith is expressed by those who are regenerated. And yet, the conclusion that regeneration is the cause of ongoing faith is hard to escape from the use of the Greek tenses.

verse. Everyone who *loves* God, loves His children. The word for love here is agape. It only makes sense that as we love the Father, then we will love those in His family. I have even heard some people say, "If you want to show love to me, then show love to my children!" Love me? Love my children! The two go together. True faith produces love for God, but it also produces love for His children. John goes on to write regarding this love we should have toward the children of God.

Love for God's Children
1 John 5:2

> By this we know that we love the children of God, when we love God and keep His commandments (1 John 5:2).

John is once again saying what he has said many times, but this time he seems to say it backwards. He usually says something like this: this is how we know we love God when we love His children. But now he says this is how we know we love God's children, when we love Him. You might be wondering, as I did, "Why is he now saying it like this?" That's a good question! Perhaps he reverses the order to answer the question we all have had at some time or another: "How do I know for sure that the love I have for others is motivated by God's love and not some warm fuzzy feeling or the fact that I just love people, or that I just like to socialize?" Have you ever asked yourself those questions? I have. John gives us the answer. He uses the words *by this*, or in this way, or this is how we *know that we love the children of God*. How can we *know*? *When we love God and keep His commandments*. You know, when you think about it, it's one big cycle. Love God, love others, keep His commandments; keep His commandments, love God, love others; love others, keeps His commandments, love God. This three-part cycle really goes along with what Jesus said to the lawyer in Matthew 22:35-40:

> Then one of them, a lawyer, asked Him a question, testing Him, and saying, "Teacher, which is the great commandment

> in the law?" Jesus said to him, "'You shall love the LORD your God with all your heart, with all your soul, and with all your mind.' This is the first and great commandment. And the second is like it: 'You shall love your neighbor as yourself.' On these two commandments hang all the Law and the Prophets" (Matthew 22:35-40).

Simply put Jesus says to the lawyer, "Love the Lord; love your neighbor; and on these two commandments hang all the law and prophets."

John tells us that we don't have to go around guessing if we love others or not. John says we can *know*, which means absolutely know, that we love God's children when we love God and keep His commandments. In order to love God's children we must be around them right? We must spend time together. With the recent rise of social networking, we are neglecting this huge need of being together. With the recent trend toward worship at home via satellite we are neglecting the need to be together. Our culture is producing individuals who are becoming very isolated, and we are setting ourselves up for some real dangers. Proverbs 18:1 states that, "A man who isolates himself seeks his own desire; he rages against all wise judgment." Not only does isolating oneself bring about more selfishness, but neglecting the assembling of believers is against the Word of God. Look at Hebrews 10:24-25: "And let us consider one another in order to stir up love and good works, not forsaking the assembling of ourselves together, as is the manner of some, but exhorting one another, and so much the more as you see the Day approaching." Ladies, we need to sharpen one another and exhort one another and love one another. I am always encouraged and edified when I meet with the local body of believers. We need each other. So John says we keep on loving God and we keep on keeping His commandments, and by this we know that we love the children of God. In case his readers didn't get what he was saying, John repeats himself again in verse 3 but adds a new twist to what he has said. Here we see that true faith produces a love for God's commandments.

Love for God's Commandments
1 John 5:3

> For this is the love of God, that we keep His commandments. And His commandments are not burdensome (1 John 5:3).

John has already mentioned in 1 John 4:8 that God is love, and so it makes sense that God passes that loving nature on to His children. His love in us will manifest itself, and it will manifest itself in the keeping of His commandments. This is how we show our *love of God*: *we keep His commandments*. By the way, this is the last time *love* is mentioned in 1 John. It has been mentioned 33 times and this is the last time. So here is how we show love to God, and it is by keeping His commandments. What does it mean to keep His commandments? It means to hold them fast, to keep our eye on them, and to guard them. John has already made many references in 1 John to keeping God's commandments: 1 John 2:3-5; 3:22, 24; 5:2, 5:3. In this verse, however, John adds a phrase that is new to his readers: *and His commandments are not burdensome*. What does this mean? It means that His commandments are not annoying, not severe, not irksome, not difficult to carry and not too hard to keep. His commandments are not heavy, not oppressive, and not demanding. Ladies, our Father, who loves us ever so much, does not give us any commandments that are too heavy or too hard to obey.

Now, in the "Questions to Consider," you were to write down 15 commandments and ask yourself if they were too burdensome to you, but did you know that there are actually 613 commandments in the Bible? Are any of them burdensome to you? You know, it is interesting that in Proverbs 13:15 it says that the way of the transgressor is hard. But for God's children the keeping of God's commandments should not be hard. Even Moses, when he was instructing the children of Israel in Deuteronomy regarding the commandments of God, said in Deuteronomy 30:11, "For this commandment which I command you today is not too mysterious for you, nor is it far off." The Hebrew words for not mysterious mean it is not hard, it is not difficult. God's commands are not too difficult, even though some of us try to make them difficult. Jesus said in Matthew 23:4 that it was the Pharisees who put heavy burdens on men that were too grievous to bear. But ladies, God's commandments are not too heavy to bear, especially when we have His enabling power to work in us. God never commands us to do anything that He will not enable us to do. Paul is clear about this in Philippians 2:12-13: "Therefore, my beloved, as you have always obeyed, not as in my presence only, but now much more in my absence, work out your own salvation with fear and trembling; for it is God who works in you both to will and to do for His good pleasure." Jesus Himself says in Matthew 11:28-30, "Come to Me, all you who labor and are heavy laden, and I will give you rest. Take My yoke upon you and learn from Me, for I am gentle and lowly in heart, and you will find rest for your souls. For My yoke is easy and My burden is light." This really is a call to salvation. Jesus says, "All who are laboring, all who are heavy, come to me!" Why do they labor? Why are they heavy laden? It's because of sin. So Jesus says, "Come to me and I will give you rest." In other words, He Himself will give you rest. All your laboring and burden will be over as you yoke yourself to Him and He removes the guilt and load of your sin.

In biblical times, the yoke was used on an ox in order that he would carry a load. Christ is saying that as you yoke yourself to Him, as He becomes the Master of your life, you will find His load not to be heavy and oppressive but easy and light. Yoking ourselves to the Master is not a burden; yoking ourselves to sin is a burden. God's commandments are not burdensome. If you do find the Lord's commands to be a burden, I would encourage you to ask yourself why, since Christ Himself said in His gospel message that as we yoke ourselves to Him His commands will not be a burden but will be easy and light. One man has said of this, "Grievous! O my redeeming God, my loving Father, the loving Father of my Lord! Grievous that you should command me! Grievous that I should be under you! Grievous that I am not independent of you! Left to choose for myself, instead of having you to choose for me, left free to do my own will and not thine! No, I will not, I cannot any more take exception to your rightful rule over me, O thou loving God and Father who so lovingly makes me your own!"[90] Would that we all had the response of Paul in Romans 7:22, where he says, "For I delight in the law of God according to the inward man."

Perhaps there are some of you who are finding the Lord's commands to be a burden. May I say to you that they shouldn't be? I would like to share with you three things that might help you with this. First of all, *God never gives us a command that is not for our good.* God is a God of love, and what He asks of His children is only because of His great love and desire to see them behave as His children. It is just like a parent does with a child. We give our children commands because of our great love for them and our desire for them to be decent human beings and people who follow Christian principles. Let me give you a practical example of this: submission. The Bible says wives are to be submissive to their own husbands, as unto the Lord. I will tell you from first hand experience that this command used to be a big burden to me. Of course, part of the reason was that I was not a believer when I got married. And there was no way anyone was going to tell me what to do! But by being rebellious I created a myriad of problems very early in my marriage. That was a burden! Marriage was hard, and I contributed a great deal to that burden. But after Christ saved me, I learned that true freedom comes from being submissive; it is no longer a burden. Secondly, *our burdens are nothing in comparison to the joy which lies ahead.* It may seem like some things are hard, especially when suffering or persecution occurs because of our obedience.

We may feel like loving God more than we love our family is a hard or burdensome command because it separates us from those we love. Or we may think that loving our enemies is a hard command because we might incur more suffering. Or perhaps sharing the gospel is a hard command because of the persecution that it might

[90] R. C. Candlish, *Commentary on First John* (Mulberry, IN: Sovereign Grace Publishers, 2002), p 197.

bring. But Paul encourages us in Romans 8:18: "For I consider that the sufferings of this present time are not worthy to be compared with the glory which shall be revealed in us." Thirdly, *our love for our Lord should make His commands a joy*. He has saved us from the pit of hell, so why wouldn't we want to do something tangible to show our gratitude? Obedience is the proof of that love for Him. I think of Jesus talking to Peter in John 21:15-17: "So when they had eaten breakfast, Jesus said to Simon Peter, 'Simon, son of Jonah, do you love Me more than these?' He said to Him, 'Yes, Lord; You know that I love You.' He said to him, 'Feed My lambs.' He said to him again a second time, 'Simon, son of Jonah, do you love Me?' He said to Him, 'Yes, Lord; You know that I love You.' He said to him, 'Tend My sheep.' He said to him the third time, 'Simon, son of Jonah, do you love Me?' Peter was grieved because He said to him the third time, 'Do you love Me?' And he said to Him, 'Lord, You know all things; You know that I love You.' Jesus said to him, 'Feed My sheep.'" Three times Jesus asked Peter, "Do you love me?" to which Peter replied, "Lord you know I do." "Then prove it," Jesus is saying, "Feed my sheep. Peter, do something that proves your love; serve me, obey me." And we know that Peter certainly did obey Him, as we read the accounts in Acts and Peter's own words in 1 and 2 Peter. Peter showed His love to God by his obedience to His commands. He certainly fed the Lord's sheep; in fact, in 1 Peter he admonishes the elders of the church to feed the flock which is among them (1 Peter 5:2).

What if Noah had not obeyed God's command to build the ark? What if he had said, "No thanks, God! I don't do arks, and I don't do rain or animals"? What if Abraham had found God's command to get out of his country and away from his family and go to another land to be a burden? What if Abraham had said, "No thanks, God! I don't do moves. Do you realize what a hassle it is to move my family and all my stuff?" What if Moses had found it annoying that God commanded him to lead the children of Israel out of Egypt and into the Promised Land? What if Moses had said, "No thanks, Lord. I don't do Pharaohs and I don't do mass migrations"? What if Ruth had not been a virtuous woman and did not have a heart to minister to her widowed mother-in-law? What if Ruth had said, "I don't do mothers-in-law, and I don't lay at the end of a strange man's bed at night"? What if Esther did not have a passion for God's chosen people, the Jews? What if she had said, "Who cares if they die and perish? I don't have time to fast and worry about them. Give up food? No way!"? What if Peter had disobeyed the Lord's command to take the gospel to the Gentiles? What if he had found that command to be irksome? What if Peter had said, "No way, God! I don't do Gentiles—they're dogs, they're a despised race"? What if Mary had disobeyed the Lord in carrying God's Son in her womb? What if she had found that command to be too hard to carry? What if she had said, "No way, God! I don't do virgin births, and I am not going to be publicly disgraced"? What if the Apostle Paul had not submitted to the Holy Spirit in writing the 14 books we have authored by him in the New Testament? What if he had found that command to be too demanding? What if Paul had said, "No way, God! I don't do correspondence. It's too much work; I might get carpel tunnel!"? What if our Lord had disobeyed His Father in going to the cross and carrying the burden and weight of all the sins of the world? What if Jesus had said, "No way, God! I don't do crosses, and I don't do suffering and mocking and that crown-of-thorns stuff. That's a command too difficult to bear"?

Summary

What about you? What commands of the Lord are you finding to be too difficult? Maybe for you it is the command in Titus 2 to disciple younger women. Perhaps you're thinking, "Lord, I don't do discipling, and I don't have the time to fulfill that commandment. I need to have time to do my aerobics and shopping and art classes." Or maybe you are the younger woman mentioned in Titus 2 and you're saying, "Sorry, Lord, I don't do older women. I don't want anyone to know my struggles." Perhaps you're finding Colossians 3:18 to be too burdensome, where wives are commanded to submit to their husbands. Maybe you're thinking, "Lord, I don't do submission. And, by the way, that husband you gave me does not love me as Christ loved the church, so why should I submit to him?" Maybe for you it is that command in Matthew 5:44 which says we are to love our enemies: "Lord, I don't love anyone except those select few and my family. I don't do loving enemies." Or maybe James 1:27 is the commandment that you balk at, which tells us that true religion is to visit the fatherless and widows in their affliction and to keep oneself unspotted from the world: "Lord, I don't do orphans and widows; I mean, really, they are too much work. I have enough to do just keeping my own home intact. And keeping myself unspotted from the world—why, Lord, have you seen all that good stuff on TV lately?" Hebrews 10:25 is a command that a lot of professing believers find very hard to bear: "Not forsaking the assembling of ourselves together, as is the manner of some, but exhorting one another, and so much the more as you see the Day approaching."

Perhaps you're in that group, thinking, "Lord I don't do faithful church attendance. I mean, that pastor goes past 12:00 noon, and those people at that church are always asking me religious questions like, 'What is God doing in your life?' and 'What are you learning in your daily Bible reading?' And then there's that conflict with my kids' sports on Sunday. And all the good sports on TV—they're always on Sunday!" For us, as women, perhaps we don't like the command in James 1:26 that tells us that real religion is to keep our tongues bridled, and that if we don't then our religion is fake: "Lord, I don't do bridles! I mean, really, Lord, bridles are for horses!" What commandments are you resisting today, and why? And what is going to happen if you continue to resist them?

My dear friends, true faith produces *Love for God* (v 1); *Love for God's Children* (v 2); and *Love for God's Commandments* (v 3). Let us also, by way of closing, remind ourselves of our precious Lord's words in Matthew 16:24-26: "If anyone desires to come after

Me, let him deny himself, and take up his cross, and follow Me. For whoever desires to save his life will lose it, but whoever loses his life for My sake will find it. For what profit is it to a man if he gains the whole world, and loses his own soul? Or what will a man give in exchange for his soul?" My friends, please do not say, "No way, God!" to what He is asking, but say, "Yes, Lord; whatever you say Lord, that I will do."

Questions to Consider

God's Commandments, a Joy or a Burden?

1 John 5:1-3

1. (a) Read 1 John 5:1-3 and summarize what John is saying in one sentence. (b) Where else in 1 John has John written things that are similar to what he writes here in 1 John 5:1-3? Memorize 1 John 5:3.

2. (a) Find someone in Scripture who found God's command(s) to be a burden. (b) Which command(s) did they find do be a burden and how do you know? (c) What happened as a result? (d) What do you learn from their example?

3. (a) Make a list of at least 15 commandments that you can find in the New Testament. (b) Now go back and write beside each commandment either the words "burdensome" or "not burdensome," depending on which is true for you. (c) If you wrote "burdensome" beside any of those commands, ask yourself why they are a burden to you. (d) As you observe Christendom today, what commands do you see that are commonly viewed as burdensome?

4. (a) Read Psalm 119 and discover what responses we should have as believers toward God's commandments. (b) Are these your responses?

5. How would you use what you have learned in this lesson to instruct someone who finds God's commands to be burdensome? (For example, they might say, "Loving my husband is a burden; coming to church is a burden; being joyful in trials is a burden.")

6. Why do you think John says this is how we know we love God's children, when we love God and keep His commandments (1 John 5:2)?

7. Why do you think God gave us commandments? (Back up your answer with the Word of God.)

8. After contemplating questions 4 and 5, what attitudes need to be changed in your life regarding God's commands? Come with a prayer request to share.

Chapter 20

The Evidence that Jesus is the Christ

1 John 5:4-8

I must confess to you that in my opinion we have come to the most difficult passage to interpret in the epistle of 1 John. It reminds me of several other passages in the Word of God that I've studied. For example, when studying 1 Peter, you come to 1 Peter 3:19 and scratch your head wondering, "What did Peter mean when he wrote about Christ preaching to those spirits in prison?" What is so interesting is that Peter writes in 2 Peter 3:15-16 that Paul has written things which are hard to understand. And I would add to Peter's comment that both Peter and John have also written some things that are hard to understand. Actually, many of the Old Testament and New Testament writers have written some things that are difficult to understand. So as we begin this lesson in 1 John, pray with me that God would grant you insight into His Word and discernment as to what His Word actually says.

In our last lesson we saw that true faith produces *Love for God* (v 1); *Love for God's Children* (v 2); and *Love for God's Commandments* (v 3). We also saw that John adds a new twist to the test of obedience—that obeying God's commands should not be burdensome to us. Now, there is a reason that God's commandments are not a burden, and that reason is found in verse 4: "For whatever is born of God overcomes the world. And this is the victory that has overcome the world—our faith." Those of us who are born of God have the power to overcome the world, and therefore following what God has asked us to do is not a burden. We have overcome the world, and because of that the world no longer has a pull on us. We are overcomers; we are not burden-bearers! In this lesson our outline will include:

Who is Born of God? (vv 4, 5)
Who Bears Witness of Jesus? (v 6)
Who Bears Witness in Heaven? (v 7)
Who Bears Witness on Earth? (v 8)

Let's read the passage we'll be endeavoring to unpack.

1 John 5:4-8

For whatever is born of God overcomes the world. And this is
the victory that has overcome the world—our faith. 5Who is he
who overcomes the world, but he who believes that Jesus is the
Son of God? 6This is He who came by water and blood—Jesus
Christ; not only by water, but by water and blood. And it is the
Spirit who bears witness, because the Spirit is truth. 7For there
are three that bear witness in heaven: the Father, the Word, and
the Holy Spirit; and these three are one. 8And there are three
that bear witness on earth: the Spirit, the water, and the blood;
and these three agree as one (1 John 5:4-8).

Who is Born of God?
1 John 5:4, 5

For whatever is born of God overcomes the world. And this is the victory that has overcome the world—our faith (1 John 5:4).

John begins this portion by letting his readers know who it is that *is born of God*. Now, you might be wondering, "Why does John say *whatever*, instead of whoever?" He shifts from the Greek word teknion, which he has been using, to another Greek word for children, teknia, which is a neuter and means male or female. Remember what Paul says in Galatians 3:28? "There is neither Jew nor Greek, there is neither slave nor free, there is neither male nor female; for you are all one in Christ Jesus." So whatever is born of God, John says, *overcomes the world*. He has used the term *overcome* before in this epistle: 1 John 2:13, "I write to you, fathers, because you have known Him who is from the beginning. I write to you, young men, because you have overcome the wicked one. I write to you, little children, because you have known the Father." 1 John 2:14, "I have written to you, fathers, because you have known Him who is from the beginning. I have written to you, young men, because you are strong, and the word of God abides in you, and you have overcome the wicked one." 1 John 4:4, "You are of God, little children, and have overcome them, because He who is in you is greater than he who is in the world." So what does it mean to overcome the world? It means to subdue or to get the victory. [91]As believers, we do not give in to the world's temptations—those John has already mentioned in 1 John 2:15-17: the lust of the flesh, the lust of the eyes, and the pride of life. We are overcomers of these things. World lovers cannot be God lovers! James makes this very clear in his epistle as well, in James 4:4: "Adulterers and adulteresses! Do you not know that friendship with the world is enmity with God? Whoever therefore wants to be a friend of the world makes himself an enemy of God."

John then goes on to state how we have overcome the world. He says, *and this is the victory that has overcome the world—our faith*. The Greek word for *victory* is nike, which is symbolic of ultimate victory or of conquering power. (In our world, nike has become a symbol for athletic attire.) John is saying that we have victory or power over the world, and the reason for that victory is what he has already said back in 1 John 4:4—He who is in you is greater than he who is in the world. John says we have *overcome the world* by *our faith*; our faith is the victory. Our faith, our salvation, is the means by which we overcome the world. In fact, when you

[91] cf. Revelation 2:7, 11, 17, 26; 3:5, 12 and 21. The term translated *overcome* (Greek, nike) is used 24 times in the New Testament and 21 times by John, expressing overwhelming success. Inherent within the term is the fact that the victory is demonstrable, i.e., a public display of victory. Paul even uses the term with a preposition to give further emphasis, i.e., "more than conquerors" or "super-conquerors" (Greek, hupernikomen) in Romans 8:37. The implications of the overcoming life of the believer are wonderful. The believer has the promise of God that victory will be experienced over the world (cf. 1 John 4:4-5) and Satan himself (cf. 1 John 4:4; Revelation 12:10-11). All believers experience this, not simply some greatly dedicated, for the promise is that, "whatsoever is born of God overcometh the world: and this is the victory that overcometh the world, even our faith."

read through Hebrews 11, the great faith chapter, you will find the word faith used 23 times (NKJV)! These men and women overcame the tests in their life by faith. The Greek word for *faith* is pistis, which refers to our salvation. When you and I became believers in Jesus Christ, we became overcomers of the world. Believers are overcomers. Unbelievers, however, cannot overcome the world because it is impossible for them to be victorious over it. When God saved us the power of sin was broken, and because of that we have victory over the world. We have overcome the world and all its temptations. We have overcome the evil in the world; it no longer has a hold on us. John goes on to say the same thing again, but this time he states it in the form of a question.

> Who is he who overcomes the world, but he who believes that Jesus is the Son of God? (1 John 5:5).

It's as if John is saying, "It is impossible to be an overcomer, unless you are a believer in Christ." The Greek tense here indicates that those *who believe that Jesus is the Son of God* are habitually overcoming the world. It is an ongoing process. To *believe* means to entrust one's spiritual well being to Christ. John is really just repeating in verse 5 what he has stated already in verse 4, that those who overcome are believers in Jesus Christ. So, who is born of God? Those who believe that Jesus is the Son of God and have overcome the world! And as he is speaking of Jesus, John reminds his readers again of the incarnation of Christ in verse 6 and answers our second question.

Who Bears Witness of Jesus?
1 John 5:6

> This is He who came by water and blood—Jesus Christ; not only by water, but by water and blood. And it is the Spirit who bears witness, because the Spirit is truth (1 John 5:6).

Now ladies, I am going to take an interpretation of this verse that I only saw mentioned twice in all my studying. And you may find yourself thinking, "She has finally lost her mind!" The view I'm taking of this verse is the one that, to me, has the least problems.[92] So, what does John mean when he says that Jesus *came by water and blood*? Some scholars think the water refers to His Baptism and the blood to His death on the cross. Another view explains that the water refers to baptism and the blood refers to the Lord's Supper. And yet another view states that both refer to the blood and water that came from Jesus' side when He was dead on the cross; John states in John 19:34 that one of the soldiers pierced Jesus' side and immediately there came out blood and water. So I had to ask myself, "How could Christ come in His baptism? How could He come on the cross, or at the Lord's supper?" I think we can come to the clearest interpretation of this verse when we define the word *came*. The word came means by or in. Jesus came by or in water and blood. Since John is writing to combat Gnostism, which denied that Jesus came in the flesh, then it seems to me that he is speaking of Christ's birth. I believe John is speaking of Christ's human birth. Jesus was born of water and blood, amniotic fluid and blood. Now we don't need to get into the details of human birth, but simply to state that there is both blood and water present in human birth. In fact, I discovered that the human body is made up of 72% water, and included in that 72% would be blood. And we know Jesus' body had water and blood because of John 19:34, where it states that when

92 There is a more popular view, which Tertullian was the first to commend, which is also popular among many modern commentators, i.e., John MacArthur; Lenski (pp 524-526); Marshall (pp 232-233); Brooke (pp 131-134); Stott (pp 177-179). Chronologically, Jesus was baptized by John the Baptist and three years later put to death by Pilate, hence He "came by water and blood." This might be John's intended meaning, as he sought to refute the Cerinthian Gnostics who claimed that the Christ spirit descended on the man Jesus at His baptism and departed before His sufferings. Law describes the terms as "a kind of verbal shorthand, intended merely to recall to his readers the exposition of those themes which they had heard from his lips" (p 95). The meaning of "He that came" (Greek, ho elthon) refers to the whole span of Jesus' ministry (i.e., from baptism to death) including the beginning of His public ministry to the close of His public ministry. Hence John gives emphasis to His coming not by "water only" (which the Gnostics would affirm) but "by water and by blood," which of course the Gnostics would deny! cf. 1 John 2:22; 2 John 7. No other reason for the precise order of the nouns makes sense. God has given testimony concerning the fact that Jesus is the Son of God or the Christ, at both His baptism and His death.

the soldier pierced Jesus' side, out came water and blood. So, why does John make it clear that it was *not only by water, but by water and blood*? Why is the *blood* also important? It's important because of the heresy of Gnostism, which stated that Jesus did not come in the flesh. The Gnostics claimed that Christ descended upon Jesus during his baptism but left Him before His death on the cross. John says no, *Jesus Christ* came by water and by blood. The blood was also important because it was the blood of Christ that took away our sins. John has already made this clear in 1 John 1:7 and 1 John 2:1, 2. So, why does he now add *and it is the Spirit who bears witness, because the Spirit is truth*?

The phrase *bears witness* means to testify. The Holy Spirit bears witness that Jesus is the Son of God, that Jesus came in the flesh. In fact, remember that the angel told Joseph in the Luke 1:35 that Mary's conception of Jesus would happen as the Holy Spirit would come upon Mary and overshadow her. Matthew also states that Mary was found with child by the Holy Spirit in Matthew 1:20. (The Holy Spirit was bearing witness not only at the birth of Christ, but also at His baptism. All of the gospel accounts tell of the Holy Spirit descending from heaven like a dove and lighting upon Jesus as He was baptized by John the Baptist: Matthew 3:16; Mark 1:10; Luke 3:22; John 1:32. Jesus, Himself, tells the disciples in the Upper Room, in John 15:26, that when the Holy Spirit comes after Christ's death on the cross, that He, the Holy Spirit, will testify or bear witness of Christ.) The Spirit bears witness to the fact that Jesus came in the flesh. He was bearing witness at the birth of Jesus, at the baptism of Jesus, and continues to testify of Him after His ascension into heaven. John adds that *the Spirit is truth*. He is part of the trinity and He does not lie. What He testifies to is true; you can count on it. Jesus refers to this in John 16:13, "However, when He, the Spirit of truth, has come, He will guide you into all truth; for He will not speak on His own authority, but whatever He hears He will speak; and He will tell you things to come." So, who bears witness of Jesus? The Holy Spirit does and He is true.

John writes next not only of the Holy Spirit bearing witness to this marvelous truth, but of the other two members of the Godhead. He writes concerning the three who bear record in heaven.

Who Bears Witness in Heaven?
1 John 5:7

> For there are three that bear witness in heaven: the Father, the Word, and the Holy Spirit; and these three are one (1 John 5:7).

There are three that bear witness in heaven, John says. They are testifying or giving witness to the fact that Jesus is the Christ.[93] Who are these *three*? They are *the Father*, *the Word* (whom we know is Christ, from 1 John 1:1, "That which was from the beginning, which we have heard, which we have seen with our eyes, which we have looked upon, and our hands have handled, concerning the Word of life," and John 1:1, "In the beginning was the Word, and the Word was with God, and the Word was God."), and *the Holy Spirit.* John says *these three* that bear record in heaven *are one.* This is a wonderful verse here, which not only gives validity to the fact that Jesus is the Christ but also to the doctrine of the Trinity.

---

[93] Before looking at the whole text in detail, there is a textual problem needing clarification. All major English translations (i.e., KJV, NKJV, NASV, NIV, RSV) give at least a marginal note, explaining that a scribal gloss adds the words "in heaven … in earth" (vv 7-8). Our English text retains those words but they have very poor manuscript evidence, and there is almost universal agreement that this passage was added later. Bruce Metzger, of the United Bible Society, gives a helpful summary of evidence against these words being in the original text. That these words are spurious and have no right to stand in the New Testament is certain in the light of the following considerations: 1) The passage is absent from every known Greek manuscript except four [12th through 16th centuries], and these contain the passage in what appears to be a translation from a late recension of the Latin Vulgate. 2) The passage is quoted by none of the Greek Fathers, who, had they known it, would most certainly have employed it in the Trinitarian controversies (Sabellian and Arian). 3) The passage is absent from the manuscripts of all ancient versions (Syriac, Armenian, Ethiopic, Arabic, Slavonic), except the Latin; and it is not found in the Old Latin in its early form (Tertullian, Cyprian, Augustine), or in the Vulgate as issued by Jerome. Apparently the gloss arose when the original passage was understood to symbolize the Trinity (through the mention of three witnesses: the Spirit, the water, and the blood), an interpretation which may have been written first as a marginal note that afterward found its way into the text.

Now, I hope you had fun with that homework question (in the "Questions to Consider") about the Trinity and how you would explain it. I remember hearing the illustration of an egg when I was growing up. The yoke, the white, the shell are all different parts of an egg, they are three in one. I've also heard of another illustration, that of being a woman. All at the same time, I am a wife, a mother, and a daughter. These are three different roles that I have, and yet all make up who I am as a woman. The Father, the Son, and the Holy Spirit are three in one, and they give testimony to Jesus coming in the flesh. So, who bears witness in heaven? The Father, the Word and the Holy Spirit. John now talks about another threesome in verse 8, but it is not the Trinity.

Who Bears Witness on Earth?
1 John 5:8

> And there are three that bear witness on earth: the Spirit, the water, and the blood; and these three agree as one (1 John 5:8).

Now, the views on this verse are the same as those in verse 6, so I won't repeat them here. I believe John is just reaffirming what he has already stated in verse 6. (As you've probably discovered throughout the epistle of 1 John, John does a lot of repeating of certain truths. This is great, since we learn by repetition!) The Trinity bears record in heaven; on the other hand, *there are three that bear witness on earth: the Spirit, the water, and the blood*, as John has already mentioned in verse 6. And *these three agree as one*. What does John mean when he says that they *agree as one*? Literally, it means that the three are for the one thing. What is that one thing? Jesus Christ. What do they bear witness to? Jesus Christ. They agree concerning the fact that Jesus is the Christ. In these verses, John is again combating the heresy of Gnostism. Throughout this letter, John has emphasized the fact that Jesus is the Christ and he continues to further prove that point with these words. Now, an interesting but important note before we go on: There seems to be some significance in the number *three* that John mentions in verses

7 and 8. According to the Mosaic Law (Deuteronomy 17:6; 19:15; Matthew 18:19, 20; 2 Corinthians 13:1), there had to be two or three witnesses to convict a person of a crime. John is saying that there are adequate witnesses here, three to be exact, not to convict of a crime, but to prove that Jesus is the Christ. So who bears witness on earth? The Spirit, the water and the blood.

Summary

In this lesson we have answered several questions: *Who is Born of God?* (vv 4, 5): Those who believe that Jesus is the Son of God and have overcome the world. *Who Bears Witness of Jesus?* (v 6): The Holy Spirit, who is true. *Who Bears Witness in Heaven?* (v 7): The Father, the Word, and the Holy Spirit. *Who Bears Witness on Earth?* (v 8): The Spirit, the water, and the blood. So, as difficult as this passage may be to interpret, it contains some wonderful truths that should encourage our hearts:

1. Those of us who are born of God are overcomers of the world. Sin has no longer any mastery over us—praise be to God! As John has said, we no longer practice sin and we can't do so, because God's seed is in us.

2. Jesus Christ really came in a human body as He was born by water and by blood. And just in case you are in doubt about those facts—don't be! The Holy Spirit testifies to these facts and He is true; He does not lie!

3. There are also other witnesses to the coming of Christ in the flesh: His Father, Himself, and the Spirit.

   May our lives testify to the fact that Jesus is the Christ, the Son of the living God!

Questions to Consider

The Evidence that Jesus is the Christ

1 John 5:4-8

1. (a) Read 1 John 5:4-8 and then rewrite it in your own words. (b) Why do you think John emphasizes in verse 6 that Jesus came not by water only, but also by blood? Memorize 1 John 5:4.

2. How do the following verses help you understand what John means by overcoming the world? (In other words, what things does the believer overcome?) Matthew 13:18-23; 1 Corinthians 10:13; 1 John 2:15-17; 1 John 5:18, 19.

3. (a) How did the heroes listed in Hebrews 11 overcome their temptations and trials? (b) Pick one example from Hebrews 11, and read the Old Testament account of his/her walk of faith. (c) Write down what you have learned from their example of how to overcome the world by faith. (d) How does this help you in your walk of faith?

4. John states in 1 John 5:7 that there are three who bear witness in heaven. (a) Who are these three that he is speaking about? (b) Of what are they bearing witness?

5. John then writes in 1 John 5:8 that there are three who bear witness on earth. (a) What three is he referring to? (b) What are they bearing witness to? (c) What does John mean that these three agree as one?

6. How would you explain the doctrine of the Trinity? (You may use illustrations that you have found helpful, but in your explanation also use Scripture.)

7. (a) How does a believer's faith manifest itself in overcoming the world? (b) In what ways do you see Christians overcoming the world?

8. Are you an overcomer? What is your prayer request as you consider your walk of faith? Be prepared to share.

Chapter 21

Receive the Son and Live; Reject the Son and Die!

1 John 5:9-12

As I walk through my pilgrimage here on planet earth, I observe the paths of many people—my friends, my neighbors, my physical family, and my church family. I find it interesting and amazing to see the things, the people and the circumstances in which many people spend the bulk of their time. For some, their whole life centers on their children. They take them here and there, making sure they get the best of this and that, and catering to to their every whim, ever fearful of offending them. Other people are wrapped up in material possessions. They are always shopping for things they can't afford or don't need, buying new houses, new boats and cars, and making sure they have the latest gadget on the market (I-phone, I-pad, I-pod, etc). Some individuals' lives are wrapped up in entertainment. I'm amazed when people start rattling off the names of actors and musicians from Hollywood, and the latest gossip on their personal lives, or what programs they're starring in, or who they just divorced. They seem to know every movie and every tidbit of information about those who are in the entertainment world. Even some, sad to say, are wrapped up in just being busy. Running here, running there, involved in this and that, volunteering for everything and anything. People's lives are wrapped up in things, people, and circumstances! But as I observe and contemplate, I see few—yes, even believers in Jesus Christ—whose lives are wrapped up in the Son of God, Jesus Christ. I ask myself, why is this? I don't have all the answers for you, but this one thing I know, the Holy Spirit through the apostle John says in 1 John 5:11, "God has given us eternal life, and this life is in His Son." This eternal life that has been given to us is not just some promise for a future in heaven with Jesus, but it is life that is given to us now. This life that we as believers possess is in His Son. John puts it this way,

1 John 5:9-12

If we receive the witness of men, the witness of God is greater; for this is the witness of God which He has testified of His Son.
[10]He who believes in the Son of God has the witness in himself; he who does not believe God has made Him a liar, because he has not believed the testimony that God has given of His Son.
[11]And this is the testimony: that God has given us eternal life, and this life is in His Son. [12]He who has the Son has life; he who does not have the Son of God does not have life (1 John 5:9-12).

In our last lesson, we considered several questions: *Who is Born of God?* (vv 4, 5): Those who believe that Jesus is the Son of God and have overcome the world. *Who Bears Witness of Jesus?* (v 6): The Holy Spirit, who is true. *Who Bears Witness in Heaven?* (v 7): The Father, the Word, and the Holy Spirit. *Who Bears Witness on Earth?* (v 8): The Spirit, the water, and the blood. John has just written regarding the three witnesses in heaven and the three witnesses in earth, and now he adds three more witnesses that prove that Jesus is the Christ. He also writes regarding the outcome for both those who receive and those who reject the witness that Jesus is the Christ. In this lesson we'll see:

The Outcome of Those Who Receive the Witness that Jesus is the Christ (vv 9-12)
The Outcome of Those Who Reject the Witness that Jesus is the Christ (vv 10, 12)

The Outcome of Those Who Receive the Witness that Jesus is the Christ 1 John 5:9, 10a

If we receive the witness of men, the witness of God is greater; for this is the witness of God which He has testified of His Son (1 John 5:9).

Why does John say *if we receive* here? It is in the indicative mood in the Greek, so that it means as we do receive. The word *witness* refers to the evidence that has been given. John is referring here to the witness, or the record, that has been given which proves that Jesus is the Christ and that eternal life is in Him. The *witness of men* that John mentions was the very foundation that John set forth in this epistle when he began writing in 1 John 1:1-3. We saw then that John and the other apostles were eyewitnesses of Jesus. They saw Him; they touched him; they bore witness to the reality of who He is. So we have the witness of men, in addition to the witnesses we saw in our last lesson: the three witnesses in heaven: the Father, The Son, and The Holy Spirit; and the three witnesses on earth: the Spirit, and the water and the blood. We have been given a multitude of witnesses that Jesus is the Christ, and yet John says *the witness of God is greater*. What does John mean?

Remember in our last lesson we learned that according to the Old Testament Law, there had to be two to three witnesses to establish the fact that a crime had occurred. John says that if you will receive the witness of men, who are mere mortals, then you ought to receive the witness of God, who is immortal. He is greater in every way! God is greater or larger than any witness! John has already mentioned in 1 John 3:20 that God is greater than our heart and knows all things; he has already mentioned in 1 John 4:4 that He who is in us is greater than he who is in the world; and now he tells us that the witness of God is greater than the witness of men. John doesn't tell us why the witness of God is greater, but do you think he really needs to tell us? What is the witness of God? John answers that in the next phrase, *for this is the witness of God which He has testified of His Son*. Do we need any other witness than Almighty God Himself? When I was contemplating this phrase, my thoughts went to Christ's baptism when God's voice spoke from heaven, saying, "You are My beloved Son; in You I am well pleased" (Luke 3:22). I also thought of the Mount of Transfiguration when, again, God's voice spoke from heaven, saying "This is My beloved Son, in whom I am well pleased. Hear Him!" (Matthew 17:5). God has certainly testified of His Son. And so John continues on with the outcome for those who receive this witness that Jesus is the Christ, in verse 10.

> He who believes in the Son of God has the witness in himself; (1 John 10a)

John says those who believe in the Son of God have the witness in themselves. To *believe in the Son of God* means to entrust one's spiritual well being to Christ. The Greek tense is such that it means this belief in the Son of God happened at one time and has lasting results. It is a belief that is continuous, not sporadic. If one believes in the Son of God, then *he has the witness in himself.* What does that mean? It means we have the witness within our heart. It's what Paul describes in Romans 8:15-16: "For you did not receive the spirit of bondage again to fear, but you received the Spirit of adoption by whom we cry out, 'Abba, Father.' The Spirit Himself bears witness with our spirit that we are children of God." Ladies, those of us who have received the witness that Jesus is the Christ have assurance that we are children of God. This witness is in ourselves! The Spirit bears witness to this! This is the first outcome for those who receive the witness that Jesus is the Christ—they have the blessed assurance within themselves that they are children of God.

In a future lesson we'll be going over some valid tests from John's epistle that bear witness to the fact that we are redeemed, but in these verses we see that we do have the promise of the inner witness within ourselves. I am often asked if I ever doubt my salvation, and I can honestly say to you that since I truly committed my life to the Lordship of Jesus Christ, there has only been a time or two that I have questioned that commitment. Those occasions were the result of areas in my life where I needed to shore up my commitment to live right or because I had become absorbed in self-pity or some selfish desire. Before I committed my life to Christ, however, I often doubted that I was a believer. I should have listened to that inner unrest. Now, however, I have the inner witness in my heart that I am God's child. And in contrast to those who believe and have that assurance, John goes on to describe the outcome of those who do not believe.

The Outcome of Those Who Reject the Witness that Jesus is the Christ 1 John 5:10b

> he who does not believe God has made Him a liar, because he has not believed the testimony that God has given of His Son (1 John 10b).

The one who believes has the witness in himself, but *he who does not believe God*, John says, *has made Him a liar*. The Greek tense here indicates that this is a deliberate refusal to believe. This would indicate that the person has heard the truth but rejected it. Throughout Christendom, mankind has heard the Gospel. And there has always been one of two responses: reject or receive. Now, I know that many of you will say, "What about the doctrine of election? What about Acts 13:48, which states that, 'as many as had been appointed to eternal life believed'?" Certainly God is sovereign in election and salvation; however, man does have responsibility to hear and receive. The following passages are excellent for looking at the rejection of Christ that some had:

> Then He began to rebuke the cities in which most of His mighty works had been done, because they did not repent: "Woe to you, Chorazin! Woe to you, Bethsaida! For if the mighty works which were done in you had been done in Tyre and Sidon, they would have repented long ago in sackcloth and ashes. But I say to you, it will be more tolerable for Tyre and Sidon in the day of judgment than for you. And you, Capernaum, who are exalted to heaven, will be brought down to Hades; for if the mighty works which were done in you had been done in Sodom, it would have remained until this day. But I say to you that it shall be more tolerable for the land of Sodom in the day of judgment than for you" (Matthew 11:20-24).

So when Peter saw it, he responded to the people: "Men of Israel, why do you marvel at this? Or why look so intently at us, as though by our own power or godliness we had made this man walk? The God of Abraham, Isaac, and Jacob, the God of our fathers, glorified His Servant Jesus, whom you delivered up and denied in the presence of Pilate, when he was determined to let Him go. But you denied the Holy One and the Just, and asked for a murderer to be granted to you, and killed the Prince of life, whom God raised from the dead, of which we are witnesses. And His name, through faith in His name, has made this man strong, whom you see and know. Yes, the faith which comes through Him has given him this perfect soundness in the presence of you all. Yet now, brethren, I know that you did it in ignorance, as did also your rulers. But those things which God foretold by the mouth of all His prophets, that the Christ would suffer, He has thus fulfilled. Repent therefore and be converted, that your sins may be blotted out, so that times of refreshing may come from the presence of the Lord, and that He may send Jesus Christ, who was preached to you before" (Acts 3:12-20).

"You stiff-necked and uncircumcised in heart and ears! You always resist the Holy Spirit; as your fathers did, so do you. Which of the prophets did your fathers not persecute? And they killed those who foretold the coming of the Just One, of whom you now have become the betrayers and murderers, who have received the law by the direction of angels and have not kept it." When they heard these things they were cut to the heart, and they gnashed at him with their teeth (Acts 7:51-54).

And when they heard of the resurrection of the dead, some mocked, while others said, "We will hear you again on this matter" (Acts 17:32).

But when they opposed him and blasphemed, he shook his garments and said to them, "Your blood be upon your own heads; I am clean. From now on I will go to the Gentiles" (Acts 18:6).

Men and women were rejecting the gospel then and they still are today.[94] And John says those who reject Christ make God *a liar*. This is the first outcome for those who reject that Jesus is the Christ—they make God a liar. What does it mean to make God a liar? We know from Scripture that God does not lie, and so to deny the witness of His Son, which He has given record to, is to reject the truth which He has given. If you reject His Son, you have essentially said, "God, you are a liar! Your witness of your Son is not true and I don't believe you!" And we know from Revelation 21:8 that all liars will have their place in the lake of fire. By the way, John has already mentioned in 1 John 1:10 that we make God a liar when we say we have no sin. So, why does he make God a liar? *Because*, John says, *he has not believed the testimony that God has given of His Son*. John R. Stott explains, "Unbelief is not a misfortune to be pitied. It is a sin to be deplored. Its sinfulness lies in the fact that it contradicts the Word of the one true God and thus attributes falsehood to Him."[95] What is the *testimony* that John is referring to? He answers that question in verse 11.

The Outcome of Those Who Receive the Witness that Jesus is the Christ 1 John 5:11

> And this is the testimony: that God has given us eternal life, and this life is in His Son (1 John 5:11).

---

[94] Two kinds of professing Christians exist. One has actually rejected the Spirit's ministry of bearing witness concerning the Person of the Lord Jesus Christ and, hence, lacks the further confirming or deepening verification by the Spirit within him. But the other has received the record God has given concerning His Son and enjoys a maturing, deepening, enriching, comforting and assuring validation of what he initially believes. This is why, as the Apostle John said previously, those who depart from their faith that Jesus is the Christ, with the result of departing morally from obedient living and then departing physically from the local fellowship (cf. 1 John 19-19), prove that they were never genuine believers in the first place!

[95] John R. Stott, *Tyndale New Testament Commentary: The Letters of John* (Grand Rapids, MI: Eerdmans, 1988), p 185.

Here is the testimony: *that God has given us eternal life.* What is *eternal life*? Eternal life "includes both life after death and the full life in the present for those who are united to Christ by faith."[96] And John says this quality and quantity of life is available by only one way: *this life is in His Son.* Jesus made this very clear in the High Priestly Prayer in John 17:3: "And this is eternal life, that they may know You, the only true God, and Jesus Christ whom You have sent." John is speaking here of a personal relationship with Jesus Christ. This is the second outcome for those who receive the witness that Jesus is the Christ—they have eternal life. The wonderful thing about this eternal life is that it is not only in the future, but it is now. John continues these thoughts on eternal life by writing a statement that is basic but profound.

The Outcomes of Both Those Who Receive and Those Who Reject the Witness that Jesus is the Christ 1 John 5:12

> He who has the Son has life; he who does not have the Son of God does not have life (1 John 5:12).

This statement is pretty simple to understand. Having been given the witness or record of men and of God, then there is a choice to be made. Have the Son and have life, or reject the Son and reject life. The one *who has the Son has life*, and the one *who does not have the Son does not have life*. The *life* here is referring to a relationship with the Father and with His Son that is based on an embracing of Jesus as the Christ. Life here refers to a continuation of life. It is not just future but it is present. We have life now! This is the third outcome for those who receive the witness that Jesus is the Christ—they have life. This is also the second outcome for those who reject the witness that Jesus is the Christ—they don't have life.

---

96 Ibid, p 183.

Summary

We have considered *The Outcome of Those Who Receive the Witness that Jesus is the Christ* (vv 9-12): they have the blessed assurance within themselves that they are children of God; they have eternal life; and they have life now. And we have considered *The Outcome of Those Who Reject the Witness that Jesus is the Christ* (vv 10b, 12): they make God a liar; and they don't have life eternal or life now.

Wouldn't it make sense that if we have eternal life now and this life is in His Son that the Son should be our life? As I meditated on these verses, I recalled my observations in the introduction of this chapter as I reflected on people whose lives are wrapped up in things, people and circumstances. And I asked myself, "Why aren't the children of God wrapped up in the Son of God?" If God spared not His Son for you and for me, and gave us life eternal, then I would ask, "What are we doing with that life?" I'd like to close by looking at some very important and challenging passages. I'd like to leave you with four challenges for how to make sure that your life is wrapped up in the Son of God. This will be in the form of an acrostic, LIFE.

Live like Christ. "With Your hand from men, O LORD, from men of the world who have their portion in this life, and whose belly You fill with Your hidden treasure. They are satisfied with children, and leave the rest of their possession for their babes. As for me, I will see Your face in righteousness; I shall be satisfied when I awake in Your likeness." The Psalmist says, "Lord, men of the world are caught up in the world. Their lives are consumed with this earthly life. But as for me, Lord, I want to be consumed with You, to the point that I will be satisfied only with being like You!" (Psalm 17:14-15). Dear friends, are you consumed with this earthly life, or are you consumed with being like Jesus?

Invest in the eternal. "For bodily exercise profits a little, but godliness is profitable for all things, having promise of the life that now is and of that which is to come" 1 Timothy 4:8). Life, in its truest enjoyment, Paul explains, is not in going to the gym to work out but in pouring your life into what is yet to come. The eternal is what will last; the temporal will be gone tomorrow. Do the weekly activities you find yourself doing count for eternity, or will they be burned up in the end?

Fixate on Christ. "If then you were raised with Christ, seek those things which are above, where Christ is, sitting at the right hand of God. Set your mind on things above, not on things on the earth. For you died, and your life is hidden with Christ in God. When Christ who is our life appears, then you also will appear with Him in glory" (Colossians 3:1-4). Paul says that we should be dead to the world and all its temptations and pleasures. Our life is different; our life is hidden with Christ in God; our life is concealed or locked together with Christ. None of those others things should be able to break through that relationship we have with Christ. Again, I would ask you, "Is your life dead to the world and all it has to offer? Are you so tight with Christ that nothing the world has to offer can break through that relationship with Him?"

Escape the world's temptations. "No one engaged in warfare entangles himself with the affairs of this life, that he may please him who enlisted him as a soldier" (2 Timothy 2:4). Paul reminds us that no man or woman who is a soldier for Jesus Christ entwines or wraps himself or herself up in the affairs, the businesses and occupations of this life. Why? Because they want to please Him who has chosen them to be a good soldier. Would others view your life and say, "There goes a woman who is out to please the Lord and it manifests itself by what she is involved in"? Or, "There goes a woman who is so wrapped up in the affairs of this life, that she barely can give God a minute of her day"? Do you desire to live a life that is wrapped up in the Son? If you do, then live like Christ, invest in the eternal, fixate on Christ and escape the world's temptations.

Ladies, to know and to live for Jesus Christ is the greatest thing there is. What or who are you living for? What is your life wrapped up in this day? Why not wrap up your life in Jesus, God's Son? He is your life today; He is your life eternal.

Questions to Consider

Receive the Son and Live; Reject the Son and Die!

1 John 5:9-12

1. Read 1 John 5:9-12. What do you learn about God, the Son, and eternal life from these verses? Memorize 1 John 5:12.

2. (a) John mentions three witnesses in this passage. Who are they? (b) Jesus mentions five reliable witnesses in John 5:30-47. Who or what are they? (c) What reasons did Jesus give the Pharisees in John 8:12-27 that He could indeed bear witness of Himself? (d) Why do you think the witness of God is greater than the witness of men, as John mentions in 1 John 5:9? Prove your answer with Scripture.

3. (a) What do you think "witness" means? (b) Do you have the witness within yourself that you are a child of God?

4. (a) How do we make God a liar, according to what John says in 1 John 5:10? (b) In what other way do we make God a liar, according to 1 John 1:10? (c) What do you think it means to make God a liar?

5. How do John 3:36 and Mark 16:16 correlate with 1 John 5:12?

6. (a) Write down at least five reasons you can think of for why an unbeliever might reject the witness God gave in His Son, Jesus Christ? (b) Now write down your rebuttals to these reasons. (c) How can you use these when giving a defense of the Gospel to an unbeliever?

7. If others were to examine your life closely, how would they conclude that you believe the witness of God, and that you have the Son of life?

8. (a) Is there someone you know who has rejected the witness of God, and will you share with them again their need of a Savior? (c) Come with a prayer request for that soul.

Chapter 22

Three Absolutes

1 John 5:13-15

Modern technology, through the internet and television, has made the world to appear smaller, bringing the latest international news into our living rooms. This information has brought many uncertainties into our lives, especially relating to the Middle East. Nations are rising up in rebellion and overthrowing their governments, and you might be wondering, "Could the same thing happen here in the US?" There are also uncertainties about our economic future. The economies of many nations around the world are crumbling; people are losing jobs everyday. Many have lost millions in the stock market. So you might find yourself asking, "What about my future? Do I have enough to live if the Lord tarries?" There are also uncertainties about our family relationships. What about our husbands and our children? Will they die before we do? Will they get some dreadful disease? For those of you who are single, you might be wondering, "Will I ever get married?" For those who are childless, you might be asking, "Will I ever have children?" These and many more questions come to our minds when we think about our future and what it holds. There are even uncertainties about today, are there not? These questions—these uncertainties—cannot be answered, at least not by mortal man. But for the believer in Jesus Christ, there are certainties; there are things we can be certain of, things we don't have to wonder about. As we come to our text in 1 John, we will discover three certainties, three absolutes. Let's read the text and discover what they are.

1 John 5:13-15

> These things I have written to you who believe in the name of the Son of God, that you may know that you have eternal life,

> and that you may continue to believe in the name of the Son of God. [14]Now this is the confidence that we have in Him, that if we ask anything according to His will, He hears us. [15]And if we know that He hears us, whatever we ask, we know that we have the petitions that we have asked of Him (1 John 5:13-15).

In our last lesson we considered *The Outcome of Those Who Receive the Witness that Jesus is the Christ* (vv 9-12): they have the blessed assurance within themselves that they are children of God; they have eternal life; and they have life now. And we considered *The Outcome of Those Who Reject the Witness that Jesus is the Christ* (vv 10b, 12): they make God a liar; and they don't have life eternal or life now. Our outline for this lesson will include three absolutes:

We Can Know We Have Eternal Life (v 13)
We Can Know He Hears Our Prayers (v 14)
We Can Know He Answers Our Prayers (v 15)

John is continuing on with his theme of those who reject Jesus as the Christ and those who receive Him. Those who receive the witness that Jesus is the Christ not only have eternal life but they can also be absolutely sure about three things. Let's look together at absolute #1.

We Can Know We Have Eternal Life
1 John 5:13

> These things I have written to you who believe in the name of the Son of God, that you may know that you have eternal life, and that you may continue to believe in the name of the Son of God (1 John 5:13).

Verse 13 is the purpose statement of the epistle.[97] This is the main purpose for which John wrote 1 John. He wants the readers to know for certain that they have eternal life. *These things* would be the things John has written about in this epistle. He has already mentioned other reasons for which he writes, but verse 13 of chapter five states plainly the main reason for his writing this letter (see 1 John 1:4; 2:1; 2:13, 14, 21, 26). It is also interesting to note that John also has a purpose statement in the Gospel of John, in John 20:31, where he says, "But these are written that you may believe that Jesus is the Christ, the Son of God, and that believing you may have life in His name."

Notice in our text that John says he has written to those *who believe in the name of the Son of God.* This book is written to believers. So, why then did John write this book? The reason is actually two-fold. The first reason, he says, is so *that you may know that you have eternal life*. The Greek order is peculiar; it literally reads, "you may know that life you have eternal." The adjective *eternal* is added as an afterthought. Westcott has translated it: "that ye have life—yes, eternal life."[98] The word *know* does not mean "I hope so"; nor does it mean you have a growing assurance of your salvation. Instead, it is a word which indicates that this is an absolute assurance; you can know for sure you have eternal life. You need no longer doubt. This is Absolute Number One—we can know we have eternal life!

You might be asking, "Well, how can one know they have eternal life?" By the valid tests John has given! By self-examination, as Paul says in 2 Corinthians 13:5: "Examine yourselves as to whether

---

97 Commentators have differed on the connection of 1 John 5:13 with the paragraphs surrounding it. Actually, there is a good case for verse 13 being the concluding point of 1 John 5:6-12, along with being the summary theme of the whole epistle. English translators have differed: the KJV and NKJV contain verse 13 in the previous paragraph; the NASV, NIV and RSV place verse 13 at the beginning of a new paragraph. Perhaps it is best to see the passage as concluding the paragraph, beginning a new paragraph and summarizing the theme for the whole epistle.

98 *Vincent's Word Studies of the New Testament*, PC Study Bible Software.

you are in the faith. Test yourselves. Do you not know yourselves, that Jesus Christ is in you?—unless indeed you are disqualified." You might also be asking, "If John is writing to believers, then why do they have to examine themselves? Wouldn't those reading this epistle be believers?" John would hope so—just as I would hope that all of you who are doing this ladies' Bible study are believers. You would think that doing a Bible study would be a good indicator that they know God. But I can't assume that, just as John cannot assume that of those he's writing to. You and I should not presume that those who read the Word or study the Word know the Author of the Word. Scripture is filled with examples of those who did those things, and yet the Gospel accounts record where Jesus calls them blind leaders of the blind, hypocrites, fools, and names like those. Our Christianity is never proven by reading or studying the Word, or even by praying, but it is proven through a current examination of our lives. This is a good time to stop and do some self-examination in light of what we've learned in the epistle of 1 John, since we're nearing its end. As I've studied through 1 John, I've come up with 20 tests of self-examination.

1. *The test of joy*—1:4.
2. *The test of partnership or fellowship with Christ and the Father*—1:3.
3. *The test of confessing our sins*—1:9.
4. *The test of broken pattern of sinning*—2:1; 3:4-6; 3:8, 9; 5:18.
5. *The test of obedience*—2:3-5; 3:22-24; 5:2, 3.
6. *The test of walking as Christ walked*—2:6.
7. *The test of loving the brethren*—2:9-11; 3:10-18; 3:23; 4:7-12; 4:20-5:2.
8. *The test of overcoming the wicked one*—2:13, 14; 5:4, 18.
9. *The test of not loving the world*—2:15-17; 4:5.
10. *The test of persevering to the end*—2:19, 24.
11. *The test of the indwelling Holy Spirit*—2:20, 27; 3:24; 4:13.
12. *The test of belief*—2:23; 3:23; 4:2, 15; 5:1, 4, 5, 10, 13, 20.
13. *The test of abiding in Him*—2:27, 28; 4:16.
14. *The test of holy living*—2:29; 3:3, 7.
15. *The test of hatred from the world*—3:13.

16. *The test of answered prayer*—3:22; 5:14, 15.
17. *The test of overcoming false teachers*—4:4.
18. *The test of no fear in judgment*—2:28; 4:17, 18.
19. *The test of loving God*—4:19-5:2.
20. *The test of keeping ourselves from idols*—5:21.[99]

So John says, I have written to you—those who believe on the name of God—so that you might know for sure that you have eternal life. And then he adds his second reason for writing: *that you may continue to believe in the name of the Son of God.* At first this statement may sound strange, but the tense in the Greek renders it this way. John is saying, I'm not only writing to you that you might know for certain that you have eternal life, but I'm also writing that you might continue on believing in the name of the Son of God. *Believe in the name* refers to God's name, which is His authority or character. John is writing so that they will continue on in their belief in the name of Christ. John then moves from Absolute Number One to Absolute Number Two—God hears our prayers!

We Can Know God Hears Our Prayers 1 John 5:14

> Now this is the confidence that we have in Him, that if we ask anything according to His will, He hears us (1 John 5:14).

What does John mean when he says *the confidence that we have in Him*? The word *confidence* means outspoken, blunt, frank, and bold. Now ladies, this does not mean we can come to God commanding Him to do things, like I've heard some televangelists do. I once heard a man command God to give him something in the name of Jesus! I've seen things like that and I've been horrified! We petition, yes, but we must never demand! There is nothing in the meaning of the Greek word that would solicit such behavior. Bluntness, yes; demanding, no! There should be reverence when

[99] An expanded treatment of these tests of assurance can be found in my booklet, Assurance: *Twenty Tests for God's Children* (Bemidji, MN: Focus Publishing, 2012). www.focuspublishing.com

we approach God's throne. But even in our reverence we can come boldly. We must tell Him what is really on our hearts. We shouldn't even think we can hide things from Him—as though we really could! Hebrew 4:15, 16 reminds us that "we do not have a High Priest who cannot sympathize with our weaknesses, but was in all points tempted as we are, yet without sin. Let us therefore come boldly to the throne of grace, that we may obtain mercy and find grace to help in time of need." For example, your boldness might sound something like this: "Lord, you know I'm having a very hard time loving this person, especially after what they did. God, please help me!" Or it might sound something like, "God, it grieves me so that my family member remains in their lost condition. Lord, I can't stand the thought of them in hell. Please save them, Lord. Open their eyes!" John says this confidence or this boldness that we have is *in Him*. It actually is boldness toward God, and it is the idea that we are face to face with Him. What a wonderful truth! I don't have to go through a priest, and I don't have to go through Jesus' mother, but I can go directly to Him, face to face! (See also 1 John 2:28; 3:21; 4:17.) In the same way, Paul tells his readers in Ephesians 3:12, "in whom we have boldness and access with confidence through faith in Him."

So John says if we have confidence in Him, the result is *that if we ask anything according to His will, He hears us*. First of all, notice we have to *ask*. I've been in many counseling sessions with women where they're sharing about this or that problem, and at some point I ask, "Have you prayed about this?" And they will give me this look like, "Wow! I never thought of that!" Usually, I challenge even those who have prayed to fast and continue praying about their situation. Many want help or relief from their problems but don't want to do the hard work of prayer. As Elisabeth Elliott once said, "Prayer is irksome; we are reluctant to start and delighted to end." Many of us just want to complain about what we don't have, or how hard our lives are, or that God doesn't answer our prayers, but do we even ask? And how often do we ask? And how earnestly do we pray? And do we fast?

So let's first define what it means to ask. The word ask means to beg or to crave. It's a word that is used to describe the attitude of one who is an inferior toward someone who is their superior. For some of its scriptural usages, consider looking at the following passages: Matthew 7:7-10; Acts 3:2; Ephesians 3:20; James 1:6; 4:2, 3. In addition to these, it is also used five times in 1 John: 1 John 3:22; 5:14, 15 (twice), and 16. John says if we ask *anything*, and that is where too many people stop. They think, "Ask for anything?! Cool! I'll ask for a million dollars and I'll get it! I'll ask for perfect health and I'll get it! I'll ask for a new home and I'll get it!" But notice that John says if we ask anything *according to His will*, He'll hear us. So let's also define what according to His will means. *His will* means His pleasure or His desire. In my humble opinion, the problem with our modern day prayers is that we try to bring God's will down to our will, instead of lifting our will up to His.[100] Do we really ask according to His will? Do we ask, "Lord, this thing I'm asking You for, is it Your will? If it's not, then don't grant it, because Your Word says You will give good things to those who ask." I remember several years ago talking with a woman who shared with me how God had given her the home of her dreams—everything she asked for! And then she made a statement I have never forgotten; she said "God gave me my request but sent leanness to my soul." Of course, she borrowed that phrase from Psalm 106:15, where the Psalmist is talking about the Israelites, who were sick of the manna God was providing for them, and they cried and complained to Moses, to give them some flesh to eat. So God said, "Ok, I'll give them flesh," and so He sent quail to them. In fact, He said He would send the quail for an entire month and they would get so sick of it that it would come out of their nostrils and become loathsome to them! (Numbers 11). God gave them want they asked for but sent leanness to their souls, which means that their souls wasted away or were destroyed.

[100] "In Johannine writings there is frequently a condition attached to asking God. In John 14:14-16; 15:16; 16:23-26 the asking is to be done in the name of Jesus. In John 15:7 the petitioners must remain in Jesus and have His word remain in them. In 1 John 3:21-22 the basis for receiving is because we are keeping His commandments and doing what is pleasing in His sight." cf. Raymond E. Brown, *The Epistles of John* (Garden City, NY: Doubleday, 1982), p 609.

Ladies, is having that thing you're praying for more important than having a soul intent on Christ? It's something to think about, for sure! Jesus asks in Mark 8:36, "For what will it profit a man if he gains the whole world, and loses his own soul?" Zero! Ladies, there is no profit in that! The very day I was working on this lesson, I was asking the Lord for something that we had been asked to pray for, and while I was asking, I said, "Lord, You know what is best. If this is Your will, Lord, then grant it." Who are we to presume we know the mind of the Lord? As Paul says in Romans 11:34, "who has known the mind of the Lord? Or who has become His counselor?" His ways and His thoughts are certainly far above our ways and our thoughts.

You might be wondering, "So, why should I pray, anyway? I mean, how do I know if something is God's will or not? If God is sovereign, then why pray? Why does He need my feeble attempts?" Well, we pray because it is a command. It is simply not an option for a believer. Paul tells us in 1 Thessalonians 5:17 to pray without ceasing—which is a command! In fact, I don't know how Christians survive without it. We also pray because prayer is communion with God. Prayer is not just to be a "give me" time; it is worship and fellowship and communion with the living God. I like what one man has said, that perhaps will help us to understand why we should pray: "Through prayer we make ourselves instruments of God's will, and at the same time, in a manner that lies beyond human comprehension, he is able to act powerfully to answer our prayers."[101] And if none of that helps you, perhaps a quote by C.S. Lewis will: "I pray because I can't help myself. I pray because I'm helpless. I pray because the need flows out of me all the time—waking and sleeping. It doesn't change God—it changes me."[102]

So if we ask according to His will, John says, *He hears us*. Wow! What a deal! The God of the Universe hears our prayers. What does it mean that He hears us? It means that He listens

[101] I. Howard Marshall, *The Epistles of John* (Grand Rapids, MI: Eerdmans, 1978) p 245.

[102] Quote from the film *Shadowlands*, the story of C. S. Lewis and his wife Joy, who becomes ill with cancer and dies.

attentively and favorably and considers our requests seriously—just like a parent would consider a child's request, if it was reasonable. I remember as our children got to be teenagers that they would often petition us, as their parents, regarding certain things they wanted to do. And as parents we listened to them, considering what they said. Sometimes we granted their petitions, if we felt led to do so and if it would not endanger them in any way; other times we said no, being convinced it would not be a wise decision. That's the idea here. God hears our prayers if we ask according to His will. I remember once speaking to someone who was going through a very difficult trial, and she said, "Susan, I don't even know how to pray for so and so." And I said, "You can always pray for the will of the Lord to be done." I'm comforted by the following verses: John 9:31, "Now we know that God does not hear sinners; but if anyone is a worshiper of God and does His will, He hears him;" and Psalm 34:17, "The righteous cry out, and the LORD hears, and delivers them out of all their troubles." So, Absolute Number Two—God hears our prayers! Its one thing to realize that God Almighty hears us, but then John tells us something that is equally incredible: not only does He hear us, but He also grants our petitions!

We Can Know God Answers Our Prayers
1 John 5:15

> And if we know that He hears us, whatever we ask, we know that we have the petitions that we have asked of Him (1 John 5:15).

John is saying since *we know that He hears* our prayers, then *whatever we ask*, we have! *We have the petitions*, the requests, *we have asked of Him*; we have obtained them. Now the Greek word here is pretty exciting; it is in the present tense, which means that God has granted our request even though the answer may not be immediately revealed. We have the thing we've asked for now, though it may not be granted until a future time. Literally, it reads, "We know that we possess the asked-for things that we asked for from Him." This is one of the reasons I am a big advocate of keeping a prayer journal; I like to record certain things I am praying for on a daily basis and then go back and record answers and see what God has done. You know, many times the Lord does not answer those petitions immediately, but much later, sometimes even years later. But He does answer. And so I would encourage you to do that! We have prayers recorded for us in the Scriptures and we can see where God heard and answered. Doesn't that encourage you? It encourages me, and it gives me hope as I see God answer prayer in my own life. Now, I know some of you might be thinking, "Okay what's the deal? I do pray, and I think I'm asking in accordance with the will of God, and yet I can say that He hasn't granted my petitions. Why?" Let me give you four reasons why God may not be answering your prayers. They all start with the word know.

1. *Know God.* Make sure you know God. Remember John 9:31? "Now we know that God does not hear sinners; but if anyone is a worshiper of God and does His will, He hears him." God is not obligated to answer the prayers of those who are not His children.

2. *Know the conditions of answered prayer.* I would encourage you to go back over question number four in the "Questions to Consider" and make sure that your prayers are in line with the conditions God has set forth in His Word.

3. *Know that God sometimes says "no."* God sometimes says "no," just as parents sometimes tell their children "no." And perhaps, just like children, you aren't content with "no." Remember Christ in the garden of Gethsemane asking the Lord if it would be possible to let the cup pass from Him? But then He said that He wanted the Father's will and not His own (Mark 14:36). I'm grateful that the Father did not answer the Son's request to have the cup removed; if He had, none of us would have eternal

life. Or what about Paul, in 2 Corinthians 12:7-9? He had some thorn in his flesh, and we're not sure what it was, but He asked God three times to take it away. God said "no." But he didn't leave Paul with "no" only. He said, "My grace is sufficient for you, Paul. My strength is made perfect in your weakness, Paul." God's grace was sufficient for Paul just as God's grace was sufficient for Christ on the cross.

4. *Know that God's timing is perfect.* Perhaps you are praying for something, but it isn't the right time. Are you trying to sell a house? Are you praying about it? Perhaps it is not happening on your timetable but it will happen on God's timetable. As the writer of Ecclesiastes says, in Ecclesiastes 3:11, "He has made everything beautiful in its time." Instead of selling your house right away, God might want to teach you trust or patience first. Perhaps He has answered your prayer, but you haven't yet seen it, or perhaps it hasn't been answered in the way that you expected. And that is where I would encourage you to keep a prayer journal and continue to trust in Him. But ladies, absolutely, you can be sure that God answers your prayers! This is Absolute Number three—God answers prayer!

Summary

In these uncertain times, we can be certain about three things. First of all, *We Can Know We Have Eternal Life* (v 13). Are you assured of your eternal destination? If not, why not make sure of that today? Secondly, *We Can Know God Hears Our Prayers* (v 14). Do you pray? Does God hear your prayers? If not, why not? Thirdly, *We Can Know God Answers Our Prayers* (v 15). Does God answer your prayers? What prayers has He answered this week? If He hasn't answered your prayers, have you paused long enough to ask yourself why? There is no reason for you and me to be uncertain in these uncertain times! Why? Because God has made these three promises to us: the promise of eternal life, the promise that He hears our prayers, and the promise of answered prayer—all given by a God who does not lie!

Questions to Consider

Three Absolutes

1 John 5:13-15

1. (a) According to 1 John 5:13-15, what three things can we be certain about? (b) Are you certain about these things?

2. Memorize 1 John 5:13.

3. John says in 1 John 5:13 that we can know we have eternal life. (a) What evidences has John given so far in 1 John whereby we can know for sure that we are children of God? (b) What are some other ways we can know for certain that we are born of God, according to Romans 8:15-17, Galatians 4:6 and 2 Peter 1:4-11?

4. John indicates, in 1 John 5:14 and 15, that we can be assured that God answers prayer. (a) According to the following passages, what might be some of the reasons that God does not answer prayer? Proverbs 21:13; Proverbs 28:9; John 9:31; John 14:13; John 15:7; James 1:5, 6; 4:1-3; 1 Peter 3:7; 1 John 3:21, 22. (b) What changes do you need to make, in light of these passages, in order for God to hear and answer your prayers?

5. Read at least *two* of the prayers from the following passages: 1 Samuel 1 and 2; 1 Kings 8:22-53; 2 Chronicles 20; Nehemiah 9; Daniel 9:3-19; Matthew 6:9-13; Ephesians 1:15-21; Ephesians 3:14-21; Philippians 1:9-11 and Colossians 1:9-14. (a) How do these prayers compare with the way we pray today? (b) In what way(s) do you think your own personal prayers need to change after looking over these prayers?

6. From *one* of the above prayers, answer the following questions: (a) What petitions were made? (b) Were they granted? (c) What principles will you apply to your own prayer life?

7. (a) Write down at least 10 things you are asking the Lord for. (b) How has the Lord answered these requests? (If He hasn't answered yet, keep this list so that you can record later how and when He has answered them.)

8. (a) Do you know for sure that you are a Christian? (b) What assurance do you have? (c) Do you know for sure that God hears your prayers? (d) How do you know that? Does He answer your prayers? (e) What is at least one prayer He has answered this week?

9. What do you desire from God? Write it down in a prayer to Him to share.

Chapter 23

Final Wonders! Final Warnings!

1 John 5:16-21

Most of us have engaged in conversations in which someone will say to us, "I've got some good news and some bad news …" and then they usually follow it up with the question, "Which one do you want first, the good news or the bad news?" As we come to our final lesson in 1 John, John has some good news for us and some bad news for us. But he doesn't ask which one we want first. Instead, he mingles the good and the bad news together. See if you can discover these as you read the text.

1 John 5:16-21

> If anyone sees his brother sinning a sin which does not lead
> to death, he will ask, and He will give him life for those who
> commit sin not leading to death. There is sin leading to death. I
> do not say that he should pray about that. 17All unrighteousness
> is sin, and there is sin not leading to death. 18We know that
> whoever is born of God does not sin; but he who has been born
> of God keeps himself, and the wicked one does not touch him.
> 19We know that we are of God, and the whole world lies under
> the sway of the wicked one. 20And we know that the Son of
> God has come and has given us an understanding, that we may
> know Him who is true; and we are in Him who is true, in His
> Son Jesus Christ. This is the true God and eternal life. 21Little
> children, keep yourselves from idols. Amen (1 John 5:16-21).

In our last lesson we discovered three absolutes: *We Can Know We Have Eternal Life* (v 13); *We Can Know God Hears Our Prayers* (v 14); and *We Can Know God Answers Our Prayers* (v 15). Instead of calling our final lesson, "Good News, Bad News," I've entitled it, "Final Wonders! Final Warnings!" because in our text we'll find:

Four Final Wonders (vv 16, 18-20)
Four Final Warnings (vv 16, 17, 19, 20)

John has just been talking about prayer in verses 14 and 15, and now he gives us something specific to pray about—a brother who is in sin! Prayer is not just about us; it is also about others. And this is one way we show love to the brethren, as John has admonished us to do numerous times. Let's look at the first final wonder, as well as the first final warning.

First Final Wonder and First Final Warning
1 John 5:16

> If anyone sees his brother sinning a sin which does not lead to death, he will ask, and He will give him life for those who commit sin not leading to death. There is sin leading to death. I do not say that he should pray about that (1 John 5:16).

The Greek word for *brother* is adelphos, which means a Christian brother, one who is alike or of the same kind.[103] So John is saying that if you see your brother sinning a sin which is not unto death, you shall *ask, and He*, meaning God, *will give him life for those who commit sin not leading to death.* The word *sees* means that you know this brother is in sin; you are not just guessing he is, but you know it for a fact. This means, ladies, that you don't take your best friend's word for it, but you have investigated the fact that this person

---

[103] Identifying the sinning one as a *brother* (Greek, adelphon) suggests this is a believer. cf. Westcott, p 198; Nicoll, Vol. 5, p 198; Thayer, p 11; Brown, pp 617-618; MacArthur, p 1974 of *MSB*. Nowhere in the Epistles of John does he ever use adelphos to refer to the unbeliever or to a professing believer who simply has a spurious faith. Others see adelphos in 1 John 5:16 as simply a professing Christian, who is not necessarily regenerate. They see *life* (Greek, zoen) as eternal life, speaking of their conversion; they also claim that John uses adelphos to refer to unsaved professing believers, in 2:9, 11; 3:10, 17; and 4:10. This is similar to Paul's reference to the "so-called brother" (cf. 1 Cor. 5:11) and "false brethren" (cf. 2 Corinthians 11:26; Galatians 2:4). The weakness of this view is that nowhere is adelphos a reference to a spurious believer in the Epistle of First John or in all of Johannine literature. The motivation for the spurious Christian view seems to be to harmonize it with 1 John 3:4-10.

is sinning or you have personally seen them sinning. Evidently, this is a sin that has not been repented of, one in which the individual is continuing.[104] And John adds that this is *a sin which does not lead to death*. Evidently, there are sins which lead to physical death and there are sins which do not lead to physical death. The Jews would understand this. Consider the following passages: Leviticus 10:1-7, Numbers 15:30-36; Deuteronomy 21:18-22; 22:25, 26; Joshua 7:25, 26. And even when we come to the New Testament, we have the account of Ananias and Sapphira, in Acts 5:1-11, who together lied about money they had kept back from the sale of some of their land, and they were both struck dead for their sin. In addition to that, 1 Corinthians 11:30 is specifically about people who have died for taking the Lord's supper in an unworthy manner. So there are *sins leading to death*, and there are sins *not leading to death*.[105]

Now, how does one know if they are sinning unto death or not? That I do not know. But I do think that's why John reminds us in verse 17 that all unrighteousness is sin. Some might be tempted to think, "Oh well, God would only take me home for the big ones, like adultery or murder." But John says no, all unrighteousness is sin. Ladies, we should never be comfortable with sinning, and we should never tempt God. As John Owen once said regarding sin: "Do you mortify? Do you make it your daily work? Be always at it while you live. Cease not a day from this work; be killing sin or it

---

[104] The Apostle affirms that genuine believers do not continue practicing sin; spurious believers practice sin. Even Charles Ryrie admits that sin may enter the experience of the saved person but it is not the rule of his life. If sin is the ruling principle of a life, that person is not saved. (cf. *Ryrie Study Bible,* p 1019) The distinction here is between acts of sin or its ongoing practice.

[105] The Old Testament made a distinction between deliberate sins and undeliberate sin. There were sacrifices for sins offered for undeliberate sins (cf. Numbers 15:30-31; Leviticus 4:13, 22, 27; 5:15, 17; Deuteronomy 17:2; Psalm 19:13). But for willful sinning, there was no sacrifice or possibility of atonement, so they were known as "deadly sins" (cf. Hebrews 6:4-5; 10:26-31). This is the Apostle John's intended meaning, as he assumes that the praying believer may have some confusion concerning the state of this sinning brother, i.e., he/she has no idea if the sin is a willful or high-handed persistence in sinning. God reads the intent of the heart and knows the willful persistent mind set to sin, calling upon his temporal judgment of death, which is His perfect will.

will be killing you."[106] (Remember the guy in Numbers 15:36 who was stoned for gathering sticks on the Sabbath day?!)

So we have the responsibility as believers to ask or pray for the believer who is sinning. The person who knows his brother is sinning prays and asks God for his brother's repentance. By the way, this is a prayer we can pray in confidence as we saw in verse 14, as this is a prayer that would be according to God's will, as we know it is not His will for His children to be sinning. This is the first final wonder—you and I have the awesome privilege to pray for a sinning believer.

So you pray, knowing it to be God's will, and if he or she repents, then he is restored to *life*. In fact the word for life here refers to physical life; God doesn't take their physical life. In other words, he or she repents and God does not take him home. Now John is talking about *praying* for the sinning brother, but I want to bring out that according to Galatians 6:1, 2 and Mathew 18:15 we should also *go* to the brother or sister who is sinning. Prayer is a part of the process and it is important, but so is our going to the person and lovingly confronting them. However, John continues by saying *there is a sin leading to death. I do not say that he should pray about that*. Now you might thinking, "That seems like a contradiction. First, John tells us to pray about it, and then he says don't pray about it!" It is not a contradiction when we look more closely. The first word, ask, means to pray: he will ask, and He will give him life. The second word, pray, means to inquire: I do not say that he should pray about that. The literal rendering is, "Not about that do I say that he should ask." We have no right to question a Sovereign God when He says enough is enough. It's like Ananias and Sapphira. Some might think that God was unfair to kill them, wondering why He didn't give them a chance to repent. John is saying we don't have a right to ask regarding that, the sin unto death. He's saying don't question

[106] William H. Good, Editor, *The Works of John Owen*, "On the Mortification of Sin in Believers" (Edinburgh: Banner of Truth Trust, 1981), p 9.

God about that. God is God and He can do as He pleases. Who has known His mind or who has been His counselor? Evidently, there are times when God has had enough with a sinning brother, and this sin leads him to physical death. This is the first final warning—there is a sin unto death! Speaking of sin, John goes on to give us the second final warning in verse 17.

Second Final Warning and Second Final Wonder 1 John 5:17, 18

> All unrighteousness is sin, and there is sin not leading to death (1 John 5:17).

The second final warning is that all unrighteousness is sin! Just in case there might be some who are reading this epistle and thinking, "Oh, this little bit of gossip isn't so bad; God wouldn't kill me for this." Or, "Not submitting to my husband in this area, that isn't so bad; God wouldn't take me home for that." Or, "Just because I don't obey God in this one little area that no one knows about, that isn't so bad." John says no, it is bad; all unrighteousness is sin. Or, as James says in James 4:17, "Therefore, to him who knows to do good and does not do it, to him it is sin." Now, this would be a rebuke to the Gnostics, who said that it didn't matter what you did in the body because you weren't responsible for it. But John reminds them that, yes, you are responsible for what you do in that body and it is sin and it could lead to your physical death. And then he adds *and there is sin not leading to death*. Obviously, we all sin, and we all will die. But those who keep on sinning are heading for a physical death as a direct result of their sin. John is perhaps reminding his readers here of the terrible reality and awfulness of sin but also the mercy of God, in that there is sin which is not unto death. God does forgive and restore us. If it weren't for the grace of God we would all be dead. So, after the reminder that all unrighteousness is sin, John reminds them again, as he already has in this letter several times, that those who are born of God do not remain in a sinful habit of life. And here we have our second final wonder.

> We know that whoever is born of God does not sin; but he who has been born of God keeps himself, and the wicked one does not touch him (1 John 5:18).

John has already mentioned earlier in his letter that those who are born of God do not sin (1 John 3:4-10). He's very clear that the person who claims to be a Christian and yet has an ongoing pattern of sin in their life proves to be a spurious Christian, one who does not have a regenerated heart. Instead of remaining in a pattern of sin, John says, *he who is born of God keeps himself.* God keeps us; we do not keep ourselves. The word *keep* means to watch, guard, and not allow to escape. How does God keep us? Well, according to John 17:11, He keeps us through His name. And according to 1 Peter 1:5, He keeps us by His power. Ladies, this is a marvelous truth! As Jude 24 states, He "is able to keep you from stumbling, and to present you faultless before the presence of His glory with exceeding joy." The one who is born of God is not only kept by Him, but also, John says, *the wicked one does not touch him*. The *wicked one* we know is Satan. John has already spoken of him in 1 John 2:13, 14 and 1 John 3:12.

So, what does it mean that the wicked one *cannot touch us*? It means he cannot attach himself to us or harm or injure us. It is actually the strongest word you can use for *touch* in the original language. It means to set on fire like rubbing two sticks together to start a fire. And the tense in which it's written gives it the meaning of constantly touching. Satan cannot touch us; it is impossible. Now, he can tempt us, and we are told that in the Scriptures, just as he tempted Christ in the wilderness. He can also deceive us, just as he deceived Eve in the garden. He is even allowed to afflict us, even as he was allowed to afflict Job. But he does not have power over those who are God's children. This is the second final wonder—we are kept by the power of God and Satan cannot touch us! John has already told us, in 1 John 4:4, that greater is He who is in us than he who is in the world. Satan is not in us; he is in the world. Believers can be influenced by Satan, but we cannot be possessed by Satan.

We are kept by God and sealed with the Holy Spirit of promise until the day of redemption. John continues on with this idea, and here we find the third of his final wonders and final warnings.

Third Final Wonder and Third Final Warning
1 John 5:19

> We know that we are of God, and the whole world lies under the sway of the wicked one (1 John 5:19).

John's third final wonder is that we can know we are of God. And his third final warning is that the whole world lies in wickedness. How do we *know that we are of God*? John has given us numerous reminders of how we can know for sure that we are of God, which we covered in our last lesson. Each one of us should know for sure if we are of God. We already have seen from verse 13 of this chapter, that this is the reason John wrote this epistle—that we might know that we have eternal life. And then John adds *and the whole world lies under the sway of the wicked one*. In contrast to those who know God, we have the *whole world* that lies in wickedness. What does this mean? It means that the complete world lies outstretched in wickedness. *Lies* is an interesting word; it means to put or to place, and it entails that the thing put or placed is there because someone else put it or placed it there. It is used of Jesus lying in the manger. Someone else, namely Mary or Joseph, put Him there. In other words, the whole world is lying in wickedness because of Satan. The world is helplessly held under the influence of Satan. This is a sobering statement—that the world is lying in wickedness. John continues on with his fourth final wonder in verse 20!

Fourth Final Wonder and Fourth Final Warning
1 John 5:20, 21

> And we know that the Son of God has come and has given us an understanding, that we may know Him who is true; and we are in Him who is true, in His Son Jesus Christ. This is the true God and eternal life (1 John 5:20).

John says *we know that the Son of God has come.* John is saying that the Son of God has arrived and the effects of His arrival are still present. Of course, we know that John is speaking of the incarnation of Christ. This is nothing new, as John has been expressing this truth throughout his epistle (see 1 John 1:1-4; 3:5, 8; 4:2, 9, 10, 14; 5:1, 6-8). And not only has Christ come, but He also *has given us an understanding, that we may know Him who is true.* The Son of God has given us the *understanding*, or the deep thought, to know that God is true. Now this would go against what the Gnostics taught, as they claimed that knowledge of God could only come from some elite group of people who were in the know about these things. They taught that knowledge of God could not come from Christ! Never! But John says to them, "Nope! Sorry, guys. It came from Christ, the One whom you deny even came in the flesh." This is also a rebuke to the watered-down gospel theology of today, which says that I'm clever enough to believe in God, and that I've mustered up this faith I have. But ladies, it is not of us. The understanding that you and I know the One who is true came from the One who revealed Him, and that is Jesus Christ. You and I did not open our eyes and turn from darkness to light. Salvation is of God and God alone.

Now, this would also have a secondary meaning, as we know and have learned in 1 John that the one who knows God will also understand spiritual truth. We are given the capacity to understand spiritual truth by God. It is God who gives us the understanding to know that He is true. The word *know* here that John mentions in verse 20 is a continuing and progressive knowledge. We are continuing to grow in that knowledge of who God is. We can know Him who is true! What a wonderful blessing, especially in light of the wicked one and the wickedness that John has mentioned in verses 18 and 19. Well, not only do we know Him, but we are also *in Him who is true. In Him* represents a relation of rest; it speaks of the intimate union we have with Christ. John adds that this relationship is *in His Son Jesus Christ*. And then John states that *this is the true God and eternal life*. What is the true God and eternal life? God the Father is true. And God the Father is eternal life; He is perpetual life. What a marvelous final wonder! The fourth final wonder is that God has come and given us the ability to know Him and to have eternal life! And with that, John turns his thoughts to the false gods, the idols, and ends his letter with his fourth and final warning!

> Little children, keep yourselves from idols. Amen (1 John 5:21).

Note the tenderness in John's words: *little children*, little teknion, little born ones of God. John uses this term of endearment one more time before he ends with his final words to them. And then he gives the fourth and final warning—keep yourselves from idols. John says *keep yourselves*; watch, be on guard regarding idols. What is an *idol*? And idol is an image, a heathen god, a form, an appearance. Anything that takes the place of God or occupies your heart is an idol. Anything that cools your affection for God is an idol. Anything that keeps you from making a full commitment to Christ is an idol. By the way, this is a command and it is given in a firm tone, as represented by the aorist tense. Now the question comes to mind, "What idols is John talking about? Is he talking about literal idols?" That is a possible interpretation. In Acts 19, we have the account of a certain idol that is in the city of Ephesus, the city in which John's original readers were living. John is writing 1 John to the church at Ephesus, a city known for its idolatry. Ephesus had hundreds of idols, and the Temple Of Diana, one of the great wonders of the ancient world, was there. Diana was not regarded as a virgin but as a mother and foster-mother, as was clearly displayed by the multitude of breasts with which she was commonly depicted. She was a representative of the same power over fertility that was adored in Israel in the worship of the goddess Ashtoreth, mentioned in 1 and 2 Kings. Her worship was frantic and fanatical, in the same way that it was in Asia, and it was traced all the way back to the Amazons. Her temple at Ephesus was one of the wonders of the world, but its great glory was the "image which fell down from heaven." Ephesus was a city of astrology, sorcery, exorcism and magic. Those who were the original readers of 1 John lived in this city, so it would be especially difficult for them to keep themselves from idolatry when it was so predominant in their community. Nonetheless, John says they are to keep themselves from idols.

Now, there is a second possible interpretation. The idols that John is mentioning could be not only the literal idols in Ephesus but also the false gods or false idols which are represented by the Gnostic teachers. John has already warned them about the false teachers in 1 John 2:18-27 and 4:1-6. The Gnostics were false teachers and thus represented false gods or idols. In fact, throughout the epistle John has referred to the Gnostics as being in darkness, of the evil one, unrighteous, liars, antichrists, seducers, deceivers, sinners, transgressors of the law, children of the devil, murderers, false prophets, and of the world. Sounds like idolatry to me; does it to you? John says keep yourselves away from them; you are in a dangerous situation if you listen to them and follow their teachings. So John could be saying keep yourself away from the literal idols in Ephesus, like Diana. But he could also be saying keep yourself away from the Gnostics and their idolatrous teaching. Both are true and both should be heeded.

There is also a third possibility, that an idol is anything that replaces God or anything from which one seeks happiness, other than God. Ezekiel talks about idols of the heart in Ezekiel 14:3. Evidently, the elders in Israel to whom Ezekiel writes not only had idols in their houses and in their streets but also in their hearts. So there are other forms of idolatry. Anything that keeps you from being fully committed to God is idolatry. Some possible idols of our hearts are: pleasure, a successful career, a goal, a desire, business, wealth, fame; material possessions like a fine house, furniture, cars, boats, or jewelry; friendships, family relationships; self-love, pride, good health, physical appearance; having a Christian marriage, being treated fairly, having a hurt-free, pain-free life; worldly pleasures such as drugs, alcohol, sex, children, money, success; another person, the approval of others, being in control, have your needs met; sleep, work, television, reading, food, shopping, sports, exercise, recreation, hobbies; or even ministry as an escape. Now you might be thinking, "Woe is me; I am undone!" You might even be wondering, "How can I know if my heart is centered on Christ or if I am an idolater?" Well, perhaps the following questions would be helpful to ask yourself when determining whether or not you're committing idolatry.

1. *What is on your mind most of the time?*
2. *What do you long for or wish for?*
3. *What is really important to you?*
4. *What do you have your heart set on?*
5. *What or who has your deepest affection?*
6. *What is your ultimate priority?*
7. *What is your greatest fear?*

I also believe that a heart centered on Christ will have an attitude of repentance. What I mean by that is that you and I will be continually turning away from these idolatrous things. Also, there will be an ongoing faithfulness to the things of Christ. There will be faithfulness to the means of grace, i.e., the church, prayer, reading the scriptures, and fellowship with God's people. You might be thinking, "Well, what do I do if I realize I have an idol in my heart? What should I do if I am committing idolatry?" Ladies, idolatry is a very serious matter, and you must repent of it. There must be a turning away from these things. As Paul says in 1 Corinthians 10:13-14: "No temptation has overtaken you except such as is common to man; but God is faithful, who will not allow you to be tempted beyond what you are able, but with the temptation will also make the way of escape, that you may be able to bear it. Therefore, my beloved, flee from idolatry." Too often we quote verse 13, but leave out verse 14, where Paul says to flee from idolatry. Paul is saying, "Run away," which is perhaps what some of us literally need to do. Some of us need to take drastic measures to get away from the idols that are taking away our devotion to Christ. Idolatry is a very serious matter, and John makes it very clear as he closes his letter.

Why do we cling to these things when we can know the true God, as John says in verse 20? Idols are passing; God is eternal! And then John ends by saying *Amen*, which means firm or trustworthy. It's interesting to note is that all the New Testament books end with Amen except Acts, James and 3 John.

Summary

As John brings his epistle to a close, he gives his readers and us *Four Final Wonders* (vv 16, 18-20) and *Four Final Warnings* (vv 16, 17, 19, 20). As we close our study of John's epistle, let's consider how we might apply the truths we've learned in this final lesson. Do you want the good news or the bad news first? Let's take the bad news first, and then I'll close with the good news!

Let's take the final warnings first. *The first warning is that there is a sin unto death.* So I ask you, are you walking in obedience? How tragic it would be to end your life sooner than planned because of sinning unto death. I've known people that I believe have sinned unto death. It is a very sobering reminder to me. We should also ask ourselves, do we know someone who is sinning? What are we doing about it? Have we prayed for them? Have we gone to them to lovingly warn them? If God has taken someone's life whom you know was sinning, did you question God's actions? *The second warning is that all unrighteousness is sin.* Do you view sin as ugly and abominable? Do you wink at sin? Do you think there are sins that God doesn't care about—little white lies, cheating a little, laziness, and the like? John says all unrighteousness is sin. *The third warning is that the whole world lies in wickedness.* What are you doing to protect yourself from the evil one? What about your husband or your children? Do you protect them from the wickedness that is in the world? Are the things you read wholesome and godly? What about your viewing habits? Do you protect your eyes from watching things that are ungodly? What about your relationships? Are they godly? Are they wicked? Who do you spend the bulk of your time with? Would that we all had the attitude of David in Psalm 101, where he vows that he will set no wicked thing before his eyes and that he will destroy all the wicked of the land. *The fourth warning is to keep ourselves from idols.* Is there anything or anyone that is keeping you from being fully devoted to Christ? Run, my dear sister, run!

Now for the final wonders! *The first wonder is that you and I have the privilege of praying for sinning believers.* Prayer is such a privilege and one that we often take for granted. I would encourage you to spend time in prayer, and especially for those whom you know are sinning. Remember the individual mentioned in James 5, who was evidently sick because of sin? James writes to the elders of the church and exhorts them to pray for him that he might be healed. The effectual prayer of a righteous man avails much. And I would add that the effectual, red-hot, fervent prayer of a righteous woman avails much! Do you know someone who is in sin, and are you praying for them? *The second wonder is that believers are not under the power of sin or of the wicked one.* Ladies, the power of sin has been broken. We have been made servants of righteousness and of God. We are no longer servants of sin and of Satan. Do you believe that? Does your life show it? *The third wonder is that we can know we are of God.* You no longer have to doubt about your eternal state. You can know beyond a shadow of a doubt that you are of God. Do you have that absolute assurance that you are God's child? *The fourth wonder is that God has come and has given us the ability to know Him and to have eternal life!* The incarnate Christ has come and given us the ability to know Him and to have eternal life and live with Him forever! It is my deepest desire that, as we have been with the Master before the mirror, you have looked into the mirror of His Word and discovered that you know Him, the only true God and Jesus Christ!

Questions to Consider

Final Wonders! Final Warnings!

1 John 5:16-21

1. Read 1 John 5:16-21. (a) What are the sober reminders that John mentions in these few verses? (b) What do you think they mean? (c) What are the encouraging reminders? (d) What do you think they mean? Memorize 1 John 5:21.
2. (a) What do you think "sin leading to death" means? (b) Give some biblical examples of those who you think sinned unto death. (c) What do you learn by their examples?
3. John says, in 1 John 5:18, that the wicked one does not touch those who are born of God (a) What do you think this means? (b) Do you think a believer can be possessed by demons? Prove your answer biblically.
4. (a) What kind of wickedness is the world involved in, according to Romans 1:28-32, Romans 3:9-18, Ephesians 2:1-3, Titus 3:3 and 1 Peter 4:1-3? (b) What type of power does Satan have over the world, according to Ephesians 2:2 and 6:12? (c) In what ways do you see the world today "lying in wickedness"? (d) How do you protect yourself and those you love from "the evil one"?
5. (a) What "idols" do you think John is referring to 1 John 5:21? (b) Why is it imperative that we keep ourselves from idols, according to the following passages? Exodus 20:3-5; Psalm 106:36; Psalm 115:4-8; 2 Corinthians 6:16; Galatians 5:19-21. (d) Do you think idols are only images made with one's hands? Prove your answer biblically.
6. (a) What are some "idols" that tempt you to not be committed to Christ and Christ alone? (b) What practical steps can you take to overcome them?
7. (a) Are you aware of anyone who is in sin? (No names please.) (b) What will you do about it after this lesson?
8. (a) How do you know God is true? (b) Do you know Him who is true? If not, please make sure of this most important commitment today!
9. (a) What has this final lesson taught you? What changes do you need to make? Write your need in the form of a prayer request.

Appendix A

Two Major Interpretations of 1 John 1:9
By Douglas V. Heck

First John 1:9 is a much discussed passage with two major interpretations: The *Fellowship View* of confession of sin. This view is probably the most popular today, and sees this verse as a remedy for broken fellowship with God. This view holds that the contrast in 1 John 1:5-2:1 is between Christians who are in the light and Christians who are in darkness. However, this paragraph is not a contrast between different types of Christians, but between those who claim to have eternal life and those whose lives pass the test of genuine faith. They hold that the theme of First John is temporal fellowship with God, and John is giving the steps to maintain this temporal fellowship. In order to hold this view, there is an emphasis on an eternal as well as a temporal fellowship and an eternal as well as temporal forgiveness.

The weakness of the Fellowship View is the demand that fellowship is the theme of First John, which cannot be supported by internal evidence. They also are forced to give a contemporary definition of *fellowship*, and ignore the New Testament and historical meaning of the koinonia word group. If fellowship simply means an activity of intimacy or communion between man and God, then the purpose statement of 1 John 1:3 offers some (although weak) support for this position. For this view to have validity, fellowship must have a temporal aspect, which is not supported by the uses of the koinonia word group in the New Testament.

The *Descriptive View* of confession of sin sees 1 John 1:9 as describing a characteristic fact in the life of a true believer. First John's theme statement is mentioned toward the close of the epistle (5:13), similar to John's style of theme identification in his Gospel, toward the close of the book (John 20:30-31). The theme concerns tests to validate genuine faith, resulting in the assurance of eternal life and continual faith. Just as *continual faith* is an evidence of eternal life (cf. 1 John 5:

1, 5, 10), so *confession* is a necessary evidence of eternal life. Confession of sins is characteristic of the Christian life! A characteristic of an unbeliever is their denial of sin. This confession is continuous, whether conscious or subconscious. There is no condition to God's forgiveness and cleansing of the believer's sin, as 1 John 2:1-2 suggests there are no conditions for the advocacy of Christ. Notice that the verb is not in the imperative mood of command; instead, John is declaring a characteristic of a true believer. This second view is the intended meaning of the Apostle John, according to the governing main point of 1 John 5:13.

Appendix B

On the Extent of the Atonement
(See Chapter 3)
By Douglas V. Heck[107]

We recognize the phrase, "And He Himself is the propitiation for our sins, and not for ours only but also for the whole world", 1 John 2:2, has been one of the great theological battlefields of the New Testament. While we do not believe that in the Apostle John's day this was a debated passage, since at the time there was no argument concerning the extent of the Atonement, we do believe that it is necessary in our day to reflect upon it. Those who champion a *limited atonement* (i.e., Christ's death was particular, i.e., for the elect only) have needed to interpret this passage in view of their system.[108] Those who champion an *unlimited atonement* (i.e., Christ's death was general, i.e., for all mankind) have sought to use this passage to establish their point.[109] Without seeking to establish a particular theological system, the honest expositor must exegete the passage within its context. Both views are here presented with their arguments:

1. Some suggest that "the world" (Greek, tou kosmou) refers to the world of the elect, allowing for a limited atonement. It is argued that because the advocacy of Christ (v 1) is for believers only (cf. John 17:9), so the propitiation in 2:2 must be limited to

107 In each of the final Appendices, scripture quotations will be taken from the King James Version.

108 Lewis Berkhof summarizes the Limited Atonement view: "The Reformed position is that Christ died for the purpose of actually saving the elect, and the elect only. This is equivalent to saying that He died for the purpose of saving only those whom He actually applies the benefits of His redemptive work." cf. *Systematic Theology* (Grand Rapids, MI: Eerdmans Publishing Company, 1939), p 394. Advocates of the Limited Atonement position include: John Calvin, Martin Luther, John Knox, Jonathan Edwards, John Owen, Charles Hodge, Charles H. Spurgeon, A. W. Pink, John Murray, John R. W. Stott, J. I. Packer, James Montgomery Boice, S. Lewis Johnson, John MacArthur, Jr., and R. C. Sproul.

109 Modern advocates of the Unlimited Atonement position include: Lewis S. Chafer, John F. Walvoord, Charles Ryrie, Warren W. Wiersbe, David Hocking, etc.

the same believers. A possible explanation of this view sees John as the Apostle to the Jews (Galatians 2:9), who included with this clause the propitiation of Christ for the elect among the Gentiles. Those holding this view also point out that the word "world" (Greek, kosmos), like the English "all," may in the New Testament refer to "everyone without distinction" and not "everyone without qualification"[110] Although this is true (cf. Luke 2:1; John 1:10; Acts 11:28; 19:27; 24:5; Romans 1:8; Colossians 1:6; John 7:4; 12:19; 14:22; 18:20; Romans 11:12, 15, etc,.), it must first be proved that the term means "all without distinction" in 1 John 2:2. In his recently published First John commentary, Pastor MacArthur affirms this view:

> In Christ all national limitations were abolished (cf. Acts 11:18; Romans 1:17; 2:28-29). Jesus' propitiatory death is for all classes of God's elect, which He is calling out for His name "from every tribe and tongue and people and nation" (Revelation. 5:9; cf. John 10:16; Acts 15:14-18; 26:23; Romans 9:25-26; Titus 2:14). Christ's work on the cross atoned for all those who would be sovereignly drawn by God to repent and believe (cf. Romans 5:18), not for those believers only who constituted the church in John's day. However, His death did not atone for or satisfy divine justice regarding the unrepentant, unbelieving millions who will appear before the Judge at the great white throne, from where they will be sentenced to eternal judgment in the lake of fire (Revelation 20:11-15).[111]

The weakness of this view is twofold: First, John's writings take place while he was pastor of the Gentile church at Ephesus, which accounts for the lack of Old Testament references in First John and the universal nature of the Gospel of John. John obviously

---

[110] For example: A waitress may ask you at the end of your meal, "How was everything?" She is not using the term *everything* without qualification, i.e., she doesn't want to know your opinion on everything in your life. She uses the term without distinction, i.e., she wants to know how the food, service and atmosphere was. The context must determine if the term is without qualification or without distinction.

[111] cf. John MacArthur, Jr., *The MacArthur New Testament Commentary on First John* (Chicago, IL: Moody Press, 2007), pp 49-50.

was not at that time functioning as an "Apostle to the Circumcision" but ministering to Gentiles.

Secondly, as I. Howard Marshall points out, the previous clause (i.e., "he is the propitiation for our sins") has covered the sins of the elect. At this point John advances another thought which rules out the possibility that the death of Jesus is of limited efficacy.[112]

2. Others suggest that "the world" (Greek, tou kosmou) refers to the entire human race, suggesting an unlimited atonement. The central view is that, in the Epistle of First John, tou kosmou is an expression for the hostile pagan order in which human life is organized in opposition to the will of God. (cf. 1 John 2:15-1 7; 3:1, 13; 4:1, 3, 4, 5, 9, 14, 17; 5:4, 5, 19) Of the 22 usages of kosmos in 1 John, only 5 passages do not refer to the hostile pagan order in opposition to God, i.e., 4:1, 3, 9, 14 and 17. Excluding 1 John 2:2, in none of the other 21 usages of kosmos, does it refer simply to believers, or the elect. In the above 5 passages, the kosmos may refer to "nations" (Shedd) but this is not the normal usage. Hence the normal interpretation of tou kosmou, is unsaved humanity in contrast to saved humanity.

A second reason looks at John's emphasis on an unlimited atonement, i.e., Gospel of John 1:29; 3:16, 17; 12:32. View 2 is the Biblical position, teaching that Christ's propitiation was not limited to only the elect, but extended to all humanity. This demands an answer to the obvious question: "To what extent did Christ's propitiation extend to all humanity? How can we escape the implication of universalism or that all humanity must be saved?" Perhaps the best answer is summarized by Calvin who said, "Christ suffered sufficiently for the whole world but efficiently only for the elect."[113] R. C. Sproul sheds some light on this question in his book

---

[112] I. Howard Marshall. *The New International Commentary on the New Testament: The Epistles of John* (Grand Rapids, MI: Eerdmans Publishing Company, 1978), p 119.

[113] John Calvin, *Calvin's Commentaries: First John*, translation from Latin by John Owen (Grand Rapids, MI: Baker Book House, 1981 reprint), p 173. However, Calvin rejects that this is what is taught in 1 John 2:2, "Though then I allow that what has been said is true, yet I deny that it is suitable to this passage; for the design of John was no other

Grace Unknown: the Heart of Reformed Theology, in which he comments on 1 John 2:2, saying,

> To be sure, Christ's propitiation on the cross is unlimited in its sufficiency or value. In this sense Christ makes atonement for the whole world. But the efficacy of this atonement does not apply to the whole world, nor does its ultimate design.[114]

Pastor John MacArthur in an earlier opinion further suggests that there is a sense in which a temporal propitiation is made for the whole world. He writes:

> The passages which speak of Christ's dying for the whole world must be understood to refer to mankind in general (as in Titus 2:3-4). "World" indicates the sphere, the beings toward whom God seeks reconciliation and has provided propitiation. God has mitigated His wrath on sinners temporarily, by letting them live and enjoy earthly life … In that sense, Christ has provided a brief, temporal propitiation for the whole world. But He actually satisfied fully the wrath of God eternally only for the elect who believe.[115]

---

than to make this benefit common to the whole church." The Bible does teach a limited or particular atonement. Jesus said, "I am the good shepherd. The good shepherd gives His life for the sheep" (cf. John 10:11, 15). Jesus prayed to the Father, "I do not pray for the world but for those whom You have given me, for they are Yours" (John 17:9). Jesus said, "This is my blood of the New Covenant, which is shed for many for the remission of sin" (Matthew 26:27).

114 R. C. Sproul, *Grace Unknown: the Heart of Reformed Theology* (Grand Rapids, MI: Baker Books, 1997), p 177.

115 *The MacArthur Study Bible* (Nashville, TN: Word Publications, 1997), p 1965. What is refreshing about MacArthur's note is that he writes as a Calvinistic expositor dealing with the text, without trying to force his theology into the obvious implications of the phrase in order to eliminate a difficulty. However, it appears his more recent work affirms another view interpreting "the whole world" as all classes of humanity, i.e., not only Jews but Gentiles, men and women, nations, tongues and peoples. It is important to remember that Calvinistic versus Arminian theology debates were not in the mind of the biblical author or his readers.

Appendix C

On 1 John 3:4-8: Views on a Christian Not Continuing in Sin (See Chapter 11) By Douglas V. Heck

1. ***The Perfectionist View, i.e., that children of God do not commit acts of sin.*** Obviously this isn't a serious competitor of consideration, for the Apostle has already affirmed the universality of sin, among both spurious and genuine believers (cf. 1 John 1:6-2:2). Also, if this was true, then "all" (Greek pas) believers do not commit acts of sin, which is contrary to universal Christian experience. Even on the pages of the Bible, children of God are seen as committing acts of sin (e.g., Abraham, Moses, David, Peter, etc.; cf. Romans 7:14-25; Philippians 3:12-13).

2. ***The Limited Sin View, i.e., that children of God do not commit mortal sins.*** The Roman Catholic distinction between mortal and venial sins is a reading into this passage in order to arrive at a solution to John's dogmatic statement, which sounds intimidating at face value. Both Augustine and Luther held to this view. There is nothing in the paragraph to speak of a particular class of sins in contrast to other kinds of sins. This is not to say that some sins are not more serious than other sins but rather to affirm that this passage doesn't speak to that issue.

3. ***The New Nature View, i.e., that children of God do not sin in their new nature.*** Those holding this view tend to fall into the false idea that believers are not essentially responsible for what they do in the flesh. Those suggesting this view look toward verse 9, in which John says, "Whosoever is born of God doth not commit sin; for His seed remaineth in him, and he cannot sin, because he is born of God." They claim that the Apostle is pointing to an impossibility of acts of sin committed in the new nature. However, this view

introduces a cleavage in the human constitution and it argues in opposition to this entire paragraph, where John seeks to call forth responsibility for law-breaking.

4. *The Willful Sin View, i.e., that children of God do not commit acts of presumptuous or willful sin.* Because the Old Testament and the New Testament warn about the danger of high-handed, willful or presumptuous sin, of which there is no sacrifice (i.e., the implication being that there is no temporal forgiveness but a temporal punishment), this must be what John is talking about. cf. Hebrews 10:26-30; Numbers 15:30-31 compare with 32-36, which illustrates it. Later in First John, the Apostle mentions "sin unto death" (cf. 1 John 5:16), which could refer to the same kind of willful sin. John Wesley held this view, making a distinction between voluntary sin, which a Christian cannot commit and involuntary sin, which a Christian does commit. However, there is nothing in the context nor the whole paragraph which would indicate that the author is talking about particular kinds of sins.

5. *The Abiding in Christ View, i.e., that children of God do not commit acts of sin while abiding in Christ.* Some divide genuine believers into the carnal, i.e., those who are not abiding in Christ in their backslidden condition, and the spiritual, i.e., those who are now abiding in Christ. They cannot commit acts of sin while abiding in Christ. However, when the same issue is repeated in verse 9, they are called those "born of God," which is a title used for all genuine believers.

6. *The Practice of Sin View, i.e., that children of God do not continue sinning as a practice.* That is, that continuing sin does not characterize the believer's life. Hence, there is a contrast between the present tense of hamartanei and the aorist (cf. 1 John 2:1) tense of hamarte. Also, the contrast with the present participle of "he that doeth righteousness" (Greek, ho poion ten dikaiosunen) with the present participle of "he that committeth sin" (Greek, ho poion ten hamartian), continues the ongoing contrast between the genuine and spurious. The Apostle affirms that genuine believers do not continue practicing sin; spurious believers do practice sin. Even Charles Ryrie admits that sin may enter the experience of the saved person but it is not the rule of his life. If sin is the ruling principle of a life, that person is not saved. (cf. *Ryrie Study Bible,* p. 1019). The distinction here is between acts of sin or the ongoing practice of sinning.

This last view is John's intended meaning, as it would be the normal way in which his readers would receive it. If Jesus was manifested to take away sin then there should be observable evidence of His work among the children of God. However, a difficulty arises when we consider 1 John 5:16, "If any man see his brother *sinning a sin* (Greek, hamartanonto, present participle; hamartian) which is not unto death." In other words it is possible for a brother (Greek, adelphon) to be sinning a sin. The present tense participle there would seem to contradict this *Practice of Sin* view of 1 John 3:6, if John's intent were to emphasize only the habitual action. The solution to this is that the participle tense of verse 6 could be a Progressive Present, which speaks of past action that is still in progress at the present time.[116] It looks back to a particular time, i.e., "from the beginning," (Greek, ap' arches), verse 8. In the case

[116] cf. A. T. Robertson, *A Grammar of the Greek New Testament in the Light of Historical Research* (Nashville, TN: Broadman Publishing, 1934), pp 881-882; Nigel Turner, *Syntax*. Vol. III of *A Grammar of New Testament Greek*, ed. by James Hope Moulton (New York, NY: T. & T. Clark, 1963), p 62. Sometimes this is called the Descriptive Present tense. In Daniel B. Wallace's *Greek Grammar Beyond the Basics: An Exegetical Syntax of the New Testament* (Grand Rapids, MI: Zondervan Publishing House, 1996), calls this an Extending-from-Past Present, describing it: "The present tense may be used to describe an action which, begun in the past, continues in the present. The emphasis is on the present time. Note that this is different from the perfect tense in that the perfect speaks only about the results existing in the present time. It is different from the progressive present in that it reaches back in time and usually has some sort of temporal indicator, such as an adverbial phrase, to show this past-referring element" (p 519). Other New Testament examples of the Progressive Present, Descriptive Present or Extending-from-Past Present include Luke 15:29; John 15:27 and 2 Peter 3:4. This helps us understand 1 John 5:16 and allows for us not to demand the Greek term adelphos (English, brother) to refer to either a genuine Christian or simply a professing/spurious Christian. In First John the term adelphos had become a reference to a believer.

of the congregation at Ephesus, this would refer to their beginning exposure and trust in Jesus Christ. (cf. 1 John 1:1; 2:7, 13, 14, 24, etc.) The devil goes on sinning from the beginning in uninterrupted continuity and so do his children. But in Christ Himself there is no sin (verse 5) and His children do not go on in the uninterrupted practice of sin. This is John's way of pointing out that the ongoing practice of law-breaking would be shattered at conversion. Robert L. Thomas helps clarify the Progressive Present tense of this participle.

> Spelled out in terms of this approach, 3:6a says, "It cannot be said of anyone who abides in Him that he has sinned and is still sinning." In other words, there is not an unbroken continuity of sin from the past into the present, with that continuing present characteristic in the life of the one abiding in Christ. In terms of this approach, 3:9a means, "It cannot be said of anyone who has been begotten of God that he has been doing sin and continues to do so in the present. As for 3:9c, the meaning is, "It cannot be said of the one begotten of God that he is able to have sinned in the past, continuing into the present, with sin still characteristic of his life"... He is saying that an unbroken state of sinful behavior from the past as characterizes the children of the devil (cf. 3:10), is impossible for the one who has been begotten by God. He is describing a continuous condition such as characterizes the devil, and saying that anyone who experiences that same condition has not seen Christ or known Him (cf. 3:6b). It is therefore, not habitual action as such that is depicted by the present tense of hamartanei; rather it is a prolonged, uninterrupted pattern of behavior from the past which continues in the present.[117]

[117] Robert L. Thomas, *Exegetical Digest of First John* (Copyright by Robert L. Thomas, 1984), p 260. The Apostle John leaves unanswered the practical question of the theoretical possibility of a genuine believer sinning for a time, i.e., continuing in a habitual sin as a regular practice for weeks, months or some years. His essential point is that children of God will manifest the nature of their Father and because Christ's central purpose in the incarnation was to remove sin, then the practice of law-breaking is incompatible with who they are. This is why personal obedience is such a key test of genuine faith!

In other words, ongoing sinning as a lifestyle points to a spurious faith, void of regeneration. The Apostle John concludes this point with a warning, as if anticipating that there was and would continue to be confusion here: “Little children, let no man deceive you: he that doeth righteousness is righteous, even as he is righteous” (v 7). There would be deceivers (cf. 1 John 1:8; 2:26), trying to contradict this axiom, i.e., that children of God are manifested by their practice of righteousness and children of the devil by their practice of sin. Notice also that the aged Apostle is pointing out that the person who does “righteousness” (i.e., in behavior, as a practice of life) “is righteous” (i.e., forensic righteousness or imputed righteousness). Those claiming to have exercised faith and received the imputed righteousness of Jesus Christ, like Paul emphasizes (cf. Romans 4 and 2 Corinthians 5), and yet continue in practicing sin or forbearing of righteousness, are deceived. They have a false, spurious faith which does not save. They are not children of God but children of the devil, like John explains in the next part of the paragraph.

Appendix D

On 1 John 5:13: "These things"
(See Chapter 22)
By Douglas V. Heck

There are three basic views on identifying the demonstrative pronoun, "these things" (Greek, tauta), which we shall examine in detail.

1. "These Things" refers to the Preceding Section of verses 1-12. The connection of believing on "the name of the Son of God" (Greek, pisteuosin eis to onomia tou huiou tou Theou), looks back to verses 5 and 12, where the Son has been the object of faith. Also, the demonstrative pronoun, as used in 2:26, clearly goes back to the preceding section about the false teachers, i.e., 1 John 2:18-25. cf. Brooke, p 142; A.T. Robertson, vol 6, p 242.

The weakness of this view is that there is nothing in this passage or in 1:4 (where the same demonstrative pronoun is used) to limit the "these things" to only the preceding section. As a matter of fact, it is difficult to see the demonstrative pronoun in 1:4 as a reference to what precedes it, unless it is limited to the joint partnership which is enjoyed (v 13). It seems the "fullness of joy" would be a result of concluding our assurance of eternal life, based on the objective tests contained within the epistle. Also, according to the development of the whole epistle, the Apostle has been giving tests of eternal life throughout the letter, suggesting that verse 13 could be a summarizing theme for the whole epistle.

There is a sense in which this view is commended, for 1 John 5:1-5 does summarize the three marks of genuine faith, essentially making the same conclusion as the third view, i.e., that assurance of salvation is based on the objective evidence of three characteristics in a person's life, i.e., faith, obedience and love.

2. "These Things" refers to the Immediately Preceding verses 9-12. Zane Hodges agrees with the above argument, with the exception that he would see the demonstrative pronoun as limited to verses 9-12.[118] If this is the case, then assurance of salvation is not based on objective evidence within the behavior of a believer's life but only on the promise or record of God, i.e., that He gives eternal life to those who believe on His Son.

The weakness of this view is that the whole epistle gives focus to the three objective marks of genuine faith and two of the three are behavioral manifestations, i.e., obedience and love. According to John, we know we have genuine faith with the assurance of eternal life, not only because God has promised it, but because we can evaluate honestly the direction of our lives. Also, why limit the demonstrative pronoun to the immediately preceding verses of 9-12, while ignoring the paragraph section of the wider context, i.e., verses 1-12? If John was talking about the one issue in verses 9-12 (i.e., the promise of God that believing in Jesus Christ would result in eternal life), then why didn't he use the singular demonstrative pronoun (English, "this"; Greek, touto) instead of the plural pronoun (English, "these things"; Greek, tauta)? This view has comparatively few representatives of the three possible interpretive options.

3. "These Things" refers to the Whole Epistle as a Summary Theme. Similar to 1:4, the main purpose of writing the whole epistle is summarized by John, similar to the manner in which he summarized the theme for his Gospel.

---

118 cf. John F. Walvoord and Roy B. Zuck, editors, *The Bible Knowledge Commentary: New Testament* (Wheaton, IL: Victor Books, 1983), p. 902. Hodges writes: "The words *these things* are often wrongly taken to refer to the whole epistle. But similar expressions in 2:1, 26 refer to the immediately preceding material and the same is true here. What John has just written about God's testimony (5:9-12) aims to assure his readers that, despite anything the anti-christs have said, believers do indeed possess eternal life. It may be pointed out, in fact, that the assurance of one's salvation always rests fundamentally and sufficiently on the direct promises that God makes to the believer. In other words, one's assurance rests on the testimony of God."

> And many other signs truly did Jesus in the presence of his disciples, which are not written in this book: But these are written, that ye might believe that Jesus is the Christ, the Son of God; and that believing ye might have life through his name. (cf. John 20:30-31)

In the Gospel of John the demonstrative pronoun (English, *these*) refers back to the each of the major miraculous signs of Jesus, which essentially covers the whole book. There is no debate concerning the pronoun reflecting on the entire book, as a theme passage. The same human author, John does the same in his major epistle, i.e., give a summarizing theme statement near the end of his writing. Hence, at the inception of writing his epistle John said, "these things I am writing unto you," and at the end, "these things have I written unto you," with the theme explained in between his two purpose statements.

This is John's intended meaning, suggesting the demonstrative pronoun (English, "these things") refers specifically to the three manifestations of eternal life that can be objectively evaluated, i.e., faith, obedience and love.[119] cf. Plummer, p 120; B. F. Westcott, p 188; C. H. Dodd, p 133; W. Robertson Nicoll, p 197; Henry Alford, vol 4, p 508; John R. W. Stott, p 184; I. Howard Marshall, p 243.[120] We know this because there is nothing within the context of the passage itself that would limit it, as, for example, we find in 1 John 2:26. There the pronoun tauta (English, "these things") is obviously

---

[119] Three cycles of each of the tests or marks of genuine faith have been given: The moral test of *obeying the Lord*, the Apostle John developed in 2:3-5; 3:4-12; and 5:2-5. The social test of *loving others,* the Apostle John developed in 2:6-11; 3:13-19; and 4:7-5:2. The doctrinal test of *believing that Jesus is the Christ* the Son of God, the Apostle John developed in 2:18-27; 3:23-4:6; and 5:1-12. It is important to remember that each cycle adds further detail and elements to the test.

[120] Robert Law seeks to combine all three views: "These words accurately define the governing of the whole Epistle. Contextually, however, they refer to the contents of 5:6-12, and most directly to 5:11, 12." cf. *The Tests of Life: A Study of the First Epistle of St. John* (New York, NY: T. & T. Clark, 1909), p 405. We consider Law's summarizing view with favor as a helpful summary of the Apostle John's authorial intent.

limited to what precedes but here in 5:13, there is no such contextual limiting issue. If, as Hodges suggests, the demonstrative pronoun is limited to the single issue mentioned in verses 9-12 (i.e., that God has promised eternal life to those who believe), then John would not have used the plural demonstrative but the singular, i.e., "this thing" (English, touto). Yes, assurance of salvation is based on the record/ promise that God has given concerning everyone who believes that Jesus is the Christ, but it is also based on a profession that results in obedience and love. The purpose of the epistle is that John's readers would partnership with God and others in the possession of eternal life and so experience full joy (cf. 1 John 1:3-4) and "that you may know" (Greek, hina eidete) you have eternal life, i.e., have assurance of salvation.

> At the opening of the Epistle S. John said, "These things we write that our joy may be fulfilled" (1:4). The context there shows what constitutes this joy. It is the consciousness of fellowship with God and His Son and His saints; in other words it is the conscious possession of eternal life (John 17:3). Thus the Introduction and Conclusion of the Epistle mutually explain one another.[121]

The Greek verb (English, "that you may know") appeals to a settled intuitive knowledge that is certain, gained by careful reflection. This is not experiential knowledge (Greek, ginosko) but oida knowledge, i.e., knowledge gained by reflection. cf. 2 Corinthians 13:5. With such belief in the Son of God and the assurance coming from objectively evaluating the characteristics of genuine faith, the end result is the continuation of believing that Jesus is the Son of God. For John, assurance of salvation causes his audience to continue in their profession of faith and not leave, as the Gnostic heretics had done (cf. 1 John 2:18-19).

---

[121] Alfred Plummer, *The Epistles of S. John: Cambridge Greek Testament* (Cambridge, 1894), p 120.

About the Author

Susan Heck, and her husband Doug have been married for over 40 years. She has been involved in Women's Ministries for over 30 years. This includes teaching Bible Studies, counseling, and leading Ladies with the Master women's ministry at Grace Community Church in Tulsa, Oklahoma. (www.gccoftulsa.net)

Susan is a certified counselor with the Association of Certified Biblical Counselors (ACBC, formerly NANC). She is the author of "With The Master" Bible Study Series for women. Previously published books in that series are,

- With the Master on the Mount:
  A Ladies' Bible Study of the Sermon on the Mount
- With the Master in the School of Tested Faith:
  A Ladies' Bible Study of the Epistle of James
- With the Master in Heavenly Places:
  A Ladies' Bible Study on Ephesians
- With the Master on our Knees:
  A Ladies' Bible Study on Prayer
- With the Master in Fullness of Joy:
  A Ladies' Bible Study on the Book of Phillipians
- With the Master Before the Mirror of God's Word:
  A Ladies' Bible Study on First John

She is also the author of five published booklets:

- Putting Off Life Dominating Sins
- A Call to Scripture Memory
- A Call to Discipleship
- Assurance: Twenty Tests for God's Children
- The Liberating Gospel: A Call to Salvation

Susan's teaching ministry is an outgrowth of her memorization work on the Bible. She has personally memorized 23 books of the New

Testament word-for-word (The Gospel of Matthew, The Gospel of John, Romans, Second Corinthians, Galatians, Ephesians, Philippians, Colossians, First and Second Thessalonians, First and Second Timothy, Titus, Philemon, Hebrews, James, First and Second Peter, and First, Second, and Third John, Jude, Revelation), one book of the Old Testament (Jonah), and several other portions of Scripture.

Susan and her husband have two grown children and seven grandchildren. Both children and their spouses are in full-time ministry. Because of the enthusiasm of ladies who attended Susan's Bible studies, she has been invited to speak to ladies' groups both nationally and internationally. (www.withthemaster.org)